T0196154

MEMOIRS OF A
BACK UP DIVA

MEMOIRS OF A
BACK UP DIVA

KUDISAN KAI

This book is a work of non-fiction. Unless otherwise noted, the author and the publisher make no explicit guarantees as to the accuracy of the information contained in this book and in some cases, names of people and places have been altered to protect their privacy.

Archway Publishing books may be ordered through booksellers or by contacting:

Archway Publishing
1663 Liberty Drive
Bloomington, IN 47403
www.archwaypublishing.com
1 (888) 242-5904

Because of the dynamic nature of the Internet, any web addresses or links contained in this book may have changed since publication and may no longer be valid. The views expressed in this work are solely those of the author and do not necessarily reflect the views of the publisher, and the publisher hereby disclaims any responsibility for them.

Any people depicted in stock imagery provided by Getty Images are models, and such images are being used for illustrative purposes only. Certain stock imagery © Getty Images.

ISBN: 978-1-4808-6305-7 (sc)
ISBN: 978-1-4808-6304-0 (e)

Library of Congress Control Number: 2018905596

Print information available on the last page.

Archway Publishing rev. date: 5/24/2018

PREFACE

Everybody loves that classic hero's story, depicting how someone came from humble beginnings and, fought through all kinds of adversity, only to rise like a Phoenix out of the ashes into stardom and acceptance.

As a singer arriving in the highly competitive town of Los Angeles, arguably the center of the music, television, and film industries, I sought out every article and self-help book, every biography and autobiography, studying them to keep me encouraged and inspired to continue my pursuit of success in the music business. I believed it was imperative that I know these stories in order to realize that I was not alone in my struggle and that, yes, it was possible to make a living singing. Those books and magazine articles were all that I had not only to confirm my identity as an artist deserving to be heard but also to reaffirm my sanity, since I was taught as a child that it was crazy to even consider such a career. The spiritual and self-help books assisted me in identifying the synchrony of events that meant I was destined for musical greatness, piecing the creative moments of my life together like a puzzle. It was awesome to witness its unfolding.

Success, as it was defined by some, soon arrived as I achieved what many aspired to do only in their dreams: sing professionally. However, this was not exactly my entire dream. Yes, I made my living as a professional background singer in the music industry, touring and recording with artists whom, as a child, after everyone was asleep, I would sneak to watch on TV's "Don Kirshner's Rock Concert" late at night. They were some of the biggest music icons in the world. Working as a singer in the music industry was an exciting life, but being a successful "background singer" was not my initial goal.

The career of a professional backing vocalist is one that few people really know or understand. It was not until the Academy Award-winning documentary "20 Feet from Stardom" was released that the profession really got any recognition. I knew and had worked with many of the singers in that movie and was even interviewed to be featured at one point. However, my portion ended up on the cutting room floor, which I understood. Unlike many session/tour singers who were a bit put off by the film, I knew there was only a small amount of time allotted to tell such a multi-faceted story and, trust me, there are so many stories to tell, spanning from touring to television to film to making records. The career of a backing vocalist can encompass all of these industries, with gigs in all of them on a regular, sometimes daily, basis. It would have been impossible to stuff all of that information into one movie. The producers' choice to take the "All About Eve" approach was a familiar and dependable formula, as it is true that most singers who aspire to success in this industry have the intention of one day becoming the solo artist. The road it takes to make that shift from singing background to foreground, is fraught with stories worthy of several movies. I hope that there will at least be a sequel to the film. Regardless, session/tour singing remains a full-service career, filled with travel, drama, one-of-a-kind experiences, hopes, and dreams.

Three years ago, while vacationing in Silver Spring, Maryland, for the Thanksgiving holiday, I ran into a friend from my college days. Formerly a recording artist, he was now an accomplished poet who, together with his wife, also started a book publishing company. We went out for sushi that evening, and it was there that he approached me about writing a book.

"I know you've got some road stories to tell," he said. "You should share your journey with people, as there are so many singers out there who want to know how you got started and what it was like."

Having also had the opportunity to teach at Berklee College of Music in Boston, Massachusetts, for ten years by this time, I knew where he was coming from. It was true. Many of my students inquired about my experiences working in the studio and touring with famous icons all the time.

At this point, in the fall of 2012, I returned to touring with Chaka Khan and by 2014, I was in the midst of moving back to Los Angeles full time to pursue the next levels in my career. Getting back in touch with old producers, singers, and instrumentalists and meeting new ones, letting them know I was in town and ready to work, was reminiscent of my first days arriving in LA back in 1985. Only this time, the landscape of the music industry had changed significantly. The events that took place as I began this next leg of my journey were so extreme and dramatic – from one end of the spectrum to the next – that I decided to journal everything just to maintain some clarity amidst the craziness. Certainly, something good had to come as a result of all of this activity. The words seemed to flow organically from the pages of my journal into this book, aligning my past experiences with my present ones. I hope you like roller coasters, as this story is quite a ride!

First of all, I thank God for this journey, as it has been a challenging one. After surviving so many ups and downs, I felt an obligation to share these stories. Eventually, I understood that these experiences were a necessary part of my life on the planet, preparing me for an even larger purpose that I had yet to imagine. Thanks to my friend, Poet Truth Thomas, for encouraging me to write down my story and supporting my need to be heard. To Maxayn Lewis, I owe my life, because she was an integral part of my survival during my return to Los Angeles. I thank my family for taking me through a hell I thought I'd never survive, because it made me the person that I am today: resilient and successful amidst extraordinary adversity. Last, but certainly not least, I give thanks to every singer, every instrumentalist, and every artist who ever pursued this adventure called the music business as a career, as we inspired and encouraged one another, becoming family members when many of us had no support and no one. Know that my love and prayers are ALWAYS with you all. To be in this business, you have to love it and WE are in this love together, forever. To be an artist in any profession, you have to be vulnerable to the Powers That Be, allowing them to speak through you. As singers, we are channelers for our music comes through our gift from this Higher Source. I truly believe that.

My purpose on this planet is to heal people through the sound of my instrument, which is my voice. I pray that what you learn in these memoirs serves as a healing for you, inspiring you to continue your journey, whatever that is, wherever it may take you.

At our best, we are all healers. We are all artists . . .

Kudisan Kai
Sunday, 23 July 2017
(At the Wi Spa in Koreatown, Los Angeles)

PROLOGUE

I am surrounded by pictures of Audrey Hepburn. Two pictures, actually. Both are from the film "Breakfast at Tiffany's," of "Holly Golightly" with the little black dress, pearls, and tiara. One of the pics is simply a portrait. The other has her blowing a large aqua bubble, obviously from chewing bubble gum. Perhaps this represents a sense of innocence or audacity. But why is a picture of Ms. Hepburn – excuse me, Golightly – hanging in a Korean spa and at a hotel bar/lounge? It speaks to the seemingly "grounded in unreality" culture of a city known to be the home of wealthy movie stars and other members of the music, movie, and television industries.

OK, the aqua bubble gum picture hangs in the bar of The Crescent, which is a boutique hotel in the heart of Beverly Hills. It is a favorite spot of mine on Monday nights, a place filled with sometimes wealthy, sometimes eccentric, sometimes creative, and many times weird wannabes living on the periphery of life. It's quite a collection of personalities, really. Come to think of it, it's the perfect place for Holly Golightly to be portrayed: A lot of drunk people in Gucci and Chanel perpetrating celebrity, trying to be hip and more important than they really are. They try in vain to dance and groove with a funk/rock/pop/R&B/jazz band comprised of Maxayn Lewis, a former Ike and Tina Turner Ikette; bassist Bobby Watson, former member of the '70s R&B

group Rufus featuring Chaka Khan; Allen Hines, former guitar player for Natalie Cole; and Donald Barrett, former drummer with Toni Braxton. They call themselves The Cookies and they are "kicking ass," by the way.

Mixed in with the wannabes are the real celebrities and/or used-to-bes in the music industry. The combined résumés of every musician in that room would read like a Grammy Encyclopedia, representing every star in every music genre you could dream of. There is Skooter Warner, drummer with Cyndi Lauper; Doc Gibbs, former percussionist with Al Jarreau; Valerie Pinkston, singer with Diana Ross and former singer with Whitney Houston. At times the place has hosted rock star Gene Simmons from KISS, recording artist Randy Crawford, known for her hit "Street Life" with the iconic jazz group The Crusaders, and recording artist/bassist Me'Shell Ndegeocello, who came on the scene in the '90s doing the duet "Wild Nights" with John "Cougar" Mellencamp. Because the level of musicianship is so high, all of these celebrities love to jam with The Cookies. It's always a great hang for good music. Like the line from Forrest Gump about a box of chocolates, "you never know what you're gonna get."

And then there's me, back in Los Angeles once again, fresh off the road from touring with Chaka Khan for the third time in my career. I haven't lived in L.A. for more than 15 years but here I am, back in town, trying to re-establish myself, this time as a recording artist and songwriter. I have never been either in this town. When living here before, my jobs included session singing for recordings, television, and film, and touring as a backing vocalist for major recording artists.

Being a session/touring backup singer is an art form unto itself, with its own unique skill set. In addition to singing, technique, and chops, a backup singer must have the gift of the "ear" to do this job. While a singer may have technique and chops, not every singer has the ear to execute the skills of background singing. Most people aren't aware of the intricacies of the profession. Being gifted with a good ear, perfect pitch, classical training and sight-reading skills made me the perfect candidate for this career. But so much had changed in my artistic life that I needed to make some adjustments.

Crescent Hotel picture of Audrey Hepburn

So, here I am back at The Crescent. I walk into the place with Prada sunglasses perched on my blonde punk rock Mohawk, dressed all in black with vintage '90s tall Doc Martens boots, approach the bar and order a vodka and pink grapefruit juice and a veggie burger. Before the night is over, I am reacquainted with several musicians, some of whom I've known for more than 20 years. We have worked together on television shows like Oprah Winfrey, "The Tonight Show," Arsenio Hall, and Rosie O'Donnell, or done live performances, movies, and of course records with some of the world's most famous music icons. There's drummer Jonathan "Sugarfoot" Moffett, with whom I toured with Elton John. There's singer Sandy Simmons, my former band mate with Anita Baker and Natalie Cole. There's drummer Alvino Bennett, from my first tour with Chaka Khan. It feels like I'm back home with people who know me and really "get" me – fellow working musician/artists who, like me, made the choice to fully commit to this music business for a living. This is a good feeling, for acceptance is a major concept for most human beings and definitely in the top three necessary emotions of an artist like myself. Hmmm ... "artist." More on this later.

I was returning to Los Angeles from a non-consecutive ten-year teaching stint at Berklee College of Music in Boston, where many in my circle believe I should have remained. My choice to leave the music business once my daughter became old enough to attend school was intentional; it was time for a change after having been on the road non-stop for years. I wanted to be an "in town" parent, expanding other parts of my brain, and was lucky enough to get a position teaching at one of the most renowned music colleges and performing arts conservatories. However, after three or four years of teaching as an Associate Professor, I started to miss my artist life. I'd become conflicted about my place in the scheme of things, and about having what family and some friends deemed a "real job." That conflict in itself was troubling. Did I really want a static, stable job, or had I been programmed to want it? Friends and relatives would say "Hey, it's a real job. You'd be crazy to give up such security for happiness, following what you 'think' is your life's purpose." I would say yes, I had a full-time position with a consistent paycheck, every two weeks, which was something a musician rarely knows (except when you are on the road, which pays you at the end of each week). But, I would not go so far as to say that I felt secure. Actually, it felt suffocating being locked into an "educator only" position because the job was so consuming. There was no time or energy left to also be an artist. Further, the next and last step in my academic career would be a Full Professorship. However, the salary was not significantly higher so there was no financial expansion and the job description was the same.

Artistically, my music business experience came from Los Angeles and New York City, which included movies, television, tours, and records, in addition to live performances and plays. The music industry in Boston was basically wedding bands, clubs, and some theater. These wedding bands/club gigs were known as "general business" or "GB" gigs. They pay well in that wedding band circuit. But in Los Angeles, GB gigs were just one of several work options available for a musician to get paid. While the cost of living was lower in Boston than in L.A. or N.Y.C., it was still quite expensive, which brought me to the final conclusion: In order to really be financially stable as a musician, you need to actively create several streams of income. In New York or L.A., it was easier to find paying gigs in the real music business: tours and recording sessions, union-governed sessions for television shows, films, TV and radio commercials, where a musician can also receive health benefits and pension plans. Even recording artists have several streams of income, ranging from voiceovers to songwriting to acting to branding with clothing lines and other products, just to name a few.

But in Boston, GB gigs are mostly how musicians get to play. However, most have to rely on non-music-related vocations to pay rent, buy a house, get health benefits and establish a pension plan. This can be problematic, especially with scheduling and nine-to-five jobs. For me as a solo artist, specifically in the rock music genre, finding work was a virtual impossibility. There were only a few venues in which to perform, and being a Black woman singing this genre only made things more challenging. There was little room for me to grow as an artist.

There's that word artist again. So, let's talk about being an artist. Whether you are a solo artist or backing musician, it can be quite a precarious life. Contrary to all the press that describes the lucrative incomes and lifestyles of music stars, most people are clueless as to how musicians and backing singers make a reasonable living. Some think of this life as poetic, fun, free-spirited, with a lot of celebrity parties; some think of music creators as not really working, which for some means that they don't have a true grasp on reality, whatever that means. They think it's like being a spiritual vagabond, or a butterfly, flitting around aimlessly from one gig to another. Most people with regular jobs think the life is crazy, irresponsible, unbalanced, reckless and unsettling. The ultimate judgement always centers around money. Most nine-to-fivers only understand the concept of getting paid every two weeks, which they feel offers that sense of security, knowing in advance what their financial situation will be, which they believe makes it easy to budget and plan financially.

While that view is understandable because it reflects the majority, there is more than one way to make a successful living and take care of bills. Artists seem to always live in a state of the consistent present. They live in the moment. They don't worry about future gigs. When an artist is in the flow, they assume there will always be another gig. All that matters is right now. Most people can't wrap their brains around how an artist can plan for a future, living in the present. Basically, artists don't plan for the future, they assume the future. For artists, all that matters is the present. However, this belief system proved well in keeping musicians "in the flow," as gigs and income were consistently coming in.

Many times, this belief system is contradictory to the belief system in which an artist was raised in. This was the case for me, and it made my life extremely challenging. And though this artist life chose me, the lessons I learned being raised in a non-artistic household were priceless. While most people, including family members, criticized artists for living day to day, for being different and dressing different, these same people idealized this life. Some would tell me they wished they had the talent to sing. "It takes balls to put yourself out there on the line," they would say. While never judging anyone for the choices they made in their lives, I took the talent that was given to me and tried to make the best of it, honoring it as best as possible. This was not the case for many around me, who were in non-artistic vocations. The judgement hammer swung fiercely and I was always ducking the blows. My non-confrontational persona would simply bury the criticism with a bag of chips or a bowl of popcorn. That would also become a problem later.

During the 15 years I spent as an artist/session/tour singer, there was always another gig. I was able to pay my rent and my bills, go out to eat, buy clothes, and even go on vacations. I had PPO health benefits and a pension plan through both unions. I was always debt-free and "security" was my middle name. Doing what I felt at the time was what I was divinely placed on this planet to do always provided me with income. Residual checks were expected every time I went to my mailbox, and what was expected was always received.

But then two things happened: I became a single parent and questioned whether to continue touring, and a union strike caused a major shift in the music business. Only then did my income begin to fluctuate.

Regardless, living a life that is constantly up in the air is not for everyone. For me, there was no other way to live. To outsiders, my life looked exciting, scary, careless, yet blissfully free. They want to know what happens on the road and how one can travel for months at a time, seemingly tirelessly. They want to know what goes on in the recording studio: Is it difficult? Can't they just auto-tune everything now, so do you really have to be a good singer anymore? Again, if you don't know when your next recording session will be, then how do you know you'll have money for rent on the first of the month? There's that money question again. More than anything, I was asked how in the world did I choose to sing rock music with my classical music background. One of my musician friends even asked me if it was because of my connection with Elton John.

At the end of the day, the question that circled around in my head was, "How do I continue to do backing vocals and sessions and pursue a successful career as a solo artist?" It was an honor to work with these great icons in the industry, but it was not my goal to be only a backing vocalist/session singer. When contemplating this question, what came to the surface was a laundry list of soon-to-be uncovered insecurities. Even with the résumé that I had, which had secured me gigs for more than 15 years, within a year and a half after graduating from Howard University, I was still insecure about my voice. I was constantly questioning whether I was worthy of being a solo artist. Scott Folks, an A&R executive from Electra Records, once asked me, "So what do you possess in your voice that should motivate me into giving you a record deal over anybody else?" At the time, I didn't have an answer. He was inquiring about me as an R&B/jazz singer, not a rock singer. I was a jack of all trades and a master of many genres – that's the job of a backing vocalist. However, this would be problematic when it came to pursuing a career as a solo artist. You have to be clear about who you are as an artist.

The next hurdle was my insecurity about my looks. Was I pretty enough? This shallow question was unfortunately tied into my singing and performance abilities, and would plague my career for decades. The age of music videos, accessible plastic surgeries, and high-definition TV complicated these issues. Having always had a weight problem exacerbated my insecurities, which in turn exacerbated my weight problem. In spite of my self-loathing, I pushed forward, continuing to pursue and excel in my career. Though I was never clinically diagnosed, I felt a deep depression about my performances and was always depressed about my looks. But at the end of the day, I put on the clothes that made me feel my sexiest, went on that stage, and did my job as best as possible in spite of my fears and low self-esteem. Deep in my heart, I believed I was fucked up.

Being raised in a family of non-artists always made me feel that I was different. Sometimes being an artist felt like a flaw, like something was wrong with me. Although I loved my family and friends, something in me knew at age four that Memphis was not the place for me. After graduating college and starting work in the music business, my relatives would even question my sexuality because I was always on tour and it didn't seem to them that I was concerned about getting married and having children. In the next moment, whenever I'd come to my hometown to perform with Chaka Khan or any other major artist, those same friends and relatives would then contact me, wanting tickets and backstage passes. On the outside, their allegations didn't bother me. But on the inside, they brought my cauldron of insecurities to a boiling point. I was not exempt from wanting the house, marriage and children. As for my sexuality, I could care less about what anyone thought. Observing the challenges of raising a family amid the abnormalities of Hollywood brought me to the conclusion that I would need to move out of the Los Angeles area to even consider doing so. With a flourishing singing career and a strong possibility of launching my solo career, I was still far from the thought of leaving L.A.

Admittedly, there were times when being a musician felt one-dimensional, as if I was a "one trick pony" of a human being, never fully committed to expanding my brain, to being versed in subjects other than music. I am smart and well-rounded. So, I took advantage of my time on the road, pursuing other areas of interest outside of music, practicing languages in the prospective countries we toured, going to museums and other historical sites. A true lover of history, these experiences expanded my knowledge and global view as a person, as a musician, as an artist.

But, several questions about my lifestyle did begin to plague me: If I do decide to have a family, then where do I live? How do I continue as an artist with these multiple streams of income, and be normal living outside the bubble of the music industry? By the time I was 27 years old, in the middle of my first big tour with Elton John, these questions came to the forefront.

In 1993 I gave birth to my daughter, the love of my life. At that point, the inner turmoil over becoming "normal" reached its peak, spouting like a kettle boiling over. There I was spilling tears as I battled through my anger and frustration with balancing life as a parent with my life as a session/tour singer and falling farther away from my original goal of being a recording artist. This was compounded with the question of where to raise my daughter. What was the universe trying to tell me? For the next few years, I vacillated between staying or leaving this music business, until I decided it was time to seek a "normal" life, full time.

I left Los Angeles and headed up to the San Francisco Bay Area to work with Narada Michael Walden, a producer who had worked with Whitney Houston and Aretha Franklin, whom I had met at an L.A. nightclub. I thought that doing sessions for him and not going on the road would be the closest thing to a regular job. At least I'd be at home with my baby. I rented a house in Mill Valley in Marin County, just five minutes from the Golden Gate Bridge. However, the collaboration lasted only six months, as Narada was not getting calls to work either. To make ends meet, I ended up returning to L.A., driving back and forth for session work, now with daughter in tow. Finally, I accepted a two-week tour in Japan with Narada and his star-studded band. Back on the road again, damn! I drove back to Los Angeles and left my daughter in the care of her godparents and the baby sitter, then headed to Tokyo, Osaka, and Fukuoka, Japan. When I returned to L.A., my 18-month-old daughter actually did not recognize me. She looked at me and I could see that, in her eyes, I was a stranger. I held her in my arms and kissed her. It took a few minutes, but she soon laid her head on my shoulders, indicating she was starting to remember. For me, this was horrifying. I knew that this could never happen again. Moving back to L.A. after my six-months stint in Marin County placed me back in the session life, but due to the changing landscape of the music industry, I was forced to tour again, bouncing between road gigs with Jeffrey Osborne and Chaka Khan for the second time in my career, living in L.A. then in N.Y.C. only to return to L.A. again between 1996 and 2001. During this time, I had to fly my daughter to Memphis and leave her in the care of my mother.

My life was completely out of balance. Again, I decided that rather than be in the center of the music business universe, I'd prefer just being "normal." After watching the 1987 Diane Keaton movie Baby Boom incessantly, being a keeper of a General Store in the middle of nowhere seemed appealing. I moved two hours away from N.Y.C. onto a 72-acre farm in Dutchess County, New York, up near a small village called Rhinebeck. While living there, I was contacted by an acquaintance whom I'd only met once. She remembered that I had expressed interest in teaching when we first met and asked if I would be interested in teaching part-time at Berklee College of Music in Boston. This was an answer to my prayer. Now, I could leave Chaka Khan's tour and be at home.

For two years, I made the four-hour commute by car to Boston to teach at Berklee twice a week. But one morning I fell asleep at the wheel, flipping my Jeep Wrangler on black ice on the Taconic Parkway, about an hour south of the Massachusetts Turnpike. Luckily, I was the only passenger and was not hurt. For me, this was a sign that it was time to make another change, as the teaching job did not provide enough money to really sustain me. I decided to return to L.A. to settle in and only do recording sessions. In the summer of 1998, I drove across the U.S.A. from New York to California on Interstate 80 with my 4-year-old daughter in tow. That trip alone is worthy of another book.

Back in Los Angeles, session work was becoming sparse. I was offered tours with Beck and with The Black Crowes, but turned them both down, trying desperately to maintain the home I had rented in Topanga, take care of my daughter, stabilize my finances, and strengthen the roots of my session career. However, it all seemed futile, as the Screen Actors Guild strike in the late '90s snatched my commercials off the air, leaving me broke and numb. I even attended the Landmark Forum, a series of life-coaching seminars. Then, like the huge neon signs that light up Hollywood Boulevard, it became clear that I should leave the music business altogether. I was finally ready to head back across the United States, this time straight to Boston, to accept a full-time Associate Professor position and hone my skills in the Voice Department at Berklee College of Music. Little did I know that my experience as a professor would enrich my life as an artist and, even more, confirm my true identity.

The first three years back at Berklee were awesome. But, by the fourth year, the artist in me would not remain held up in a corner of my heart, choking. I escaped from Berklee back to Mill Valley, California, of all places, via marriage to a guy I had met 12 years prior, only to divorce him and return to Boston for five more years. My daughter's graduation from high school prompted me to ask myself if I had enough energy left to return to the music business for one more try at my ultimate goal, being a solo artist. This return would include pursuing a career as a songwriter. I solicited help from the Universe and so it was decided. If an opportunity came up to return to singing anything, then I would seize it.

Once again, like the neon lights on Hollywood Boulevard, the Chaka Khan/David Foster Hitman Tour shined down on me like a beacon in the night in the fall of 2012. Here was my chance to get back into the music business. However, the age-old questions returned: What about your solo artist career? Are you returning to another decade of background singing? Really? Isn't this going backwards? This time, being older and wiser and more strategic, listening to my heart and not my head, I did the tour. In 2013, I resigned from Berklee and returned to Los Angeles to sing my music and pursue my dreams. Everyone told me "but the music business has changed." I knew this. I was there when it all changed. Perhaps, I play a role in this newly changed music business.

Maybe that is my destiny, my reason for being back here. To some people, that sounds crazy and naive. Some believe there is a mixture of innocence and audacity here. At this point in my life, having acquired more self-confidence and honed some priceless skills that have afforded me several careers, I know that the Divine – which is all knowing – speaks through my heart. This journey is fraught with a level of homelessness I had never known before and was not certain I would survive. The invaluable lessons learned during this time were humbling and transformative. These have been the most difficult experiences of my life, but they made me into the person, the singer, and the artist that I am today. Over and over, the question would return, "What kind of singer are you?" To fine-tune who I am as a singer meant I needed to be clear about the answers to other questions: Who am I as a human being? What kind of artist am I specifically? What are my contributions to the world? Why am I here? That title "Artist" weighs heavy, sometimes like a crown of thorns. But, it is a crown nonetheless. The Divine prepares us for a higher purpose not only as celebrities but as human beings. On this journey, I found out what that higher purpose was.

I learned that surviving to tell one's story is an example of how God does not give you more than you can bear. I believe the Divine places us on courses to survive all of these experiences as a witness, to reveal to others what possibility is and what resides on the other side of hopes and dreams: Our heart's desire. Imagine how productive, loving, and happy everyone would feel in a world living out their heart's desire? Pursuing what's on the other side of hopes and dreams is an ageless quest. You can choose it any time. Wouldn't it be awesome if every being on this planet took that chance to pursue their dreams, relentlessly, through the pain and seemingly insurmountable opposition, to the other side of their experiences in spite of their fears? This is a significant part of being a true artist in any vocation. Many people live in fear of something. But, the difference is that successful artists continue to move forward, living their lives, pursuing their dreams in spite of their fears.

Here are the confessions of this back-up diva.

WELCOME TO THE MUSIC BUSINESS
CHAPTER ONE

There aren't many things more beautiful and relaxing than driving up the coast of California from Los Angeles to San Francisco. Most Californians who take this trip prefer to take Interstate 5 because it's quick. It's basically a five-hour drive. Personally, I have a disdain for that particular freeway, having driven it before and witnessed a horrific accident. There were bodies strewn across the road, impeding traffic. I actually had to drive around them. This experience affirmed my belief that this boring, flat, one-dimensional straightaway was unsafe and definitely not the route for me. After you get through the high elevation point, a path that leads you through the mountains down into the desert known as The Grapevine, there is nothing but flat, empty spaces for about two hundred miles. It can lull you right to sleep.

The slowest route between San Francisco and Los Angeles is Route 1, also known as the Pacific Coast Highway or PCH. It is eight to ten hours of gorgeous two-lane highway with ocean and cliff views. The only issue with this route is possibly being stuck behind a recreational vehicle, which can be a hair-raising experience on a winding, narrow road like PCH. Otherwise, it's an awesome drive, especially if you are in no hurry.

The "in between" route is Highway 101. It's about six hours of beautiful rolling hills, some ocean views, wine country, and the garlic capital of the world, the pungent town of Gilroy, California. The 101 is my route of choice. It's safe, beautiful, and relatively quick.

When you have traveled as much as I have over the years, air travel – whether it's domestic, international, or private – can be a pain in the ass. Going through security as a band can be an asset or liability. An asset is that, whether we are flying first or economy class, the road manager can make special arrangements for all of us as a band to bypass long lines and some of the security measures to get on a plane early, which is great. We get seated first, with first dibs on overhead compartment storage. Other times, security personnel may meticulously and leisurely go through every piece of luggage and equipment, which can be a very long and drawn out process. Sometimes they assume musicians are carrying illegal drugs and this is their chance to catch them. We have spent countless hours and missed numerous connecting flights over this kind of nonsense. Not once in all of my touring experience has anyone ever found drugs in the suitcase or equipment cases of any of my band mates, by the way. There have been times when we were held up in a first-class lounge until security clearance for our large group was completed. While that may sound nice in a pampering, luxurious way, it also meant we were at the airport for an extra hour or two, sitting around, which could be completely exhausting after traveling for God knows how many hours on a plane to our destination. Either way, when flying, my time is not my own. I am at the mercy of the TSA, the airlines, or an airport for days, weeks, months on end.

This is why getting in my car and being in charge of where I am going and when is a gift. For me, driving is a place of peace and meditation. Highway 101 affords me this experience in addition to getting me to my destination at a reasonable time. I never enjoy being in a hurry to do anything, having spent most of my life rushing around on jets. So, driving in my car is considered a savored vacation.

I am headed up to Marin County, which is just across the San Francisco Golden Gate Bridge, to do a gig for my friend Tracy Blackman and then scout out possible gigs for myself.

My designated stops were all plotted out. The first was Solvang, a picturesque, Scandinavian-style village that was recently made more famous in the 2004 movie "Sideways." This was my breakfast stop in case I didn't eat before getting on the road. Next was Pismo Beach, which is an all-ocean view from the freeway, for coffee. Lunch would be in Paso Robles, the wine region, accompanied by a glass of my favorite Cabernet Sauvignon of course. Then, it was nonstop until Morgan Hill, which is a suburb just south of San Jose, for gas and Trader Joe's snacks. At that point, my destination would be about an hour and a half away, depending on traffic in the city of San Francisco. Taking this leisurely drive up the coast, on my own schedule, was the luxurious side of my charmed, nomadic life right now.

As I continued up the coast, the interior of my car was quiet, as I rarely turned on the radio or my iTunes playlist. Music is usually the last thing that I want to hear, unless I'm memorizing songs for a show, which means work. The time that day was used to contemplate, to plan, and day dream.

I'd been contemplating my decision to return to the music business, to establish myself as a solo artist, songwriter, and clinician. At this point it was the summer of 2014, approximately a year since I'd quit my job as a college professor back East. In between touring with Chaka Khan, I'd been staying with friends and family in New York City, Los Angeles, and San Francisco, constantly looking for more singing work in all three places. Moving around constantly because of work, not landing in one

place long enough to warrant a permanent home, was challenging. However, it made me into the perfect guest. The tours with
Chaka had been taking me out of the country at least once or
twice a month, which was good from an income standpoint.
However, it broke my momentum toward booking consistent
work in any one town – L.A. specifically – and thus establishing
a home base, which was my ultimate goal. Meanwhile I was
juggling some live club gigs via sitting in on jam sessions, contracted recording sessions, and teaching a couple of voice students from time to time, so my schedule was relatively full. I
didn't know how all of this would play out. But it was all about
to change.

I got to my friend Tracy's house and was welcomed with open
arms. I was there to sing background for the CD release party
for her third project entitled "Mercy". I am the only other singer
on the gig. This was a paid job for me; in addition, she had asked
me to sing one of my original songs on her show, which was an
honor. This would be an opportunity for people to hear my music
and to possibly secure some club work as a solo artist, which was
my first goal. I had already done some research on places to sing
and showcase my original tunes while in the Bay Area. This was
a great start to my first day.

My second goal was to reconnect with Dina Eisenberg, a
brilliant lawyer and business strategist friend from my college
professor days in Boston. We had been discussing ways for me
to set up an online vocal music course, specifically focusing on
vocal performance. I was excited at the prospect of yet another
stream of income, one that is in alignment with my second goal:
bolstering my work as a clinician/artist in residence. This would
be great because I could manage this stream of income and gig
at the same time.

Zipping around Marin County in my Mini Cooper, I went
from Tracy's house in the little hippy, flower power town of

Fairfax over to Mill Valley for rehearsal, then into the East Bay to my Boston friend Dina's home in Berkeley. During the visit, she and I decided that the next step would be to return to the Bay Area in the near future to work more in depth on this project in order to get it up and running as soon as possible. Both prospects were exciting. It was all coming together.

I got all of my music-related business done, and before the night was over, I even connect with John and Michael, my two close friends in San Francisco proper, for a nice, non-music-related dinner.

Tracy's CD release party at Mill Valley's Throckmorten Center was a complete success as we played to a packed house. Some of the musicians who attended expressed interest in playing on gigs with me, should I ever get bookings in the San Francisco Bay area. This was exactly the response I was hoping for.

The next day, I visited several clubs as prospective performance venues, dropping off download cards and copies of my CDs. No scheduling of gigs at that point. In fact, the people who book the clubs were not available or even in the office. All that was left of these attempts was possibility. Hey, I thought, I'll take it. "Possibility is desire seeking to express itself," said the Rev. Michael Beckwith, founder and leader of the Agape International Spiritual Center in Culver City.

I drove back to Los Angeles inspired, having set some significant projects in motion, envisioning my streams of income already in flow, streams that would finally give me the foundation to set up house in Los Angeles once again, this time for good. Though this would be my third time living in LA, it felt brand new because this level in my life was new. Yet, it reminded me of how exciting it was the first time I'd moved to Los Angeles in 1985, embarking on a career as a session/background singer, which at that time was also a new level in my life.

At that time, I had never known such a career even existed

until a friend from college suggested I pursue it. Unlike the professions chosen by many of my colleagues who graduated from
Howard University, there were no entry-level jobs or internships
for singers in the contemporary music business. The closest thing
to a paid internship would be to audition for an opera company
or to be a cast member in a theatrical play or musical. Personally,
I am not a fan of musicals, and having already been a member
of the Pastiche Opera company in Memphis in my teens before
entering college, I'd already had this experience and realized
that this was not my path. Although there have been exceptions,
generally neither genres provided a direct route to getting work
as a singer in the commercial music industry. There were no
definitive answers. I had to take my chances in the field and see
what was out there.

Fast forward to today, as a seasoned professional singer in
this business re-acclimating to a new music business model,
once again, is about taking chances. Still, there are no direct
routes. Right now, the music business is in a state of transition
and no one knows how to traverse these waters. What did I
learn the first time by going out on a limb? How can I use the
knowledge so I don't make the same mistakes? Well, I've taken
the plunge yet again so I'm about to find out.

THE PAST IS PROLOGUE

In 1984, after briefly touring out of New York City as a featured
vocalist with trumpeter Tom Browne (who'd scored big R&B
hits with 1980's "Funkin' for Jamaica" and 1981's "Thighs High"),
I applied and got into the Arts Administration master's degree
program at New York University. Thinking this degree would focus on the business component of the music industry, and knowing that it was the closest degree program to do so at the time,
I applied and got accepted. But after completing one semester, I

realized this was wrong. True music business degrees were not readily available yet, which was frustrating. Although this program focused on non-profit arts administration mostly, I figured it was in my best interest to just go ahead and accumulate more degrees to "fall back on," a term learned from my conservative, non-artistic parents. I decided to finish what I started.

A friend and fellow Howard University alum, Wayne Linsey, who was also a talented keyboardist and musical director, called me up one day. He and his family had recently moved from Washington, D.C., to Los Angeles. With his usual animated, exuberant demeanor, he told me that I needed to move to L.A. as well. "Why are you getting another degree? To do what?" he asked. "Don't you want to sing? You could be making a killing out here singing!" He invited me to move in with his family on the West Coast. So, after completing that fall semester of graduate study at NYU, I went home to Memphis for the Christmas holiday, and told my parents of my choice. My father gave me $150. I packed my bags and flew west.

After arriving in LA, my first task was to join a temp agency to get work as a receptionist, secretary, or administrative assistant. My second task was to join a choir to develop friendships, maintain some kind of spiritual security, and finally learn how to sing gospel music. With no savings or car, I rode the bus. Anyone who has ever lived in Los Angeles can tell you that not having a car there is extremely challenging. This was long before the city had built out a subway system or established enhanced bus routes. Los Angeles is a sprawling city of connected suburbs for miles and miles, through deserts and mountain ranges. The places I could physically get to without a car were few. Luckily for me, the Linseys lived in an area called Ladera Heights, which was near Slauson Avenue, a main thoroughfare with a bus route that could take me to downtown Los Angeles, thus determining the area I should focus on to look for work.

I signed with a temp agency and got a secretarial job at a
company in the Wells Fargo building in downtown Los Angeles.
My job description included opening mail, inputting data into
the computer, writing letters, answering phones, and other basic
administrative duties. I learned Excel and other computer software programs on the job, which made me marketable enough
to increase my salary a bit. Every morning I got up around 6 a.m.,
had my coffee and toast or muffin, then walked three long blocks
to the bus stop. After work, I would catch the bus back to Ladera
Heights, then connect with Wayne and go to a club called At My
Place, located on Wilshire Blvd. in the city of Santa Monica.

At My Place was a hub for some of the most talented musicians in the industry at that time. They were famous players
whose names were listed in the liner notes of numerous albums.
They'd come in off the road and gather at this club to jam. It was
a place for them to reconnect and/or network with other musicians while maintaining their already ferocious "chops" (skills).
Some of the singers who regularly sang with these musicians at
the club included Will Wheaton, Phil Perry, Michael Ruff, and
Tony Warren. After each show, Wayne would introduce me to
everyone and I would hang out and talk with the lead singers and
their backing vocalists. I met Fred White and Tigger, who sang
backing vocals for Phil Perry. I met Kim Edwards-Brown, who
sang with Will Wheaton and Tony Warren. Soon, I made lifelong
friendships with these musicians and got work opportunities as
well. Some of my first gigs at this time were singing background
for Will and Tony at At My Place. This led to me singing on Will's
album as well. These small singing jobs and relationships were
the foundation-building connections that established me in this
industry.

Wayne also introduced me to producer, composer, arranger,
and conductor Benjamin Wright, a former arranger for Quincy
Jones and Michael Jackson albums who went on to do work for

Justin Timberlake, OutKast, Aretha Franklin, Janet Jackson, and was also musical conductor for Gladys Knight, to name only a few. Benjamin was the first producer to hire me in Los Angeles. My first session with him was a radio commercial for a hair product called Optimum Hair Relaxer. This radio commercial was my first job that paid "residual" income, which means that every time that Optimum radio commercial is replayed, I get paid. It was a national commercial, which meant that it played all over the U.S., possibly several times a day.

Fortunately, I'd joined AFTRA before leaving New York, which made me eligible to do this radio commercial. I'd had to join the union in order to do vocal work on Tom Browne's Tommy Gun album, which was the last music project that I completed before leaving N.Y.C. The union – the American Federation of Television and Radio Artists – governs performers' rights on all sound recordings; all work on videotaped television like soap operas, game shows, and late-night shows; and everything on radio, among other things. Commercials generate residual income, and residual income is the foundational salary of all session musicians and singers. It is work that you do only once, and you continue to get paid each time that spot is broadcast, which could last for years. Equally important, each union job that one does counts as credit towards eligibility for full medical and dental health benefits and payment toward my own pension plan. Every year, members who make a designated amount within that year are eligible to receive or continue receiving health benefits. Doing union work is as close to a regular job as it gets in the music industry. Within a year of making the minimum required amount, which was $10,000 at the time, I received full PPO, Blue Cross/Blue Shield health insurance.

It was on this session that I met singer/songwriter Phyllis St. James, now known as Eyvonne Williams. She had previously been signed to Motown Records as a solo artist, and now toured as a backing vocalist with Australian stars Helen Reddy and The Bee Gees, and she became a valuable and trusted friend. Phyllis (Eyvonne) would call me to do demos for songwriters and other small jobs. I became a working singer who continued to work temp jobs whenever possible. In between temp jobs I would collect unemployment from my session work. If the temp jobs interfered with any singing work, I would cancel or tell the agency I was not available. This would become an issue later.

After living with Wayne's family for a few months, I lived with another friend and Howard alum, drummer, Land Richards, and his wife in Pasadena for about three months. Soon after this move, I was finally able to save every bit of cash and get my first apartment in the Mid-Wilshire district of Los Angeles, in an area now known as Koreatown.

As for my second task, I chose to join First A.M.E., a Methodist church near South Central Los Angeles. I heard one of their Sunday services, which in those days were broadcast on the KJLH radio station. The music and the preaching caught my attention. Dr. Cecil L. "Chip" Murray was a prominent figure and active change agent in the community. In addition to being an eloquent speaker, Pastor Murray was committed to serving the people, where his actions spoke as many volumes as his words. He built schools and senior citizen homes as well as many other businesses in the surrounding neighborhood. He was down-to-earth and well educated, with a brilliant mind, and I made several appointments to speak with him one on one about my life and the Bible. He was always available. His knowledge of many religions, expansive thinking, and liberal, all-inclusive teaching made him the perfect connection for me.

Not being a fan of religion at all but a believer in God and coming from an ultra-conservative Baptist church background with overtones of a Catholic school education, I was looking for a gospel music experience, which was something new for me. The choirs at First A.M.E. were renowned. Both Joe Westmoreland, Minister of Music, and Rickey Grundy, Director of the Unity Choir, were icons in the gospel music industry. I joined the Unity Choir, which was comparable to a young adult choir. The friends that I made during my time in the choir include the godparents of my daughter today. Our friendship now spans 30 years.

One day, I received a phone call from Shelton Becton, a singer and musical director in New York City and another Howard University alumnus. I had met him through some other alumni while in graduate school in N.Y.C. He was working with Phylicia Rashad, the star of the huge television hit "The Cosby Show," where she played Claire Huxtable, the mom on the show. She had also been doing some live performances in clubs and Shelton was her musical director. This time, he was in Los Angeles recording the music for a television commercial titled "Disney World with the Cosby Kids." Ms. Rashad was pregnant at the time and could not make the plane trip to L.A. to do the recorded portion of the spot, so. Shelton needed female voices to sing lead and backing vocals for the session. He knew that I had just moved to L.A. and asked if I could sing the lead and contract another background vocalist for the session. A contractor contacts and hires singers for a session on the producer's behalf. In return, the contractor gets an extra fee, or scale, when the contracts go to the union. This is also included in residual payments. My first call was to Phyllis St. James. It was my chance to return the favor for all the work that she had called me in to do when I was getting my start in L.A.

In addition, Shelton asked if I could do Phylicia Rashad's speaking part in the commercial in her absence. This meant reciting a spoken line, known as a voiceover. A voiceover is considered a separate job that includes another set of residuals as well. This was a monumental opportunity. At the time, I didn't understand the financial ramifications of his offer, until I received my first set of residual checks.

This Disney World spot was a filmed television commercial, which fell under the criteria of the Screen Actors Guild union. I was not a member at the time. However, anyone who works their first union session is allowed to do so as a non-member under Taft-Hartley, which is an Act that allows you to do a one-time union job without joining SAG right way. It was in my best interest to join SAG as soon as possible to be eligible to do more work on television and movies, so I joined as soon as I received my first session check. As a member of AFTRA, I was eligible to join SAG at half the price. Back in the day, the cost was $1,000, so half price was $500 to join each union. (The current fee to join the newly merged SAG-AFTRA union is a $3,000 flat fee.)

To my surprise, this Disney World TV commercial paid great residuals. Residuals are monies that are paid to the performer for the continued "usage" of the music on radio, television, and in movies past the original broadcast date. They are calculated and paid out every 13 weeks. For this commercial, I would receive four sets of residual checks, first as the general contractor for the session; then for singing the lead (Phylicia Rashad's part); then, a solo/duo rate for backgrounds with Phyllis. The small speaking part or voiceover, was yet another residual. The commercial was national, which meant it was shown all over the United States. So, it generated hefty residuals every quarter (which was approximately 13 weeks) for a while. The day that I received my first set of checks was mind blowing. I was on my way to pick up my friend Cristi Black, background vocalist for Stevie Wonder and Tom Jones, for a songwriter demo session, which paid us each $50. Thrilled to make $50 that day, I picked up Cristi, then decided at the last minute to stop and check my mailbox.

Now, a private mailbox is an expense that most musicians incur. It was necessary, especially if you were a touring musician who was on the road all the time. While I hadn't gotten a road tour at this point, I felt that getting the mailbox would create the energy to make touring work flow from being a dream to a reality. There was no designated day that residuals were mailed out every 13 weeks, they could come at any time, so it was best to have an address at a post office or private mailbox company (comparable to a Mailbox Etc.) to prevent checks from sitting, vulnerable to theft or loss, in your home mailbox while you were out of town.

That day, I opened my mailbox and had at least eight or nine checks from AFTRA totaling more than $10,000 in residuals. I opened check after check after check. It was crazy! I sat in my car, stunned by this windfall. Cristi was stunned, too. I drove straight to the bank and deposited my checks and continued happily to my $50 session. At the end of that year, that single Disney World commercial netted me over $30,000, which was a hefty sum at the time.

Now, here's where I had that issue regarding the temp agency. As I explained, I would do temp work in between music jobs but if any music work or recording sessions came up, whether they paid or not, I would cancel or not be available to do temp work. This was my way of putting out energy into the universe that I would soon make singing my one and only vocation. Finally, this one day the temp agency got upset with me for being unavailable for a temp secretary job, so they contacted the Employment Development Department in an attempt to cut off my unemployment benefits. I was subpoenaed to attend a hearing at the EDD office to determine my fate. It didn't make sense to me that after receiving excellent recommendations for my work with this agency, they would attempt to stop my income because of my unavailability to do a single job. After all, it was a "temporary" agency. In the end, the hearing was decided in my favor for the following reason: I was registered at the EDD as an unemployed singer, not an unemployed secretary. So, there were no grounds to stop my benefits for turning down work that was not in my specified vocation. No matter what I did, my music always came first.

After that experience, it was clear that my temping days were numbered. It was time to trust that singing alone would sustain me. Soon, this turning point in my career cleared the way for a new job to show up and reveal itself in the form of my first major tour. This happened a year and a half after I'd moved to Los Angeles. From that point on, every day felt like CHRISTMAS!

MY FIRST MAJOR TOUR

It was tough at times, but for the most part, I was able to maintain the basics like food, water and shelter. My rent on the Koreatown apartment was $500 per month at the time. In addition to doing temp jobs, I booked record sessions, demo sessions for songwriters, and I did live gigs as a backing vocalist for two actresses who also sang, namely Sheryl Lee Ralph from Broadway's "Dreamgirls" and Lisa Raggio from the television sitcom "Private Benjamin." Most of those gigs paid from $50 to $100 per performance. My only activity outside of work was the gym. Constantly concerned about my weight, I attended advanced aerobics classes, sometimes taking two classes back to back, at a fitness chain located in downtown L.A. after work. Sometimes I would walk home, which was probably not the safest thing to do. But, coming from living in N.Y.C., L.A. was like Disneyland to me. It took at least an hour to make the trek. I saw it as a warmdown from my exercise classes and it saved my bus fare.

As the end of my one-year lease was approaching, my rent was behind by one month. At this point, strange things began to happen at my apartment. One time, my electricity went out. Noticing that no other person in my building had this issue, I called a male friend to come over, as I was freaked out by this.

Just as he arrived, the lights suddenly returned. He thought this was simply a short in the wiring.

Then, a few days later, my landline phone stopped working. I contacted the telephone company and they sent out a technician the next day. We both went down to the basement to the room that housed all of the wiring for every telephone in the building. The technician found that my phone wire had been disconnected. This was odd, as the wires were behind a locked door that could not have been jarred loose. Needless to say, I was startled and nervous. My friend offered to come and stay with me for the night. Happily, I accepted.

Then, the inevitable happened. The eviction sign/notice finally landed on my door. The court date was set, but the order gave me an extra month to remain in the apartment, as I was at the end of my one-year lease. As much as it would have been my choice to leave immediately, I had to remain through the end of my lease plus one more month, as I had no money to move or another place to go. All of the tell-tale signs had revealed themselves through that unexplained sequence of events, telling me to "get out!" However, I had to just be tough and get through this somehow. So, my focus remained on taking on every temp job that I could, exercising, and just watching my back. I survived living in New York City in the '80s when it was crazy, as the city struggled to reboot itself from garbage strikes, an economic crisis, and crack cocaine had taken its toll on the safety of most neighborhoods. Certainly, I could make it through this. Then, it happened from a chance meeting.

ANITA BAKER

I had met Ndugu Chandler, drummer for Herbie Hancock and session drummer/percussionist for Miles Davis and Michael Jackson, through some musician friends, at a gathering at his

home. At this time, I wanted to get some of my original music
recorded so that I could send out what was known as a vocal
reel, which was a five-minute audio tape of recorded singing
examples, showing versatility of one's voice, to get more singing
work. Since I couldn't afford to get a professional vocal reel,
which meant getting a producer to record and edit it, I decided
to barter by supplying my voice for sessions/demos for songwriters in exchange for getting songs produced and demoed for my
vocal reel.

Ndugu introduced me to Greg Dalton, a guitarist from
Portland, Oregon, who had recently moved to L.A. Greg was
looking for a singer to record songs he was shopping to recording artists. So, we made a deal that I would sing his songs for his
demo in exchange for him recording my original songs for my
reel. The day that I recorded his song, titled "411," his girlfriend,
Sandy Simmons. drove in from Portland to move in with him. I
met her briefly as I was leaving Greg's house. She drove a Snow
White's Apple red Volvo that she called Ruby, which I thought
was such a cool car at that time. Sandy was also a singer whom
had moved back to her hometown Los Angeles not only to live
with Greg, but to go on tour singing background for Anita Baker.

A week or so later, I received a phone call from Sandy, asking
if I could attend an audition to tour with Anita! Five days before
the tour was to start, Anita had fired one of the backing vocalists, which prompted the last-minute audition. Since Sandy had
been gone from L.A. for a while, she had been out of touch with
many singers here and was at a loss for whom to call for this
audition. It just so happened that after she'd met me at Greg's
place, he played her the music that we had just recorded. So, she
took a chance and called me.

I rented a car and drove to the audition at a rehearsal studio called The Alley over on Lankershim Boulevard in North
Hollywood. I had no idea what to do or how to prepare, since

it was my first tour audition. I was familiar with Anita Baker's music because, coincidentally, Benjamin Wright had called me a month or so before to come in for a recording session, singing the bridge to a song called "Mystery" that would be on Anita's new album, "Rapture." Evidently, when Anita came in from Detroit to record this song, she forgot to sing the bridge. The improvised melody was there, but the basic melody, which could now be construed as a background part, was not. Well, that's what ended up being my singing part. Who knew that I would end up auditioning to perform the music I had just recorded a couple of weeks prior?

I knew that if they asked me to sing a song at the tour audition, I would have several standard R&B or jazz tunes ready. I also knew that I could sing *a cappella* if necessary, with no accompaniment. If they asked me to do backgrounds on a song at the audition, that simply required me to listen and execute, and there was no preparation necessary for that. So, I felt ready for anything. Keyboardist Bobby Lyle was the music director. He had different girls come up on stage to sing on the microphone with Sandy and Tanya Boyd, the other singer who already had the gig. Bobby taught me the song and asked me to sing the top part, which I guessed was the part the former singer performed. I learned the part to the song, executed it, then left. I wasn't sure if the audition was recorded via audio or video. A day or so later, I received the call that I got the gig.

That was it! Within five days I was on my first major music tour out of L.A. It was the end of my temporary secretary career, and I never looked back. I was able to move out of my apartment, knowing that I would be able to pay my rent plus the extra month owed. It would be an experience of many life lessons. Along with it being my first major tour, it would be my first of many trips to Europe, specifically England. But, touring with Anita Baker was no day at the beach.

ANITA BAKER: THE GHOST OF CHRISTMAS NOW PAST

Touring with band members Bobby Lyle, James Bradley Jr., Gary Glenn, saxophonist Gerald Albright, Donald Griffin, Sandy, and Tanya Boyd was pure fun and entertainment. Most of the time was spent laughing and tootling around London like tourists. We were a family. Already well-rehearsed, the remainder of our time off stage was spent together going to the movies, out for drinks, clubbing and hanging out with fans.

We were creators of fun. Once, while having dinner in the designated dining area at London's Hammersmith Odeon Theater before a show, Bobby almost spilled a bowl of hot corn chowder in his lap. From that point on, he was known to us as Bobby "Sweet Corn" Lyle, which was our joking homage to that infamous incident when Al Green got scalded with hot grits by an irate girlfriend. We still laugh about that chowder to this day. Whenever I see Bobby, I yell with a southern, R&B-flavored, high-pitched tone, accented on the first word of "Sweet Corn" like an animated radio announcer. By the end of the London portion of the tour, almost everyone had a special name or comedic reference: Donald "Where My Linguini's At" Griffin, Gary "I Hate Them Motherfuckers" (referring to flies) Glenn, and Sandy and Tanya "The Dubonnet Twins," to name just a few. Pure comedy.

During the entire tour experience, Anita seemed fidgety. She was never content, constantly accusing people of undermining her, and completely obsessed with her sound on stage. It was rarely right. Sound engineers were fired regularly as no one could meet her demands. Periods of being relaxed, happy and carefree in spirit on this tour were few. It was exhausting.

We had each other's backs as well. One incident started with Anita Baker buying onstage suits for the guys in the band but refusing to buy anything for the singers. This should have been a huge red flag signaling what was to come, but it was ignored.

Then, that day finally came when the finish line flag waved fervently and yes, there was no gray area – our reality was all black and white.

Five months into the Rapture tour, Anita decided the guys needed new suits for the remainder of the tour. Once again, she refused to buy anything for the singers. The television show "Miami Vice" was a huge hit at the time, so Anita decided to get them black suits with pastel-colored wife beater T-shirts for their stage wear, similar to the style worn by Crockett and Tubbs on the television show. In the meantime, our white outfits – or should I now say "off-white" – looked dingy and worn and had started to fall apart under all the hotel basin washing. Of course, there was no budget for dry cleaning. The lesson learned here was that sweating on stage in off-the-rack clothes that were not properly laundered meant that the outfits would not last out the tour.

Sherwin Bash, Anita's manager, called a meeting with the singers and offered $800 to be split between the three of us for purchasing new outfits. This was done without Anita's knowledge.

At the time, we were in Philadelphia and had just met Patti LaBelle, who had come to a couple of Anita's shows at Radio City Music Hall in New York. She suggested that we go to her shop, LaBelle Ami, and ask the tailor who also ran the shop to make our outfits. So, the next day, we went over to her shop on South and 3rd streets in Philly. We decided that to best utilize this small amount of cash, we would build outfits for me and Sandy around what Tanya already owned, including going to the Baker's shoe store to get boots that matched hers. Patti's tailor made me a white lace tuxedo tails jacket that I wore with white tights. He made Sandy a short white lace skirt with a matching short tuxedo jacket. Tanya stood in the middle, so our outfits complimented her white bustier and flared skirt perfectly. We all wore the white granny boots and gold jewelry Anita insisted on.

Next, came the part where someone had to tell Anita about our new outfits but not disclose that she had paid for them. I was the designated mediator. Now we were in Detroit, Anita's home town, at the Pontchartrain Hotel. On this trip, she would be presented with the key to the city and a plaque from the Recording Industry Association of America because her record had just achieved gold status, meaning she had sold 500,000 copies. I made an appointment to go to her hotel room for the talk. As I entered, it was obvious that Anita was in a great mood. I explained in complete detail, describing what the new outfits looked like and that our previous outfits were turning to rags. Her only response was that the clothes didn't matter, "as long as y'all got my gold jewelry on." I assured her that we had the jewelry as well. It was all set. The next gig would be at the Budweiser SuperFest in North Carolina with Jeffrey Osborne.

Myself, Anita Baker, Sandy Simmons, and a Tanya Boyd

Now, Jeffrey Osborne was a huge success at the time. Former drummer and lead singer with the legendary R&B group LTD, Jeffrey's solo career was soaring. However, I don't recall if we were the opening act or the co-headliner of this show. Regardless, it was agreed that Anita would go on stage first. Immediately, she insisted on some rules. All banners in the coliseum with Jeffrey Osborne's name on them had be rolled up and covered while she was on stage. That was rule number one. Rule number two, which Anita announced to the band before the show, was that no band member of hers was allowed to attend Jeffrey's show, or else they would be fired. Now, of course, this sounds crazy. Everyone in the band couldn't wait to see Jeffrey's show. He and his band were the hottest R&B act at the time. So, we all agreed to go together, regardless of Anita's rule, and stick together.

When it was time to go on stage to do our show, the band and singers went on stage before Anita came out of her dressing room, which meant she did not see our new outfits before we hit the stage. The band was set up on the floor and the backing vocalists were on risers above and behind them. As the band started the show with a grand intro to "Caught Up In The Rapture," Anita came out onto the stage singing, improvising the intro to the song. When it came time for us to sing our parts in the chorus, the stage lights beamed right in on us. There we were, all sparkling under the lights in white lace outfits with gold accessories. Anita turned around and looked up. Her jaw dropped to the floor. She looked as if she had seen a ghost. Now, I know we looked good, we sounded good, and I figured she would be surprised because she had not seen what we were wearing before she entered the stage. But, given my thorough explanation of the outfits in Detroit, I thought her reaction was overly dramatic. Nevertheless, we continued the show, which was a great, by the way. We received outstanding reviews in the local paper later.

Afterward, we went back to our dressing rooms and quickly changed our clothes. Everyone got ready to do our "sneak back" into the venue to see Jeffrey Osborne's show. Anita had already returned to her hotel, so we were clear to go. The crew for both our band and Jeffrey's band were aware of this rule, so quietly and carefully, we all got escorted into Jeffrey's show with our backstage-access passes.

It was a fantastic show. Jeffrey's band was on fire. Afterward, both bands got together in the lobby bar of the hotel. We had tons of laughs and drinks and by the end of it all, we had become fast friends. We finally headed to our hotel rooms around 1 a.m. Then, it happened. There was a message waiting for each of Anita's three background singers in our prospective hotel rooms. "You have been fired and your plane leaves at 10:30 in the morning," it said. "Please be in the lobby by 9 a.m." We were shocked, upset, and confused. We tried calling Anita's room, even knocking on her door, but there was no answer. No one would give us any information. Bobby Lyle and the rest of the band were shocked as we called each of them and told them what was happening. Was it the outfits? Did she find out we saw Jeffrey's show? We didn't know. The next morning, we flew back to L.A. The next Anita Baker show was in two days, in Memphis, Tennessee – which, ironically, was my hometown – but we would not be on it.

When we got off the plane, we decided to go to Tanya's house in Alhambra, California. No sooner had we gotten settled, sitting around the kitchen table feeling exhausted and numb, Tanya's house phone rang. It was Anita Baker. "Y'all got to come back," she said. "I fucked up. We've been sitting around this table trying to learn this music." Tanya was so infuriated she would not respond. She gave the phone to Sandy, but Sandy didn't want to speak to her, either. So, once again, I was the designated mediator.

I picked up the phone. As Anita continued to speak, both Sandy and Tanya began to talk to me at the same time. "Ask her why we were fired," they prompted. "We are always on time. We do our job. It can't possibly be about clothes." So, I proceeded to ask Anita why she fired us, explaining that we could understand if she was upset that we had done something wrong and that, whatever that was, then we needed to be told so we could fix it. Then I repeated, "it can't just be about the clothes." That's when Anita lost her temper and said, "Well, if you think I'm that devious, then I don't want you here!" Abruptly, she hung up.

None of that conversation mattered to us. We were already fired. We just let it go. It had been a tumultuous time on the road with Anita Baker, save for the fact that we loved our band mates. They were sorely missed.

Two weeks later, Sandy, Tanya and I received calls from Anita's manager Sherwin, asking us to come to a meeting at his Beverly Hills home to discuss how and when we could return to the tour. We went and had a heart-to-heart discussion about our experience with Anita on the road and what had culminated in our being fired. In the end, the three of us came to an agreement: We would return to the tour under one condition. "We cannot be fired for nothing," we explained. "If we are late, if we sing badly or are disrespectful in any way, then, understandably, these are reasons to be fired."

Meanwhile, Sherwin gave us some background info on what could possibly have caused Anita to react so quickly and illogically. If she was going to fire us, it would have made more sense for her to wait two more days to finish that leg of the tour. That way, she would have had a two-week break to find and rehearse new singers for her show. But, there was nothing logical about this. There was nothing logical about her. It turned out that the night we were released, she contacted Shelton Becton in New York (yes, the same Shelton Becton that hired me for the Disney

World commercials; ironic?) and got him to suggest names of East Coast singers. Then she flew them in to North Carolina that same night on the day we were flying out, then spent time prepping them to learn and execute her show in two days. None of it made any sense.

Sherwin agreed with our terms and the meeting ended on a promising note. However, the promise would be short-lived as, in the end, we never returned to that tour. We received a call shortly after our meeting, stating that Anita Baker wanted to retain the right to fire anyone at any time for whatever reason she saw fit. That was the end of my first tour out of Los Angeles.

The good thing was, we were seen in Las Vegas by Natalie Cole. As soon as she found out that we were no longer with Anita Baker, she hired the three of us to be her backing singers. It was for $200 more per week than we'd been making. Her tour dates were scarce, as she was returning to the music business from a rehab center at this point. But hey, we had some work! Welcome to the music business.

PRESENT DAY IS NOW PROLOGUE

Recalling those first gigs in Los Angeles reminds me of the numerous times that I stepped out on faith, not knowing if the work that came my way would continue long enough to sustain me. I believed in my heart that living in Los Angeles, actually singing for a living, had solidified my purpose and was a clear indication that I was in alignment to pursue my dreams. I just had to maintain my commitment and soon even more opportunities started presenting themselves, with one thing leading into another, like a domino effect. It only took faith and trust on my part. Today I was back living in Los Angeles for the third time, regardless of the challenging circumstances in this new music business environment. Again, I took a chance.

Trusting your instincts is not an easy thing to maintain as one gets older. Multiple rejections over the years can raise all kinds of doubt, causing you to question your abilities. Soon, society factors in age as an issue for any declination, and before you know it, your main focus is on what you have lost, not on what you have achieved. When the time comes for one's re-invention – and yes, it's coming – then fear of taking chances sets in. Society allows youth to experiment, to take chances. But, when you are in what is considered middle age, like forty or fifty years old, society sees chance takers as foolish dreamers, disillusioned midlife crisis eccentrics, who are devoid of any sense of what is considered reality. People think you're crazy. Compound that with being surrounded by non-artistic, conservative relatives, friends, and colleagues who are in your ear, constantly whispering how you should be "settling down," maintaining your status quo, and prepping for retirement, which only provokes confusion, creating an ongoing battle between your heart and your mind. At the height of this confusion, life's challenges start firing away, shaking your confidence to its core. It can make you mentally, physically, and spiritually ill.

Despite my belief in the alignment of my purpose, and even after taking chances once again, the consequences of some of my actions began to manifest themselves in the form of rejection after rejection after rejection. I began to question my heart. Did I do the right thing? Following my heart, I had quit my teaching job and moved 3,000 miles back to the West Coast to pursue my music career and start a songwriting and acting career, this time around as a seasoned grownup. I had plotted and planned out a strategy, with these three options to "fall back on" (there's that term again!). If anyone asked me what my plans were, my answers probably seemed to pose minimal risk because they included some amount of teaching, which I was now established and credentialed to do. The average non-artistic person would find that this leap of faith was more calculated because it sounded "normal." Yes, I quit teaching, and already had the backing vocalist job with Chaka Khan, so the blind trust might have reflected a view through rose-colored glasses, but it wasn't so severe. Also, the possibilities of teaching at a university like USC, with my credentials from Berklee College of Music, minimized my risk a little more. However, the lesson learned this time around is that "plans have nothing to do with your ultimate destiny". In fact, plans can postpone what you were striving for in the first place. "How" you will achieve your goals is never in your hands. Even if things appear to fall in place as planned, there is always a shift. Your job is to take the initial step or chance, then let go, listen, pray/meditate, then allow yourself to be led. There are landmarks that materialize as confirmation that you are on the right path. Acknowledge them and hold them close to your heart, as very soon, these lessons will reveal themselves, *loud and clear*.

I took my chances but today, it feels as if they are not panning out. I am running out of options, falling in and out of depression. However, there was something inside of my heart that kept saying, "Don't give up. Keep going just a little longer." I would even get messages in fortune cookies saying, "You are headed in the right direction. Trust your instincts." Grasping on to those little synchronistic events, I would not give in, despite the criticism of my own family and my peers. There were a few close friends and many times strangers who would appear and give me support, holding me up, and many times carrying me through to the other side of my challenges. Many days, afternoons, and nights were filled with tears. Prayers and tears, every time was I alone in my car. My eyes were a constant shade of magenta, as exhaustion riddled my body and my brain. Yet, at each turn, I took those times as a sign from God saying, "Don't Give Up, I Got You! LET IT ALL GO."

Fortune Cookie

BACK TO 2014

After six hours of driving from San Francisco back to Los Angeles, I finally arrived on the outskirts of Camarillo on highway 101. I was on my way to Long Beach for the night, which was another hour's drive south of my location. My friend Marlena Jeter was in town from Las Vegas, visiting her sister who lives in Long Beach, and had graciously offered me the sofa at her sister's apartment for the night. Great. Food and shelter were confirmed. Perfect timing because at this point, my bank balance was exactly $1.81 with literally $1 in my purse. Hopefully, there was money in my mailbox in the form of a residual check of some sort, awaiting. Besides, the gig with Chaka Khan is coming up at the end of the week, which would give me some immediate per diem, money that is provided on the road for food and other incidentals. I can make it until then. The next day, at the invitation of my friend, singer and songwriter Siedah Garrett, I would be headed to the University of California at Irvine to a seminar given by one of my favorite writers, Deepak Chopra, who had asked Siedah to sing "Man in the Mirror," the international hit song that she wrote for Michael Jackson, as an opening to his presentation.

I decided to get off of the 101 freeway and take the scenic route in the gloaming of this beautiful Saturday. I approached the Los Virgenes exit that leads onto Malibu Canyon. While driving down the Calabasas portion of Malibu Canyon Road, I heard a loud BANG! I hadn't run over anything, but clearly something was wrong with the car. Something was flapping against my right front tire. My Mini Cooper dashboard notification said the right front lamp was malfunctioning. OK, at least it wasn't a flat tire. This front lamp must be the lower fog light closest to the wheel because the main headlights are working, which is a good sign as I approach the dark, two-lane portion of Malibu Canyon. Closer to the Pepperdine University campus, the street widens to three lanes. The guy driving behind me switched lanes and pulled up to my right/passenger side. He looked at me oddly, then made a right turn, entering the university grounds. What was that about? Did he see something? What does my car look like? When I got to the Pacific Coast Highway, I pulled into the Malibu Shopping Plaza parking lot near the Ralph's grocery store and got out to check my car. It looked as though I'd been in an accident though it sounded as though something internally exploded, forcing everything to come undone. My front fenders were loose and swinging in the air. No wonder that guy in the car behind me looked so confused. My fog light was missing, the rubber strip around my passenger side front wheel was loose and flapping, the grid in front of my radiator was loose, and my bumper was torn. Damn! But the car was still running OK, so, I continued on to Long Beach and arrived safely at my destination. What an eventful end to what started out as a quiet Saturday! I managed to have a restful sleep on the sofa at Marlena's sister's home. On Sunday morning, I woke up, had coffee with Marlena and her sister, then hit the road to Irvine to Deepak Chopra's seminar.

Siedah's husband Erik met me at the front entrance of the venue and directed me to my assigned seat. It was early and Siedah was about to go on stage to do a quick sound check before the rest of the crowd entered the auditorium. She and I have worked together on numerous recording sessions with producer Patrick Leonard for Elton John and many other artists. She is crazy and hilarious, and it is always great to see and hear her. As soon as she finished her sound check, the doors opened and the guests flooded into the auditorium quickly and the show began. Siedah was awesome and well received. Then came Deepak. His book, "Spontaneous Fulfillment of Desire," is one of my favorites. I have read it at least five times. I took some notes from his lecture and felt inspired and fortunate to have been asked to attend. Afterward, I spoke briefly with Siedah and Erik, thanking them for the tickets, then shuttled back to my car.

Driving back toward L.A., I finally face the question, "Where do I sleep tonight?" I decided to call a friend in the Inglewood section of the city, but she said it wasn't not a good night to come. She's dealing with some family stuff. So, I called my sister, who lived in Mid-City L.A. She said yes, so I drove to Los Angeles to spend the night there. My plan was to get up first thing in the morning and take the car to the Mini Cooper dealership to see what happened.

Early Monday morning, I got up and drove to the Mini Cooper dealership where my car had previously been serviced, which is about 45 minutes away in Monrovia. When I arrived, the service technicians looked at me as though I was nuts, saying, "You must have run over something or hit an animal." I explained that nothing was hit and the road was totally clear when I was driving through Malibu Canyon. There was no dent indicating a crash or debris on my car from hitting any animal. Then they noticed an interior bend in the radiator behind the fender and note that it's possible the dent was there prior to my ownership. It was a used car. They suggested I take my vehicle to where I bought it. This meant driving to CarMax, near the Los Angeles Airport, which is miles away. In addition to having some factory warranty left, I had purchased an extended warranty from CarMax when I purchased the car. So, off I went to CarMax via Malibu, where I stopped first to check my mailbox.

I got to my mailbox in Malibu and – yay! – I had a residual check. But it was for $16. Well, that was better than nothing at all. It would tide me over until Thursday when I headed out to my gig with Chaka. As I pulled out of the parking lot, my car started to drive erratically. My dashboard notification flashed "engine malfunction." I drove slowly down the Pacific Coast Highway to Santa Monica, deciding not to get on the freeway. The engine was getting worse. It sounded as if it couldn't get momentum enough to even reach 35 miles per hour. Slowly and carefully, I drove to CarMax. After a tedious hour of driving gingerly, I finally arrived only for the dealership to say that they were full and couldn't even look at the car to assess the issue for two weeks!

At this point, I started to stress. They suggested I take the car to the nearest dealership. Oh, my God! Again? The nearest dealership at this point was in Torrance, which was another 15 minutes away. I wasn't certain if the car could make it but had no choice but to try. If it stopped, it would have to be towed. Continuing on in prayer at this point, I consulted with my GPS, then got on the freeway.

I got off at the exit only to realize that in my flustered con-dition, I'd left a pile of stuff at the CarMax office: My iPad, the $16 residual check, a new bank debit card, and other really im-portant mail. This meant I had to *drive back* to CarMax. It was hot and I was panicked that the car wouldn't make it. My stress level jumped up. Tears began to roll down my face. I was ready to give up, feeling this was more than I could handle. But, sur-prisingly, I made it back to CarMax and the service rep was still there. When he saw me walk in, he immediately retrieved my things from his desk.

Once again, I drove back to Torrance. At this point, I prayed to my dad, my guardian angel, asking for help. Suddenly, the car actually started to drive a little better. I arrived at the dealer-ship and the service department technicians were helpful. They assured me that everything would be OK and that it would be a couple of days before they could assess the damage to my car, estimate the cost, and see what was under warranty.

I called Dave, the only friend I knew who lived in the area and asked him to pick me up. Dave is a good friend and a great drum-mer who used to teach at Berklee College of Music with me. He'd been in L.A. playing drums for a few years now, with Marilyn McCoo and Billy Davis, Jr., of the '60s group The Fifth Dimension. Realizing that I had not eaten a bite of food since that morning, I also asked him if he could treat me to lunch before returning me to my sister's house. Luckily, he was available, willing and able to come get me, feed me, then return me. He picked me up and we headed to the nearest Whole Foods Market. We sat in the patio area and I rehashed my story. The conversation and the food calmed me down. Afterward, he dropped me off at my sister's. What a hell of a day.

Car-less, with a residual check for $16 – basically all the money that I had in the world at that moment – the next hur-dle would be getting to my rehearsal the next day in North

Hollywood at Amp Studios on Lankershim Boulevard, on Tuesday at noon. The rehearsal is for a benefit concert that's scheduled in Valencia, California, the following week, after my return from my gig in Alabama with Chaka Khan. When Dave dropped me off at my sister's home, I told her about my car and asked if she could drop me off at Amp Studios. I knew I'd figure out a way to get back to L.A. to her house after rehearsal. I called my friend Sandy (from the Anita Baker tour), who lived near the rehearsal studio. After explaining what happened to my car, she offered to help. My transportation was all set up, and I was excited about the gig. This Valencia gig would be my first time working with these musicians, including Kat Dyson, a former guitar player with Prince. We had toured together years earlier when Chaka Khan opened up for Prince in the late 1990s. I just wanted everything to go smoothly, including being on time and prepared for rehearsal – this was foremost in my thoughts.

I thought everything was set, but no. First, my sister informed me that she had no gas or money for gas to get me to my rehearsal. I offered $10 out of my $16 check for gas. She accepted and decided that we should leave the house by 10:30 a.m. to get to the bank to cash my check, buy her some gas, then speed off to North Hollywood which is about 30 minutes away.

Tuesday morning, I was up and ready by 10 a.m. As we got into her car, my sister announced that she didn't feel like taking me to rehearsal and that she'd be dropping me off at the subway station instead. She had been having blood pressure issues, and although her pressure was getting better, she decided to go to the doctor. I didn't respond, but quietly I wondered how this was going to work. My sister didn't appear to be in any physical stress and had intimated that holistic healing solutions for her pressure were helping. My concern was whether we were leaving in enough time for me to catch a train and arrive on time. Los Angeles has an extremely limited subway system. There is only one stop in the whole of North Hollywood. I had no idea exactly where Amp Studios was. I thought, *This could be a very long walk.* Also, I didn't have enough money to get a taxi or Uber once I arrived at the subway station. I had no idea how frequently the trains run. This was not N.Y.C., where the subway comes every few minutes. My stress level soared.

After cashing my check at the bank, we proceeded to the train station. It seemed as though we were driving far out of the way. Nervously, I joked that we could have driven to North Hollywood in the time it was taking to go toward downtown L.A., which was due east. North Hollywood was north of our current location, past Hollywood and just over the hill next to Burbank. My sister remarked, in all seriousness, that this subway was closer, three miles to be exact, and that it was much closer than North Hollywood, which was close to five miles away.

It was almost 11 a.m. when we got to the subway station at Wilshire Boulevard. and Vermont Avenue. Worry has completely set in and tears quietly roll down my face as I realize I'll be late. My sister was either totally unaware or simply refused to acknowledge my emotional response to this situation. She dropped me off at the corner, instructing me to cross the street to the entrance, and before the light changed, continued her way. Choking back more tears and too upset to speak, I left the vehicle and approached the information desk to inquire about where to purchase train tickets and get schedules with red eyes, hot tears streaming down my face, visibly upset. The gentleman ignored my appearance and told me how the subway system works and where to pay at the machine.

Admittedly, it was quite easy and the train pulled in about 10 minutes after I arrived onto the platform. I got to the North Hollywood subway stop within 15 minutes, then immediately input the studio's address into my walking GPS. Again, Luck! The rehearsal studio was literally down one block and across the street from the subway station. As I walked into the rehearsal room, the band was just getting set up. It was perfect timing.

Rehearsal went well and everyone was happy with the results. These players have worked with some incredible artists, including Beyoncé, Prince, and Lalah Hathaway. Regardless of my tumultuous morning, I held my own amidst this group.

By 4 p.m., Sandy was on her way to pick me up to take me back to my sister's house. As I waited for her, a text came in from my sister. It read, "You need to make other arrangements for tonight and tomorrow night." My response was, "I don't have anywhere else to go. What happened?" Then my sister responded, "Did you contact Debi, Ray, or Sandy?" I said I had. Then my sister texted, "I have too much going on right now. Not a good time. You need to find other arrangements."

My final response was, "I don't have anywhere else to go tonight. I don't know about tomorrow. I can ask." It was true. I had been staying at my daughter's godparents' house pretty consistently, and had also spent the night at Sandy's for a few weeks, and although my schedule kept me leaving town every three to four days, I knew it would be best to spend more time with family rather than lean on friends. Still, it was rare for me to stay at my sister's house because of my allergy to her dog. Her reaction came as a complete surprise and became a defining moment in our relationship.

The only thing that came to mind was that if I had my car, I'd sleep in it. That way, no one would be inconvenienced. I simply couldn't believe she was doing this, especially under these challenging circumstances. I walked out of Amp Studios feeling numb, lost, and depressed. Sandy was almost there, according to her last text. Just as I stepped off the curb as Sandy was pulling up, one more devastating notification came in. It was from Chaka Khan's road manager: "Please be advised, the show this week has been cancelled." That was it. I fell completely apart. I felt helpless and hopeless. As I got into her car, Sandy asked me what was wrong. Trying to explain but slightly incoherent, I told her what happened as I was in that stuttering cry. She hugged me and said, "You can stay with us. Let's go to your sister's house and get your things." I simply could not stop crying. Everything that had happened up to this point, poured out of me like a waterfall.

We went to my sister's house, uncertain of what reaction would meet us at the door. As I walked in, my sister was cleaning floors and acting as if everything was fine. She had moved my things from my nephew's room, where I'd been staying, as if she couldn't wait for me to leave. I collected my suitcase, left her keys on the dining room table, turned and left. Nothing was spoken and there was no eye contact. I was so hurt. This was a new experience for me. Still the non-confrontational person, I kept my mouth shut and my thoughts to myself as I left the house.

Over the years, ever since my sister landed in to Los Angeles in 1987, I have helped her. I gave a party to introduce her to my friends to help acclimate her and her then husband-to-be to L.A. when they first arrived. I paid off all of their bills as a wedding present when they got married in Bermuda. When they returned from living in Barbados, I hosted them and their new baby in my two-bedroom apartment with my daughter, always finding a way whether or not I was financially able to do so. For her to know my dire circumstances – having no money, home or transportation, literally in the street – and to turn me away was devastating.

Once again, my friends stepped in to help. We went to Sandy's house, where I crawled onto the futon sofa and fell into a long, hard, emotion-induced sleep. The very next day, a text came in from the road manager stating that Chaka's gig was back on.

The following day, Thursday, I was on a plane to the gig with a $150 cash per diem in hand. I arrived in Montgomery, Alabama, checked into my hotel room, hopped into the king-sized bed, turned on the television and tried to numb myself from the insanity of the past few days with some stupid reality TV. Later, I went out for a bite to eat with the other two singers as if nothing had happened. Once I returned to my hotel room, I took a long hot bath and afterward – still emotionally frazzled – I climbed into bed and literally passed completely out. This is what the road addicts you to. You get to leave your problems at home and pretend everything is fine out there.

We had a great show and everyone was happy. Afterward, the band went out for a drink or two. There were always a lot of laughs with this group. We hung out until the early hours of the morning, shutting down the hotel bar. As I returned to my room, reality set in. It was time for me to go back home.

Home? What was that? I was still fighting to find "home." After a ten-year hiatus from touring by teaching in Boston, then returning to Los Angeles to find a new and even more precarious music business, this was what I got? It was too much. Just as it was at the very beginning of my first career, I was in uncharted territory. All my planning and plotting couldn't prepare me for what came next. Nothing about this was predictable. With everything that was happening – or not happening – in my life, I had to let go of all the worry or risk losing my sanity. I found myself in a constant state of prayer and meditation and this was only the beginning.

Welcome back to the music business.

YOU'VE GOT TO LOVE THE ROLLER COASTER
CHAPTER TWO

THE IMPORTANCE OF LOVE AND RELATIONSHIPS

Two of the most powerful words in the universe are "love" and "relationships." To endure the roller coaster ride of this music business, one must fully embrace the attributes associated with these words, for they are essential to your breathing mechanism. When you are making something as personal and vulnerable as music, the connection between musicians is key to the quality and message of the music that is created, felt, and heard by all whose ears it falls upon. This is powerful. The depth and quality of most of my friendships and past love relationships remain solid, loyal, and impactful to this day. However, the one constant in my life that would resurface frequently was my lack of self-love. For a long time, I did not realize this feeling existed; even when I acknowledged it, I didn't realize it could be an issue. But, time and time again, it would be proven that, on the contrary, this was yet another personal challenge. Over and over, the issue of loving myself would be revisited.

God is the spirit that resides in me, the common denominator of all creation, that started the beating of my heart, connecting everything with everything in and through the interspaces of the universe. I love God, so doesn't this mean that I love my-self? What's missing? In my relationships, I am the giver and nurturer, always putting the "nurturees" first. I was taught that "it is more blessed to give than to receive," and I believed that this philosophy made me a great friend. Wouldn't being a trust-ing, dependable, loyal person, who reflects love, also help solidify my relationship with myself?

After much deliberation, the answers to this question began to surface. It took homelessness to get me to understand that in order for me to survive the stress of my life and move forward in pursuit of my dreams, I had to truly learn how to love and take care of myself. For me to do this, I had to do two things: 1) begin putting myself first, and 2) learn how to receive. Both seemed like foreign concepts, and in the beginning, felt selfish, even arrogant. This "it is more blessed to give ..." belief, along with my "over-achiever" attitude, caused a huge chasm of im-balance and misunderstanding around the "gift of receiving." It was paramount for me to realize how arrogant it is *not* to receive. Homelessness is a hell of a way to learn a lesson, for it comes at a high price. A price that seemed, initially, impossible to pay. While embracing the gift of receiving clearly made sense in theory, it would be through a specific experience that I fully realized its value. The results were nothing short of transforma-tive. I'll explain shortly.

My return to the new music business revealed the strength and durability of the bonded friendships that I'd built years be-fore when I arrived in Los Angeles the first time through to the help and support I received now. Many of these folks were closer than my own blood kin. In fact, my relationships extended through their families: their mothers, fathers, siblings, grand-parents, etc., treated me "like family." Some of these connections remained tight, and yes, my return revealed that some friend-ships were seasonal and fleeting. Regardless, all lessons learned were priceless. As we all traverse this life, doing what we love for a living at a high level, then, as with everything in life, we experience lulls and downward spirals only to rise again with a broader consciousness and more expansive understanding. It's a cycle. How one reacts to these pendulum swings in life is everything. How we navigated these ups and downs is what my "old friends" and I had in common.

In my younger years, I'd been so focused on getting work and becoming established, I didn't think about the long-term effect of the relationships I formed at the time; it never occurred to me that they would play a part in life as we all grew older and became seasoned professionals with our own families. These same friends and colleagues have various positions in the current music industry, reflecting the reality that the entire music business is made up of relationships, which can impact one's career in a multitude of ways. These bonds can be viewed as small microcosms, with less than six degrees of separation between them, which gives new meaning to the question, "Who am I at the center of it all?" In conclusion, my relationship with "me" affects every relationship outside of me, and is played out in rich, fulfilling ways throughout my life and the lives of others. In the end, we are impactful parts of "the whole," and as always, it's all good.

A NEOPHYTE'S EXPERIENCE

There are several groups of musicians, doing various jobs, creating a number of streams of income in this network all the time. Some are playing live gigs in local clubs, weddings, and corporate parties (also known as "industrials"), and other similar events, which in Los Angeles are also known as "casuals." Other musicians are mainly known for sessions, which are mostly arranged through the union and includes playing for recordings, films, television shows, and commercials for both TV and radio. These musicians usually read charts and orchestral scores. My goal as a working musician in L.A. was to be well-versed in all genres of vocal performance, maintaining every stream of income possible. Other work that is open to union or non-union members include sessions for video games, smartphone apps, webisodes, and other Internet programming. Of course, there are the touring musicians who are constantly on the road, hopping from one tour to the other. Generally, they are not governed by a union although, these instances have been and continue to be under negotiation. Currently, SAG-AFTRA have negotiated to recognize tour income as points toward health and retirement benefits, with an agreement between the musician and the artist's company.

A session singer, depending on their skills and how well they blend vocally and personally, will always get called for work. The question that frequently comes up is, how do you pay bills when you never know when you are getting paid? Non-union sessions usually pay at the end of the session workday. Sometimes, though rarely, the producer may state that your check will be in the mail within three to five days. In general, I don't care for those sessions. However, it depends on the producer, as they may have to set up your payment after they have been compensated. Whenever singers do union sound recording sessions for artists, the contractor/session leader has to turn in the contracts to the union. This paperwork lists the number of tracks sung, song titles, hours worked, and the length of the song(s). After they submit this paperwork to the union, the record company has 30 days to pay union members before incurring any late fees. So, you can reasonably approximate when a check will arrive. Once singers are "in the queue" for getting calls for sessions per month, then it's relatively easy to know when you may receive checks. If you do one session per week, then approximately 30 days from the receipt of paperwork, you will receive your check. Before you know it, you are receiving checks every week.

My first professional recording session was actually for my friend Shelton Becton (from the Disney World commercials) in New York City, before I moved to Los Angeles. It was a rocky start, but I learned some lessons really fast.

First, coming from a classical music background, I had not developed a mix or middle vocal register, which is used in most contemporary music styles. Shelton had me singing the top vocal part with three other well-known New York singers: Deborah Byrd, Adrienne Lenox, and Nedra Neal. Being the youngest and most inexperienced one in the studio, I kept as quiet as possible, just listening for my instructions. After timidly singing my part, Shelton kept recording over and over, making adjustments. Finally, one of the other singers blurted out, "Who is singing opera?" Immediately, I was horrified, for I knew it was me. Quickly, when it was time to sing the part again, I adjusted the sound quality of my voice to mimic the girl singing the third voicing below me as best I could. Thankfully, it worked.

Once Shelton seemed confident this was the sound he wanted, he instructed me to "sing out." This was the learning curve. Rule number one in studio recording: It is better to be too loud than too soft, that way the producer can make sonic adjustments more quickly and efficiently. Time is money in the studio, which is being charged by the hour. The other lesson: I have to develop my vocal mix with a quickness to be viable in any studio recording session. When recording, the producer can "solo" each part – each voice – which exposes any flaws. So, you have to be perfect in your execution, style, and energy so your vocal will match everyone else's output, and it has to be done with feeling or emotional intent. After all, you are selling a story, an experience. I never made those first-timer mistakes ever again.

The key is to trust that if you get called for one gig, you will be called again for another. This is true for any job in any profession, really. But, for some reason our society treats everything, whether it be "that personal relationship" or "that job," as if it is the last and only job or relationship. This false belief perpetuates the feeling that you have to settle and accept your position without question, whether or not you're content or fulfilled, as if you're just lucky to have gotten that far and this is "as good as it gets." Faith, trust, and being deserving are somehow dropped from the equation. The common denominator is fear. Most people are afraid to take chances or aspire to get anything better, not believing it is possible to have what they truly want. The pursuit of a job in music seems unattainable to most. While it is true that musicians as a group generally step out and live by faith to a certain degree, many musicians fall prey to this fear-based dogma, especially those who grew up in non-artistic households. However, in the end as it is in any profession, the truly driven ones always succeed because they actively keep moving forward in spite of their fear.

Being a working musician is no different from working in any other profession. You have to adhere to those basic redeeming qualities of being on time (dependable), easy to work with (pleasant), and good at your job (smart) – all factors that secure you in your profession. The difference with musicians is that the work is so artistically personal, transient, and independently contracted that it requires you to stay in the space of frequently working with new employers. The constant movement and never-ending creativity can also exacerbate fears and insecurities. Often, we start grabbing for what is close at hand but not quite what we desire, then holding onto that situation for dear life in the event it never comes again. This is what causes so many to carry that "this is as good as it gets, so I better do whatever it takes to hold on to this job, by any means necessary" mentality into this artistic workplace. This fearful attitude only creates obstacles like worry and stress, which causes people to act in a way that can make them mistrustful and difficult to work with, not to mention inhibit the freedom to be creative. These behaviors can keep you from getting hired and can eventually get you fired.

The truth is, if you can read music, have a great ear, can become vulnerable through music, have a knowledge of several music styles and can perform them efficiently in a timely manner, you can expand your work base and become extremely marketable. Being likeable as well as easy to work and live with – especially for touring gigs – secures you a consistent and busy music career.

I always felt there was plenty of work available in the music, film, and television industries. However, my confidence in this belief was shaken to its core when the Screen Actors Guild (SAG) commercials strike hit in 2000. The industry fought the union by not hiring union members. That way, they didn't have to pay union scale, health or pension benefits, or residuals. Instead, they offered one-time buyouts, which are non-residual generating; these were one-time fees paid for doing industry work. Sometimes the fee would be high, which seemed OK, but remember, they didn't pay residuals. This was not OK, because residuals are a major source of ongoing income for musicians and actors, as they can receive these payments for the remainder of the time that program is aired, which can be years. This policy proved quite lucrative for SAG and was done at the expense of using a different, usually lower level of talent.

Union musicians sign an agreement to uphold the laws of the union, which includes not accepting rates lower than union scale. Also, doing work that does not pay into your health benefit and pension plans would increase your chances of losing them. No one working in the industry could afford that. This, along with music now being practically given away on the Internet thanks to the ninety-nine-cent downloading of songs, and technological

advances in music software that granted people who are mar-
ginally talented a chance to make music at home, worsened my
fears about the state of the industry and my survival in it. With
AutoTune – a digital audio program that enhances and changes
the pitch of a sung vocal tone so that, even if it's off-key or out of
tune, it can be digitally fixed – non-singers could make records,
even though the actual sound produced was of a more robotic
nature. This tone, ironically, soon became "the new sound" in
pop music and has since become a standard in pop music production. This technology has significantly impacted the use of
real singers in the studio. Sessions became scarce and recording
budgets were cut, leaving most artists to do their own backing
vocals, which were not always good. As stated earlier, singing
background is a specific skill set that not everyone possesses.
Great singers don't automatically make great backing vocalists. Plus, the artist is charged per hour or per day for the time
used in the recording studio. If that artist is not proficient in
recording those backing vocals in the studio, it can take a lot
more time to get them done. Time is money. That's why one hires
professionals.

   The strike ended, but since then the music business – along
with everything else we know in this world – has been reeling
in transition, struggling to find its footing in this new world
order. After the horrific disaster of 911, and the ensuing oil crisis, when gasoline prices and air fares skyrocketed, the touring
business saw a significant downturn. Shorter tours meant fewer
tour dates. Fewer tour dates meant smaller salaries. Soon, the
weekly salary devolved to the "one off" and "pay per show" pay-
days. Precarious is an understatement for the status of working
musicians, but still, as the industry transitions, new opportunities for talented music professional show up all the time. Those
opportunities are being engineered and/or exploited by the musicians themselves.

My name for this phenomenon is "vocal entrepreneurship." Actually, it's exciting and precarious at the same time. Artists have to know the ins and outs of marketing strategies, but in the end, they get something most of them never had before, which is creative control. More than ever, artists can create and release their own music without the manipulative, non-creative, under-their-thumb dictates of a record label. In the end, the artist receives all of the profit. There is no middle man. This is paramount.

From my point of view, what's happening with recording artists is similar to what is happening to mankind. It is an evolution in spirit from being followers, answering to a leader, to being the leader/the boss/the creator of one's own destiny. It seems everyone on the planet now realizes that to be happy and fulfill one's purpose is to master one's path. The answers have always been "within you."

The days of waiting for someone to "make you a star" are swiftly coming to an end. If you are a singer, you need to write your own music. It's one of the ways to make money from your art, especially now that music is downloaded freely. Also, you have to know your craft and be able to perform. Live performances are a main source of income. Creating your own persona and branding are key, which means you have to know who you are and share the things that are innately "you," creating a lifestyle and a community of people who are in agreement with "you" and will want to purchase what you sell and own what you own to be in community/sync with "you." Again, relationships.

If you write music, it also opens you up to opportunities to score music for film and television, which is another stream of income. Profits made from one source can be used to invest in other interests. Life for everyone on the planet is entrepreneurship at its best. The Internet has created new opportunities for everyone to go into business for themselves. Think of it: Everyone is their own boss. Oh, the music business! While it's a thin line between loving it and hating it, you've just got to love the roller coaster.

PRESENT-DAY POSSIBILITIES

I returned to Sandy's home from a brief gig with Chaka in Montgomery, Alabama. Her little three-bedroom house was filled to the brim with her, her husband, her daughter, her daughter's boyfriend, and their dog, to which I was allergic. There really was no room for me, so I made it a point to be up and out of the house first thing in the morning, not returning until late most nights, closer to 10 or 11 p.m.

Living in this state of homelessness, my instincts led me to adhere to some kind of a schedule, which I believe was key to keeping me sane and grounded. At this point, on most mornings my first stop would be Starbucks, where I'd sit and write, journaling for hours on end. Then, off to Whole Foods for a fresh, raw juice, then off to work out either with Robert, my personal trainer, or to yoga in Santa Monica. I knew that exercise would keep my endorphins up and my depression about my circumstances down. After yoga or weight training, I'd head to Malibu, check my mail, then off to Point Dume Beach, where I would remain through sunset. This would be my schedule.

On Monday evenings, I'd head to the Crescent Hotel to hear Maxayn and the Cookies. Afterward, we would sit up and laugh and talk with the owner of the hotel until the wee hours of the morning. Maxayn didn't have a car, so I would take her home to Marina del Rey. On the way, we'd stop at Mel's Diner on the Sunset Strip in West Hollywood, grab a bite, and hang out with the night manager and a cacophony of crazies, ranging from drunk tourists, club-hoppers, porn stars, pimps and prostitutes, homeless people, actors and comedians, young couples on dates, and regulars from the neighborhood. That place was jumping 24/7. More on Mel's later. Afterward, I would drop Maxayn off at home, then head back to Sandy's in the San Fernando Valley. Other evenings would be spent parking along Pacific Coast Highway watching Netflix on my iPad or going to Starbucks in Malibu Cross Creek Mall and reading, playing Words With Friends, or writing, until I got sleepy. Then I'd head back to Sandy's. This schedule went on through the fall.

At Thanksgiving, Sandy invited my daughter to visit from N.Y.C. My travel with Chaka had given me enough airline award miles to get her a free ticket to L.A. She and Sandy's daughter were 2 years and 3 days apart and had known each other since my daughter was 6 and she was 8 years old. Although she was only able to stay for a couple of days, the time spent was awesome. It ended up being an enjoyable holiday.

NOW, MORE ON MEL'S DINER

Mel's Diner on the Sunset Strip could spin off a movie or television series all on its own. I constantly encourage the night manager to "write the book" about what goes on there. The place was often my refuge in the wee hours of the morning, between midnight and 8 a.m., as it was open 24 hours. Guy, the night manager, and an assortment of friends he'd met from their patronage over the years, were quite the motley crew. Needless to say, there was never a dull moment.

One of the things on my list of goals is to own a restaurant. So, being in this environment and observing how a restaurant was run was valuable knowledge. Watching the restaurant staff serve these casts of characters and other music and movie celebrities was pure entertainment. One well-known rapper would come in with his entourage and order breakfast. He was very particular about his food, specifically asking that no foods touch each other on the plate. This would result in each item being on a separate plate, of course. Also, there were times when the toast was too light which meant it would be returned until it was cooked perfectly. Regardless, the servers accommodated him and he tipped them generously.

Guy had a heart of platinum. He was always in a good mood, doing whatever needed to be done, as many time, he'd take off the managerial hat, step in, and become the cook, server, dishwasher, or whatever role was needed at the time. He would allow me to park and sleep safely and peacefully in my car in the back parking lot. I could go to Mel's during those hours and just wind down, have a conversation or a laugh, go to the bathroom, and even grab a bite of food if I had the cash. Sometimes, Guy would even treat me out of his own pocket, if things were really tight. This rarely happened, as most times I had enough for one hot meal a day. But, it was the thought that counted. Thoughtful is Guy's middle name.

Another character was Jesus. His real name escapes me, as I called him by his self-given moniker, Jesus. He was a really cool guy, always dressed in a long, floor-length robe and roman sandals, with long, brown hair and beard just like the Leonardo da Vinci pictures of Jesus hanging in the living rooms of many across the U.S.A. Jesus was quite a well-spoken, intelligent guy who was always available for pictures and conversation. After all, who wouldn't want a picture with Jesus?

At the other end of the spectrum was the porn star Ron Jeremy, who most times would frequent Mel's with a small entourage of chicks, upholding his public persona, of course.

The other regulars ranged from well-known pop stars and songwriters to affluent businessmen and homeless people, whom Guy would allow inside to rest and get a cup of coffee. Sometimes, there would be women like myself, with no place to go, and some with a child in tow, which was always heart-wrenching to see.

Many times, I would just pull up into the parking lot and sleep in my car, feeling safe and at peace. I knew the workers recognized my Mini Cooper and were kind enough to leave me alone, but still watch over me. At least, that was the story I told myself. Regardless, going to Mel's was a part of my home life at this time.

Guy@Mel's Diner on the right]

I would sit at the counter most times and either play Words With Friends or write on my iPad. As the oldies music played incessantly on the jukebox there, I would find myself singing along, sometimes without realizing it.

Once, the waitress came over to me and said that a songwriter who happened to be there having breakfast had overheard me singing one of his songs and wanted to meet me. It turned out to be Neil Sedaka. I was singing the Captain & Tennille song "Love Will Keep Us Together." Sedaka invited me to come and sit at his table. He commenced to compliment me on my voice and inquired about my career. I told him that I had met him before, when I was a backing vocalist for Elton John. He then told me how Elton had signed him to his label, Rocket Records, and re-started his career with the hit record "Laughter In The Rain," then went on to write and record a duet with Elton titled "Bad Blood," which became another hit record for him. It was an awesome exchange. From that point on, any time I was in Mel's at the counter and Mr. Sedaka walked in, he would acknowledge me with a kind nod. What a sweet man.

Another time, I was again at the counter with headphones in my ears, singing away. This guy came up and tapped me on the shoulder. He was wearing silver Elton John-like glasses, and he said, "You have a lovely voice, do you sing for a living?" "As a matter of fact, I do," I answered. He went on to say that he was a musician and songwriter in a band from years back, but that he was now writing for television and film. I asked him the name of his band. "Devo," he said. Ecstatic, I told him that of course I knew who Devo was and that I was a huge fan. Then I asked him about the band, and whether they were still doing gigs. He intimated that a couple of their members had passed away and that they weren't really doing any gigs now, but that he had gotten involved in songwriting for television and film and that that was his main focus. "That's what I want to do also!" I answered.

He then said that his office was just down the street on Sunset Blvd., and that I should stop by and give my name to the receptionist and say that I was a singer looking to work on some projects. I thanked him and said that I would be happy to do so. Remembering that I had download cards of my EP on CDBaby.com in my purse, I offered him a card and asked if he also had a card. He exclaimed, "I'm not sure, but let me check." While he checked his wallet, I asked his name. He says, "Oh, it's Mark." "Awesome! Nice to meet you Mark, I'm Kudisan." We shook hands, then he said, "Oh, here it is! Found a card!" He handed me the card, we shook hands once again, then he left.

I looked at the card, then called Guy over immediately. "Do you know who that was?" Guy looked puzzled with hunched shoulders. "He was in the band Devo and he is a famous television/film music writer, whom I recognized right away," I said. Turned out it was Mark Mothersbaugh. You've got to love L.A. for that. You never know who you may run into.

Moments like those spent at Mel's Diner were quite poignant. At the end of the day, everyone has a story. That restaurant was the Encyclopedia Brittanica of stories from all walks of life. Many times, I witnessed a mother sitting quietly in the back of the restaurant, sipping coffee, with her child lying next to her on the seat, fast asleep. They would be there all night, for the duration of Guy's shift, obviously with nowhere to go. It would hurt in my heart to see this, as the only difference between my circumstances and theirs was that my child was now grown, living on her own. I knew all too well the weight of caring for yourself and your child in homelessness, and it is seemingly unbearable. But, as women do, we put on those big girl drawers and make it work somehow. No one was crying or sad at Mel's Diner. Just maintaining, as the jukebox blared "Shake Your Booty" by K.C. & the Sunshine Band. Oh, the roller coaster.

I continued to go on the road with Chaka as the fourth person in a three-person slot, basically as a sub, until my friend Lisa, who hired me, decided to finally quit the gig. She told me to never solely depend on this gig for income. She was right. Things had changed drastically, financially, since my previous gigs with Chaka Khan. This first year back, I made $14,000, which was ridiculously lower than my salaries from working with her in the past. The second year was even worse. My resources were dwindling.

Before leaving the faculty at Berklee, I had envisioned a three-tier plan for survival that included setting up several streams of music-related income on both coasts. Initially, I thought I would live between L.A. and N.Y.C. and work accordingly. Only there was no work in New York at the time, so most of my time was spent reconnecting in L.A. It seemed as though, once I committed to returning to L.A. (which was Lisa's suggestion), everything that was set up quickly fell apart.

There was a possible part-time teaching position at the University of Southern California coming available. That carrot dangled in the air for about three semesters before the chairman of the voice department finally informed me that they had decided not to hire anyone after all. The only work that came out of that stream was a two-day clinic. That was it. My online course proposal was completed, except the next step included making the videos for the classes and that cost money, so that project got postponed. Out of the blue came an offer to do a reality television series with the working title "Back Up Divas," that was loosely based on the Academy Award-winning documentary "20 Feet From Stardom." I completed the interviews for that show, along with my friends Bridgette Bryant, Lynne Fiddmont, Siedah Garrett, Sharlotte Gibson, Marlena Jeter, Mortonette Jenkins, and new friend Nichelle Tillman. While this project was hopeful, there was nothing I could do to control the time line of the production. It was still pending.

Two of my former students had asked me for voice lessons via Skype. At one point, I had three Skype voice students. But, within a year, they all either ran out of cash for lessons or simply didn't think they needed lessons anymore. All of those possibilities were gone with the wind. Meanwhile, I was doing sessions as the offers slowly trickled in, and vocal coaching whenever possible.

The very last tier in my plan was to cash in one of my two retirement pension plans early. I knew that the penalties for doing such a thing were very high and would cause me to lose a significant amount of my retirement monies, but that did not matter to me. I was only concerned with having enough money to pay for my daughter's college tuition and a little stipend for me to live on, in addition to my other streams of income. I went to the SAG-AFTRA office and filled out the paperwork, only to be informed that when I joined in the '80s, they no longer allowed lump-sum retirement withdrawals. I was devastated. What in God's name was I going to do? How was I going to help my daughter? How could I tell her that I was misinformed? This event alone would challenge my sanity, for everything I did at this point in my life was always with my daughter first and foremost in my mind. I felt that I had let her down, which propelled me into a state of pure depression. I simply could not live with this.

My life was catapulted into yet another level of survival. Every day and night I would journal, writing down what needed to be done and who needed to be contacted for work. Most of Chaka's gigs took me out of the country. We traveled to Moscow, Curaçao, Toronto, Tokyo, Johannesburg, and all points in Europe. However, these gigs were spread out, far and few between. It appeared as though work was happening regularly, but the pay was per show, not weekly, and was significantly lower than in the past. The checks weren't enough to pay my car note and my phone bill regularly. Also, I would be gone maybe three or four weekends each month. Sometimes, I would stay at my daughter's apartment in New York. Sometimes, I would stay on a sofa at a friend's house in L.A. For at least a year or so, being homeless didn't feel so "homeless," as my streams of income had me constantly moving, flying overseas or driving to San Francisco or hanging out in N.Y.C. However, as the second year was approaching, my anxiety was also.

One night, while having dinner at the Whisper Lounge at the The Grove, which is a hip outdoor shopping mall in L.A.'s Mid-Wilshire district, I was contacted by the office of Oscar-winning composer John Powell, asking me to do a session for the movie

"Rio II." A few weeks prior, I had left messages for him asking for advice about how to get started writing music for film, which was one of my listed goals. Wow, my conscientiousness and persistence paid off. While I was not up to date on my union dues, the studio allowed me to do the session under the Taft-Hartley Act, for which I was most grateful. The Taft-Hartley Act is a piece of union legislation that allows non-union or delinquent members to work on one union project without having to join. So, I did the session and connected with John about writing music. The residuals were small but helpful.

As for the songwriting, John offered to help and made some suggestions and followed through. But, after sending email after email with no response, no contact was ever made with the third party, which was a notable executive at Twentieth Century Fox Music. All of this seemed to be a reason to give up, but I simply wasn't ready to do so. The prospective jobs that I had lined up were with major players in the music industry. Everything was still in alignment with my dreams. All that was needed was for something to stick.

After returning from one of the Chaka gigs in Tokyo, I was contacted by Kevin Flournoy, the keyboard player sub, asking if I would coach a singer who was preparing for a Whitney Houston tribute. Her name was Gennine Francis, and she lived out in Temecula. The gig would entail me driving down to her house, which was nearly two hours away. This sounded feasible to me since I was fine with long drives and knew this singer had a goal, a budget, and she was serious. She wanted this tribute to be perfect for the investors who could potentially take this show to Las Vegas. This was the level of vocal coaching I wanted to do at this point. I worked with Gennine twice a week for about three months. Most times, I would spend the night at her home. She and her husband were very gracious and we soon became friends. The coaching income sustained me between the gigs with Chaka, which at this point were becoming infrequent. In addition to coaching her, Gennine hired me to do backing vocals for the show, along with Kevin Dorsey, former backing vocalist for Michael Jackson; my pal Sandy Simmons, from Anita Baker and Natalie Cole; and Valerie Pinkston, backing vocalist for Diana Ross, who also sang with Whitney Houston for twenty years. The other members of her band were also former members of Whitney Houston's band, with the exception of two. The musical director was Melvin Davis, who was Gennine's husband's childhood friend and, ironically, Chaka Khan's MD. You have to love the synchronicity of it all. The Whitney Houston tribute debuted October 14, 2014, at the Indian Wells Theater in Palm Desert, California, and it was well received.

Like a turtle, slowly but steadfastly, more work started coming in for me. Shortly after Gennine's show, I was asked to do a live performance with a choir backed by the Glendale Symphony Orchestra. It was a Christmas program, completely scored. One of the lead performers was singer/songwriter Michael Posner. His vocal coach, David Stroud, attended the rehearsal with him at the conductor's home in Los Feliz. Stroud was vocal coach to Michael Jackson and other stars, and he'd taken over many clients from Seth Riggs, who had recently gone into semi-retirement. He and I connected, as we had a couple of friends in common whom he had coached. He ended up giving me a key to one of his vocal studios, which was in a premium location in West Hollywood across from the historic Chateau Marmont Hotel on Sunset Boulevard. He said I could use his studio to teach on Saturdays and Sundays. This was awesome, as I had just begun to build up a clientele.

As December rolled around, I performed at a charity event at a mall in Valencia, California, to raise monies for homeless children during Christmas headed by Ethan Dettanmaier, Executive Director at L.A. Talk Radio, with the same women

musicians with whom I had that rehearsal at Amp Studios in
North Hollywood on that momentous day when I was officially
car-less and homeless. It went off without a hitch and the possibility of us doing more rock gigs as a female rock band looked
promising. Getting a residency, which is a regular gig night at a
club each week, would be the goal here.

My ideas for multiple streams of income were now falling
synchronistically into place. I had the vocal coaching gig, Chaka
Khan gigs, San Francisco gigs with Tracy Blackman, potential
online courses, some recording sessions, possible band residency,
and a free vocal studio to teach live and Skype lessons. I built the
railroad. Now, all I needed was for the train to come rolling in.

GHOST OF CHRISTMAS PAST - 1987

Staying in this music business can be an emotional roller coaster.
You're always fluctuating between loving it and hating it. However,
there's nothing more gratifying than those moments when work
is flowing continuously. Checks come in unexpectedly, many
times from work you've forgotten that you had done, as it takes up
to thirty days to get paid for recording sessions. Residual checks
from commercials and movies come every thirteen weeks. While
I never counted out the weeks, being more focused on getting
work every day, it was as if I had set an internal alarm clock, as I
soon developed a "feeling" that those checks were coming soon.
Still, when those residuals did arrive, they were a welcome surprise and relief. For a while the bills got caught up and paid, some
of them in advance whenever possible. But then, in the blink of an
eye, it appeared as though everything would downshift and work
would disappear. The phone stopped ringing and the savings
started to dwindle. There's that roller coaster again.

Tours made the most money. The longer the tour, the more
you earned. However, you were always at the mercy of the artist,

hoping they want to stay on the road. That is, unless you were lucky enough to be on a tour that paid you a retainer, which is an agreed amount, possibly equivalent to your regular weekly salary, that is paid during the interim the artist is not on the road. It contractually guarantees the integrity of each performance, establishing job security by maintaining the same band members for whenever the tour reconvenes. Touring could be fun and full of adventure.

By comparison, recording sessions meant possible residual income, future earnings that are guaranteed, though how much you receive is undetermined. Recording sessions were considered the most difficult work. This is where precision came into play. All ears were attuned to every single note, breath, and nuance, heard clearly through loud speakers. You had to execute in tune, with emotion, in a timely manner. Time is money and the singers that got hired to do the job were experts at getting it done fast, efficiently, and with feeling. The work could definitely be nerve-wracking if you were shy, had a hard time replicating vocally what you heard, or were slow to really get in front of that microphone and perform. Again, rule number one, it is better to be loud and wrong than to be told to sing out. That way, the producer could make corrections more quickly and efficiently, fine-tuning the blend.

Some singers preferred to do tours. They were considered hard work in a different way. You had to be in good physical shape and develop stamina to do tours, as traveling was hard on your body and you were physically exerting yourself, singing and dancing in front of thousands of people, sometimes for several nights in a row. The vocals didn't seem to be out there as naked and vulnerable to scrutiny as they were in the recording studio. Once you sang the part, it was out there, gone, not to be heard again unless the shows were recorded, which they sometimes were. Hearing recorded concert performances was always cringe-inspiring. What felt good at the time when you were dancing and singing on stage, didn't always sound good. How well you made adjustments to hear yourself through floor or ear monitors was always a huge factor impacting your performance. Add in the possibility of working through possible equipment malfunctions or bad weather, and you have more factors working against you. These problems could mostly be offset by the assistance of a good tech crew. It can be quite an adventure, but hey, that's part of the job. You learn to work through it, in spite of what you can hear. It's a valuable skill.

I loved both the studio sessions and the tours. The perfectionist in me loved doing intricate parts and getting the breaths and blends on recordings just right. On tour, I enjoyed being part of so much creativity and improvisation. Also, I love working out and exercising, which were an integral part of being on the road. Admittedly, my focus on my body only exacerbated personal issues that were already present, issues related to my weight, self-esteem, self-confidence, and my "look," all of which had to be maintained to keep my gig. Weight-loss issues were a roller coaster ride unto themselves.

Regardless, I found both lifestyles exciting and fulfilling, which only made the times when there was no work even more strenuous. I loved my job and hated being out of work, hated the ambiguity of it all, but not enough to want to quit altogether. This career defined me, as I was fulfilling my purpose. Just as the lines between the two would wear thin, something new and exciting would always pop up. This always kept my faith in this music career restored. Every day was steeped in Spirit and belief. What more can I say than, "You've got to love the roller coaster!"

NATALIE COLE

Natalie Cole attended one of the gigs that Sandy, Tanya and I had done with Anita Baker. Evidently, the impression that we made on Natalie was a good one. When she found out that we were free agents from Anita, she hired the three of us as her background singers. Natalie was just coming out of a drug rehabilitation facility, trying to re-set her career. Watching her work was a gift. Her showmanship was stellar and her voice was spot-on, every time. Natalie never, ever sang a single bad or off note. So consistent.

On our first meeting, which was a rehearsal, we talked about being "daddy's girls," how both of our dads died from cancer, and having in common the fact of being named after our fathers (my birth name, like Ms. Cole's, is also Natalie, and I was also named after my father, Nathaniel). "Jumpstart My Heart" was her new R&B single at this time, as the label was trying to test the waters to see what genre suited her the best. She could sing anything, be it pop, jazz, or R&B. The three of us appeared with Natalie on the television show "Solid Gold," which was hosted by Marilyn McCoo, former member of the iconic '60s group The Fifth Dimension. At some point, Natalie dropped the other two singers and kept me, adding her original backing vocalist, Katrina Perkins. The two of us went on to do a few shows with her, including casino gigs on the boardwalk in Atlantic City, New Jersey. However, these would become somewhat stressful times, as my finances were once again up and down, now collapsing under the strain of Natalie Cole's infrequent work schedule.

One day, out of the blue, I received a phone call from an old New York friend, singer Sandra St. Victor, who had been on the road singing with Chaka Khan. She was ready to leave the tour and was looking for a replacement. Chaka was in Los Angeles, preparing to return to the road with a band from the West Coast. I was the only singer in L.A. that Sandra knew at the time, so she called me.

Again, the irony was that I had met Chaka Khan briefly in N.Y.C. at this club on the Upper West Side called Mikell's. I had performed there with Tom Browne, and after making friends with the bartender, I would pop in from time to time to watch other renowned artists. This particular night, Chaka was preparing to go on stage and I happened to be in the dressing room area in conversation with the bartender. It never crossed my mind that one day, there would be an opportunity for me to sing with her.

Chaka's tour paid twice the salary that Natalie paid. Plus, she had three months of tour dates already scheduled. Natalie Cole could only promise two weeks of work at the time.

I called David Joyce, who was the Musical Director for Natalie Cole at the time, and explained my dilemma. He was very understanding and suggested I call Natalie's personal manager, Dan Cleary, after lining up a substitute for the gig. So, my decision was made. I would start Chaka Khan's tour a week late, after fulfilling my obligation to Natalie Cole by doing her first week gig, while the second and last week gig would be done by my sub. That way, everyone was covered for both weeks. After lining up a singer to do the Las Vegas dates, I called Dan Cleary's office. However, instead of being understanding, Dan was angry. He informed me that if I couldn't do both weeks, then I should not show up to the airport to do any gigs. I felt that was unreasonable. Instrumentalists get substitute players for their gigs all the time, with no consequences. Regardless, this was the situation. So now, I was free to start the Chaka Khan tour on time.

Still suspicious of the response from Natalie Cole's management, I decided to contact Natalie Cole personally. When I got to my hotel room, I made the phone call to her room, as I still had the tour itinerary and knew her whereabouts. She answered in a happy, relaxed mood. I explained the situation, that I never planned to leave her hanging without making the right provisions, that she was never in jeopardy of not having a backup singer to take my place and that my integrity was intact. She then informed me that it was her idea for me not to do the dates

MEMOIRS OF A BACK UP DIVA

unless I could do both weeks. She continued, saying that she was upset and frustrated that I was quitting just when she had gotten to the point of being able to afford three singers again. She was about to add Sandy Simmons back as the third singer, but then I decided to do Chaka's tour. Fortunately, there were no hard feelings. The air was cleared and as always, the show must go on.

PRESENT AND NOW - 2014

Christmastime was approaching and Sandy informed me that I could no longer stay at her home. I'd already felt that would be the case. She gave me until the 27th of December. I'd already prepped to move before Christmas any way, wanting to spend the holiday with my daughter and mother in Memphis. Though I was definitely grateful to Sandy for a place to sleep, it simply was not a place for me, for several reasons. No hard feelings. It was time to move on.

A few days before leaving Sandy's home, I decided to test out what living outside would feel like, by spending the night in my car at a beachside campsite near Ventura. Beautiful spot. Mostly everyone owned RV's or campers. I was sleeping in my Mini Cooper. Right before dusk, some guy with toddler in tow walked over to my car and offered me water. While it was appreciated, it felt a little strange and unsafe. There was something uneasy about his demeanor. I graciously declined his offer and he walked away, sometimes turning back to stare from time to time. Obviously, he was curious about my being there. His actions confirmed that the location felt too remote and uncontrolled should I have needed any help. While the feeling of being outside all night was OK, especially on the beach, overall this was an experience that would be best suited for two people, not one woman. If this were any indication of what total homelessness felt like, I might survive it.

I had two gigs scheduled before leaving for the holiday. One was with Chaka Khan and the other was in the Bay Area, again with my friend Tracy Blackman. This time, we would be joined by her sister, drummer Cindy Blackman (best known for her work with Lenny Kravitz), and Cindy's husband, music legend Carlos Santana.

I took my relaxed, regular Highway 101 route up the coast. The gig was in Mill Valley at Sweetwater's, which was a well-known club where rock icons often performed over the years. I had sat in with Jerry Harrison from Talking Heads and seen Bob Weir from The Grateful Dead there quite often. It was the perfect place for Tracy's gig with her rock icon brother-in-law, Carlos Santana. The place was sold out to capacity. Her music was well received, as Tracy is known and well-respected in this area as an uber-talented singer, guitarist, and songwriter. Having Carlos and Cindy Santana as an addition to the show was the sweetest icing on a ten-layer cake. We all had a great time that night, creating music at an unsurpassed level of musicianship.

While in the San Francisco area, I went over to my friend Dina's house in Berkeley to fine tune my online class proposal. As always, I continued working to establish these multiple streams of income.

Within days of my return to L.A., it was time to head to the airport to fly to another Chaka gig. After the show, I decided to go to Chaka's hotel room to tell her about my finances and what had been happening with my car, which was still damaged from the Malibu Canyon drive. I was hoping to get a salary advance to pay my deductible from my car insurance. Chaka assured me she could help and, in addition, offered me work on a track date in Dubai the day after Christmas. Track dates are when recording artists use recorded tracks instead of a full, live band for accompaniment, usually for private parties, clubs, and other small venues. This was great. Hopefully, I wouldn't have to dip into the auto insurance cash after all. If I did receive enough to cover my deductible, then I would take care of the damages to my car. If not, I would go ahead, dip into my insurance disbursement and pay bills. I returned to Los Angeles awaiting the money Chaka promised to hit my bank account. Nothing happened. I texted her but got no answer. There were enough awards miles on my American Airlines Advantage for me to get a one-way ticket to Memphis for Christmas, so I went ahead and booked my flight. Then, I decided to contact the manager about the Dubai date, since I should have received an email with travel itinerary by now. He informed me that he had no idea I was included. He had not been notified, and it would be too late to get a ticket for me at this point anyway. It would be too expensive. Angry, disappointed, and frustrated, I went ahead and took a big dip into my insurance disbursement, paid my bills, and bought my return airline ticket. The speed with which things were now going downhill had me off balance. OK, roller coaster, here we go.

My mother had decided to purchase a plane ticket for my daughter to come to Memphis also. Great, we would all be together for the holidays. I got to LAX, parked my car and headed straight to a restaurant for a glass of wine and a bite to eat. Then, they announced that my flight would be leaving an hour and a half late. This caused me to miss my flight connection in Dallas, which meant arriving in Memphis a day late, while the airline put me up overnight in the most disgusting hotel ever. I slept on top of the covers in my clothes with the light on.

I did finally arrive in Memphis and Christmas with my daughter was great. It was short but sweet. I went ahead and dipped into my auto insurance money once again and bought some gifts. We both left Memphis for our destinations on 26 December, with my daughter heading back to New York City and me arriving back to Los Angeles around 10 p.m. to pick up my car from the airport garage. I headed out to my daughter's godparents home to drop off their children's gifts. Afterward, I went to my sister's house to drop off my nephew's gift. This was the first time I had seen or spoken to her since the day she disallowed me from coming to her home. She came out on the porch, took the present, then went back inside. No conversation was exchanged. After dropping off my nephew's gift, I headed to Santa Monica to what would be the first time that I would sleep in my car. I was literally homeless.

Proceeding to Ocean Avenue, across from Palisades Park, I parked and slept in my car until 3 a.m., which was the time every car had to be off that street. As I lay sideways in my Mini Cooper, uncertain of where to go next, I decided to ask my iPhone Siri "where is the safest place to park and sleep in your car?" You have to love Siri. He said that "parking in front of a busy apartment building is the safest place." This made sense. People would be in and out of the building all hours of the night. There would be nothing suspicious about someone sitting in a car in front of a building. So, I proceeded to drive around to look for the right building. Constantly talking to myself out loud, praying to God to lead me to the perfect place, I happened upon Rose Avenue in Venice Beach, which is the town right next to Santa Monica. I remembered that there was a vegan restaurant that I loved to go to on this street called Cafe Gratitude. That's it! Love the word "gratitude," as it has a nice ring to it. And there were apartments above the restaurant! As I turned onto Rose Avenue, I saw that the streets in this area were filled with homeless people. Some were riding around on bikes, some were walking, pushing grocery carts with their belongings inside, and some were in their parked cars, vans, or motor homes. On one block, there were tents lined up and down the sidewalks with people sleeping in them, and cars and campers parked out in front of the tents filled with people. Two more blocks away was Cafe Gratitude. The workers were cleaning the restaurant as I pulled up and quietly parked out front. The street signs indicated that it was fine to park there for the entire night. I parked, got in the passenger side of my car, covered myself with my black sweater and jackets, then leaned over into the driver's seat. I closed my eyes and quietly cried myself to sleep.

This was my reality. Living in my car, still touring and teaching. One thing I knew was that I could not afford to be sick. I had to keep my sanity and maintain my appearance to continue to work. In essence, I had to take meticulous care of myself, emotionally, spiritually, and physically. It was time to take this belief system to the next level.

My God, the thin lines of loving and hating this music business were wearing even thinner. This roller coaster was making me dizzy! But, something in my heart would not give up. Something in my heart kept saying that it would be OK – even while something in my head said, "You are crazy and you are losing your mind." I decided to follow my heart.

POETRY IN MOTION
CHAPTER THREE

MAINTAINING THE FLOW

The definition of "poetry in motion" is something or someone that moves in a beautiful or graceful way. This was how my many friends and associates saw my life from the outside. All they could see was that I seemed to move gracefully through life, never complaining or responding dramatically to whatever the circumstances were, no matter how horrendous. This was how my name Kudisan Kai came to fruition. Up until this point, I worked under my birth name Natalie Jackson. In 1998, I decided it was time to finally change my name.

As a solo artist, I wanted to have a stage name that would create a separation between my solo career and my session/touring career, indicating that I was a "new" artist. I asked my boyfriend at the time to come up with an Afrocentric name that he felt defined me as a person. He decided on a list of African names, all meaning one thing that he believed was inherent in my existence. My last name, Kai, is from northern Gambia and it means "you are loved," which is a reminder for me every time my name is called out. As for my first name, he felt that no matter how challenging things got, I was always lucky or blessed, able to successfully move through them. This is the meaning of Kudisan. It is Eritrean for "blessed," "holy," or "lucky." A chance meeting with a young Eritrean woman gave me the idea of how to pronounce my name. While the spelling "Kudisan" suggests the "u" vowel to sound like the "u" in "music," she said the name with a clicking sound. To my ears, the "u" sounded like the American short vowel "e" as in the word "egg." I felt that most Americans would not get that clicking sound and there would be constant mispronunciation. So, I decided to sound out my name as it would be heard by an American ear. Plus, the "e"- sounding vowel in Kudisan felt more informal, which best matched my personality. Ironically, I would later research my family tree and find that my African ancestry on my father's side was actually from the country of Eritrea, formerly Northern Ethiopia. It was as if I had psychically found my African roots.

Regardless of the romantic notion of moving through life like poetry in motion, many of my non-musician friends commented that they could never live under the strain of not knowing when they were working or when would they get paid. The temporary homelessness was also an experience these friends made abundantly clear that they would never withstand, even at the expense of being an artist. It simply was not worth it for them. Of course, I understood their feelings, for this life was not meant for everyone. Even among artistic, working musicians, there were limits or certain levels to which some would aspire. Not everyone was willing to go out on a limb to be a solo artist. Many were happy with their status quo, choosing complacency and indicating comfort with their career even if it meant they were not really living their dream. My feelings were that this life chose me and my desire to live my dreams overruled everything. They would not be ignored. While my solo career got postponed while I continued working as a session/tour singer, I never relinquished my pursuit of it. In the end, I accepted my gift, with all of the consequences. What more can I say? You've got to love the roller coaster, baby. Once I realized that the negative events that seemed to block my path were really disguised lessons, then I understood the process. After I understood the role these incidents played in my life, balance appeared, giving me comfort and, ultimately, pure happiness all the time, as my life fell into a routine with consistent work coming in. At the end of the day, I felt I was honoring my craft, doing what I was placed here on this planet to do. Not thinking, just doing, listening, and moving in accordance to spirit was like a dance, like poetry in motion.

PRESENT DAY 2015

In this homeless life, there were many different levels. My level provided the comforts of a car to cover myself and sleep in a reasonable amount of peace and safety, for which I was truly grateful. In fact, from the first night sleeping in front of this vegan restaurant, appropriately named Cafe Gratitude, my new mantra was a simple "Thank You." Every moment that I was alone in my car was spent in pure gratitude. It flowed freely from my thoughts, covering me and keeping me warm. For every person that I saw literally living on the streets, every night and day a prayer for their wellbeing and safety would extend from my heart as I drove west down Wilshire Boulevard. I was fortunate to be inside of a car, which provided a feeling of safety and privacy. They were outside, vulnerable to the weather elements and unwanted advances.

The inhumanity of it all – witnessing adults, children, men, women, and their pets living this way, crawled up in a doorway, on a bus stop bench, on the steps of churches, under overpasses of freeways – cut me like a machete. Whenever I exited a freeway or stopped at a traffic light and saw a homeless person standing there with a sign, asking for money and food, it stirred up feelings of uneasiness and helplessness, as they would stare into my eyes pleading for help. How did we as human beings allow such a thing to happen to another human being? I could not understand this. Knowing that I was no better off than they were, having no money or food for myself or any to offer, driving around in a Mini Cooper, all I could do was acknowledge them with a kind bow of my head. How deceptive my appearance was!

I would see people asleep in the middle of a sidewalk, imagining that they tried to stay awake by moving, walking as much as they could until they simply passed out from sheer exhaustion and fell asleep in that very spot where their legs couldn't carry them any farther. That way, they were assured a somewhat more restful sleep, without too much anxiety about safety. The ones who could not dismiss this anxiety would simply stay awake all night and sleep in the day. At least, this was the story that would live inside of my head. It seemed that daylight hours were safer.

I was always trying to wear myself out so that once parked, I would pass out from exhaustion. Staying up those late hours/ early mornings, always in darkness, would incite feelings of suffocation, which felt as if the weight of the clouds and dark skies overhead were pressing down on my chest, deflating my lungs. Many times, I found myself longing to just feel the cool wind on my face as my eyes closed, not wanting to witness my plight. However, sleeping with my car windows open was not a safe option. Feeling as though insanity were creeping up behind my back, despotically screaming obscenities in my ear for putting myself in such a position, I would pull over my car and pray or meditate, whatever it took to calm my brain, to end those erroneous thoughts. Again, Gratitude would surface.

The energy it took to plot out and strategize where and when to sleep quickly became overwhelmingly stressful, especially at first. Very soon, I decided to choose a place to set up my temporary residence. Cafe Gratitude in Venice Beach became my sole, consistent home of choice. My choice was confirmed by a stranger I met in a bookstore over on Abbott Kinney Boulevard in Venice. As I was browsing the shelves of the Mystic Journey bookstore, this gentleman approached me with an intense gaze. He asked, "Do you live around here?" I replied rather sheepishly, "No, I don't." Then he said sternly, "Well, you should!" and walked away. It was an unusual exchange, but I felt the genuine love in his comments. From that moment on, I parked on Rose Avenue in Venice Beach in front of Cafe Gratitude with ease and peace in my spirit, knowing that this place would be OK. The word "gratitude" was such an attractive and beautiful word, and as dire as my circumstances were, I found this state of being grateful every moment of every day quite comforting. It happened so organically, and quickly became part of my breathing mechanism, reminding me that there was always hope, and that everything was going to be OK.

I began to understand how someone would choose to numb themselves with drugs or alcohol just to emotionally get through each day, when you are homeless. I spent days and weeks on end thinking, writing, dreaming, planning, and re-assessing my goals. As time passed, it still seemed as if nothing was changing for the better in my life. My concerns were that I would lose my mind, or make food my drug, as eating away feelings was the numbing vehicle that I'd contended with in the past. At the same time, I knew that I had to eat, preferably every three hours, to sustain my metabolism. Thus, came the next level of my commitment, which was to take exquisite care of my mind, body, and spirit by getting sleep, exercising regularly, and initiating a vegan lifestyle, which also happened organically.

One day I woke up and simply lost my desire to eat meat, fish, fowl, and cheese. By fervently exercising, meditating, and staying in the moment, my mantra became "What's the right thing to do today?" Thank you, Oprah Winfrey, for that sage advice, because at this stage, I could not handle thinking past a moment. The peaceful place for me was that blank canvas of thinking nothing. Nothingness soon became my guardian, my refuge.

Then, as my mind fell into a calmer space, like peeling away the layers of an onion, I was able to think more clearly. However, the old habit of reassessing my position in regard to my goals resurfaced. Over and over, I re-checked my list:

- The part-time teaching position at USC was not happening at this time. Let that go.
- The television show "Back Up Divas" was still a possibility, swaying in the wind with nothing attached to the front or back of it, just awaiting confirmation. Hold on to that.
- My proposal for my online courses was written and just needed the videos done to get it off the ground, which meant raising the money to pay for the videos to be professionally done. Hold on to that.
- The voice student bookings were fleeting, as they always are, which was OK. At this point, I was only teaching voice for the income, not for the love of it. This stream of income would soon be over. Frustrating. I'm credentialed to do it, but I didn't want to do it. Let that go.
- At this point, the only thing that I had was my gig with Chaka. This, too, I did only for the income, but it was hardly consistent and definitely not financially rewarding. Rarely did Chaka's work garner a whole week's salary; mostly, it was pay per gig. I was the fourth person in a three-person spot, which meant not always getting called to even do every gig, which made this precarious job even more precarious. Regardless, it was my job and when I got on that plane to do my gig, it was a rather

pleasant getaway from my life as a couch-surfer. Hold on to that a little longer.

For a moment, reassessing my goals felt OK. But, before I knew it, anxiety crept back in, as the next nagging question regarding the things I chose to hold on to was, "How can I make these things happen?" The answer resonated loudly from the back row of the theater also known as my mind: "You don't worry about the 'how.'" This was a statement/belief system I'd learned from in a PBS documentary based on the life of writer and mythologist Joseph Campbell. From this film, I learned that my desires were "possibility seeking to manifest, to express itself" and that these desires were my destiny. Getting out of the way, letting go, and trusting that these desires would manifest were all key to realizing my dreams. This meant, don't try to fix it, contemplate, or worry about how it would happen. It was already destined to do so. Needless to say, "don't worry about 'how'" became yet another ongoing thread that ran through my mind like a newsfeed.

One night while hanging out at my regular spot, Mel's Diner, I met a guy named Chandler. He was a friend of the night manager there. What a character. He was funny, gregarious, and a little freaky. We had a heart-to-heart one evening and he offered some advice that, instinctively, I had already activated. It was confirmation. He said, "Developing a routine is a good way to maintain your sanity under these homeless conditions." It saved him and, yes, he was right. At the very least, my routines took my mind off of the "how." Now, this felt like poetry in motion.

The new routine was:

Mondays, at some point, go to yoga class at Power Yoga in Santa Monica. On Monday nights, I would go to the Crescent Hotel at 7 p.m. to hear Maxayn Lewis and the Cookies. Afterward, I would take her home, but before doing so, we'd go grab a bite to eat, most times ending up at Mel's Diner. Then, I'd take her home and either sleep on the floor next to her bed in her room, or head to the Korean Spa, trying to get there by 4 a.m. so that I could have the entire day to rest for the discounted $15 fee that would allow me to stay there until 4 a.m. the next morning. It was Maxayn who told me about the 24-hour Korean Spa, a place that would soon become another saving grace, my lifeline. More on this later.

Tuesdays, I was at the spa all day, in the hot tub, the cold tub, all the different saunas, sleeping, catching up on emails, texts, movies, Netflix, sometimes phone calls. I would write, write, write in my journal, pages and pages of feelings. Sometimes I would write songs, and always brought my books and magazines, anything to read. Then, there was that priceless commodity called sleep. I slept like a baby on that heated jade floor.

At 4 a.m. on Wednesdays, no matter how rested I was – as it was always difficult to rise at that hour to be out of the spa so not to incur another fee – I got up, showered, then drove down Wilshire Blvd. toward the Pacific Coast Highway (a route I affectionately dubbed "taking that slow boat to China"), then on to the beach, sometimes parking out front of the Malibu Beach surfers' spot, where there was always activity, as surfers were usually up preparing to catch that first wave at the crack of dawn. Other times, I'd drive out to Point Dume next to Zuma Beach in Malibu, where I would park and sleep in my car or on the beach, depending on the weather, right in front of that beautiful ocean. Because the continental shelf was so short there, about 100 feet long, you could see pods of whales, teams of dolphins, and rafts of sea lions come close to shore. It was an amazing concerto of aquatic nature and a lovely way to start a day.

Afterward, I'd go either to the local juice shop and get my plant-based chocolate protein smoothie or to Starbucks in Cross Creek Center and get my tall soy no-foam latte and toasted plain bagel with butter, then sit and write on my iPad or relax my mind playing Words With Friends. Then, I would go by and say hello to Becky, the owner of the mailbox company I used, located inside of the P. C. Greens Organic Grocery Store. We'd chat for a while, I'd check my mailbox, then drive back into Santa Monica to the Sokkai Gakkai Buddhist Center (SGI), where I would chant, chant, chant, and pray until I couldn't chant any more for the day, then off to yoga again.

The next hours would depend on whether I had to do a recording session, teach a student, or pick up and drive Maxayn around to help her run errands. If I taught a student, I would either go to Dave Stroud's vocal studio where I rented my teaching space or go to my friend Sandy's house and teach a student online. Then, as evening approached, I would return to the beach always to catch the sunset, say prayers and meditate. Soon, it was night again. Sometimes, I'd grab a $10 bite of food at my favorite spot, Seoul Tofu in West L.A., for tofu soup with veggie dumplings, medium spicy, and water broth. Then, I'd head back to my sleeping spot, Cafe Gratitude in Venice Beach on Rose Avenue.

Thursdays, Fridays, and Saturdays were pretty much the same. If there was a gig with Chaka on the weekend, I'd park my car at the airport and board the plane. From that point on, things felt semi-normal. I'd collect my per diem when I got to the hotel, which meant having some cash on hand, then sleep and get ready for the gig. It felt like a vacation from what was becoming my "new normal." Generally, whenever I did have a recording session or had to sing live, I would sleep at the spa or at a friend's home the night before. Lack of quality sleep in my car kept my voice in a hoarse, cracked state, which made it difficult to do my job, so going to the spa on those days became mandatory preparation for work. If I didn't have to sing, I would drive over to Cafe Gratitude and sleep in my car. This would be my spot most Sundays if I was not on the road or doing a session. I'd leave Cafe Gratitude around 6 a.m., then head over to Starbucks on Main Street in Santa Monica, where I would order my tall soy no-foam latte and converse with Lou, Bill, and Gail, regular Starbucks residents at this hour of the morning. Before sitting with them, I would go to the bathroom, bird bathe with my Kiehls body wash, and brush my teeth. Then, off to yoga. After yoga I would head back to Malibu, to the beach to stretch, contemplate, and await the sunset. This was my basic routine. I believe that it kept me sane.

Though I was spending nights in Venice Beach, I felt as though Malibu had chosen me as its new resident, so I decided to drive around to see if I could get any psychic feel for the location of my next home. I came across this street with no name where the people who jogged and walked their dogs were quite friendly. They would speak or wave as I drove by, as if they knew me. In the middle of this long block was a lovely house that was for sale or rent. Immediately, I called the realtor's number on the sign posted out front and left messages, inquiring about this and other rentals on this street, but never heard back from them. I decided to contact a realtor friend of mine and inquire about "my" house. I gave him the street name, but for some reason, he could not find any information on that house or any of the other rentals I had mentioned. I continued driving until I got to the end of the road where there was a small public beach. I pulled up and parked on the water side, which for me was the driver's side, the left side, the wrong side of the street. I rolled down my window to listen to the ocean and was soon lulled to sleep.

When I awakened, there was a ticket on my windshield, on the passenger side. Unbeknownst to me, a police officer had approached my car, not awakened me, and posted a ticket on my windshield for parking on the wrong side of the street. It was unnerving to know that someone had approached and placed a parking ticket on my car, without me realizing it. I looked at the ticket. It was for $63, but as I continued to read, there it was, the name of the street: Malibu Road. No wonder there was no information on these houses I had inquired about. All this time, I had been giving the realtor the wrong street name. In a strange way, the parking ticket was a blessing.

Eventually, I gathered the nerve to call and make an appointment with the realtor whose name was on the sign posted out front of this house that caught my attention. From the moment that I walked through the front entrance that led into the atrium and moved from room to room, it felt like home. This really could be my home. I decided to take pictures of the house and make one of the pictures the screensaver on my cellphone and iPad, and from that moment on, every drive to Malibu included driving by "my" house. Sometimes, I would park at the public beach at the end of the road and watch the sun rise and set, at times drifting off to sleep, always parking in the correct direction. One night, though, I was spied on by a drone. It came right up and hovered above my front windshield. Was it a nosy neighbor? A U.S. government drone? After all, this is the western border of the United States of America. Either way, it was uncomfortable. Fearing someone was not happy with my visits, I decided to not sleep there anymore. From now on, I'd just drive by and check on "my" house.

One day, driving up PCH towards Point Hueneme in Oxnard, I saw this huge rock formation on the ocean. It is a well-known spot, visited by many who live in the cities of Ventura County, which is north of Malibu, which is in Los Angeles County. I realized that this was the place I had been coming to and spending quality time since first moving to L.A. in the 1980s. Now, recalling the numerous times I took this drive along PCH, bringing friends up here who were visiting California, I realized that I'd long felt a connection to this northern beach area. Now, the realization hit me that perhaps the whole time, even when first living in L.A. in the late '80s, Malibu was luring me. Malibu was always my destiny.

While my current nomadic life was unusual even for me at this point, it was in fact, "my life." Just as Chandler also said, once you accept your circumstances, then comes change. More of those magical moments were starting to appear to a point where it felt somewhat normal. There was some movement in my life. Yes, acceptance was key. Stop fighting. It made sense, but it was a struggle accepting these circumstances as they were. My heart told me that from this moment on, my job was to work on acceptance. Accepting the situation, knowing you are moving "through" something, still knowing your dreams are being realized, makes getting there much easier. Also, there are even more valuable, life-changing lessons to learn along the way as you stop fighting and just listen and accept.

So, if accepting my life as a homeless person would end this homelessness, then I wanted to understand and move through this quickly. Hopefully I would never revisit "this homelessness" ever again. My previous bouts of displacement would only last from three to six months, as I continued to tour or do sessions, never really being completely broke, just couch surfing periodically.

Prior to this current living experience, every house or apartment that I had ever lived in, was first envisioned in my dreams, then appeared in real time, and finally I moved in, thus ending my homelessness. Synchronistic! Magic! This time around, the pendulum had swung way left as was reflected by my circumstances. Because of my previous ups and downs, I'd learned to always remain faithful that things would change. Admittedly, even as things looked up, my concern was on high alert, as it had been not just months but almost two years since my last home, at this point. In spite of my fears, my faith kept me in check as I continued to believe that "Winter always turns to Spring" (Daisaku Ikeda).

CHAKA KHAN - 1987

I was to go to Chaka Khan's hotel room and sing for her. Sandra St. Victor gave me the address of the hotel. I arrived at the room and there was Chaka, seated on a sofa in a long, oversized shirt dress, with her manager and Tony Patler, her Musical Director/keyboard player. I stand before them all; no one gets up. Chaka asked me, "So what songs of mine do you know?" I answered, "I know all of your songs." She asks, "Do you know 'This Is My Night'?" "Yes." Then Chaka asked me which part I wanted to sing. I told her that I could sing any part. So, she had me sing top, she sang the middle, and Tony Patler sang bottom and played on the keyboard that was set up in the room. We sounded great together. Then she asked me to do another song. My recollection is that she switched me to the middle part, then she sang top, and Tony again sang bottom. Afterward, she said, "You got the job!" It was verbally accepted and agreed upon. It would be a three-month tour, opening up for Al Jarreau, commencing July 2nd. The band consisted of James Jamerson, Jr., on bass, Alvino Bennett on drums, Jeff Johnson on guitar, MD Tony Patler on keyboards, and Arno Lucas on percussion and backing vocals.

The first show was a small gig in Santa Barbara, California, before we joined the tour with Al Jarreau. The opening act was a Seventh Day Adventist Gospel Choir. One of the lead singers of the choir was a girl named Lisa Robinson, whose father was also a television evangelist and minister of a church. Chaka fell in love with her voice and asked her if she would join the tour immediately, as in, within 24 hours. Against her father's wishes but with her mother's blessings, Lisa joined the tour. This would be the Chaka Khan touring unit for the next three months, and the beginning of longstanding friendships and work relationships that would last forever. We were a family.

[Chaka and me in the '90s]

I learned a lot from Chaka. One of many things that Chaka taught me was her work ethic. She believed that "the show must go on," or, as she would say, "you got to kick it out yo ass." It never mattered how exhausted or vocally tired she was, Chaka would always get up on stage and take chances. She never held back. Her ability to know when to push the envelope with her voice given her circumstances, whether it be illness or just plain sleep deprivation, was phenomenal. She knew her parameters. She never made singing only high notes her apex. She was just as committed to her lower register. Although she was not college trained, her expansive musical vocabulary was unmatched. Our use of softness and sweetness, coupled with full-on mix singing, was what we eventually had in common as I learned how to build my "mix."

A mix is a full vocal sound comprised of a balance between a head/falsetto or high voice and chest/mid-range voice. I learned to respect and accept my own sense of vocal identity through working with her. Because of my classical training, my mix – or mid-range of my voice – was never fully developed. It was during my first tour with Chaka where I developed my mix to match her sound on stage. It took two weeks of doing shows, being hoarse, creating makeshift steam rooms in my hotel bathroom, and drinking lots of hot tea with honey and lemon, and sometimes rum or cognac, before my voice would finally acclimate. I do not recommend using the alcohol, by the way. It can dry out your voice and drinking alcohol in hot outdoor venues can make you sick, sometimes faint. My approach to singing this full mix was from a classically trained perspective, as I came from possessing a fully developed head voice to focusing my sound toward the chest, which I believe saved my voice. No vocal damage ever occurred.

After doing the first show with Chaka, my voice was completely hoarse. There was a show the next night, and needless to say, I was nervous and concerned that my voice would not reciprocate. After breathing in steam, being quiet throughout the day, and drinking hot beverages, I had to vocalize to see what my voice could do before the show. Focusing my voice from the head/falsetto region toward the chest voice range and finding that exact balance between the two was the only way I knew how to match Chaka's timbre or tone. Trusting my ear to match her and working to push only when necessary, I was able to get enough vocal sound through to finish the show. Luckily, Chaka never did more than three shows in a row, so there was time for me to rest my voice for more than 24 hours.

It was Chaka who taught me that the voice is a muscle and that you have to exercise it and acclimate it to what you are doing regularly. She assured me that in time, my voice would get used to its schedule and soon it would strengthen to meet the demands of the tour. She was right. After two weeks, my voice found its stride and was there in full force, never failing me. The repetition of singing in that mid-range built up my mix and it has been there for me ever since. I thank Chaka Khan immensely for that.

In those days, Chaka hated being alone. The road can be a very lonely place before and after a show. Many times, the three of us singers would go to her hotel room and spend the night, crowding up in her seemingly huge, double king-sized bed, with our PJs on, to watch scary movies. At this point, the backing vocal trio included singer Penny Ford, who would eventually go on to sing lead for the iconic dance music group Snap.

I can recall arriving at a five-star hotel in Madrid, Spain, after a long ride on the tour bus late one night, exhausted and hungry. It was the wee hours of the morning and everything was closed except for the neighborhood dive bar. We talked the staff into letting us into the hotel kitchen to raid their refrigerator to scavenge up goodies to eat. Just imagine us in the kitchen refrigerator of this fabulous hotel, making sandwiches with whatever we could get our hands on, cheese, cold cuts, veggies. We treated every five-star hotel as if it were our real home. It's amazing what people allow celebrities to get away with. So much fun.

On another tour in Japan, five weeks into a six-week tour, everyone was longing for some non-Asian, home-cooked food. So, we all went to a store and Chaka bought a camping burner, food, and other cooking accoutrements. She returned to the hotel and cooked in her hotel room for the entire band. She really is a good cook! My fave was her thinly sliced fried garlic chips. Delicious.

Once, we were all in Germany for what would have been Thanksgiving in the U.S. We had a Hungarian stage crew who traveled with us throughout Europe. The road manager, a black guy named Cecil, taught the crew's chef how to make fried chicken. We had fried chicken every night after the show for the entire tour. For Thanksgiving, Chaka had them make a huge turkey dinner. For some reason, there was no knife to cut the turkey at dinner. So, Chaka took her hands and just literally pulled and tore off bits of turkey, slamming them down on everyone's plate like a cave woman. It was hilarious. It was true family shenanigans. While this may seem trivial and silly to some, it was a large part of our dynamic as a working family unit. It was all in fun and we loved each other and laughed at and with each other often. Happy Thanksgiving, everyone.

Once, we girls had been in a conversation about men and missing boyfriends. This conversation evolved into talk about sex toys. For fun, we decided to each buy a vibrator, which was quite easy to come by in the drug stores in Europe as it was actually a hand-held massager. That night after the show, we all went to our hotel rooms. Then, suddenly, the power went out in the entire hotel. The next morning, as we got onto the tour bus with heads down, finally someone broke the silence with a comment about the power outage. We realized that each of us believed that we were responsible for killing the electricity in the entire hotel, since we all had been using our toys simultaneously. We laughed about that one for days on end.

One New Year's Eve in Los Angeles, Chaka was slated to sing at a hotel, except the promoter had run away with the money, neglecting to pay anyone, as was agreed upon before the show. It was two hours after midnight on New Year's Eve before Chaka finally went out on stage and explained what was happening to the raucous crowd, then we gave the show of a lifetime. The people went nuts and the band had her back. She paid us out of her pocket for that one. It was a stressful night that ended up being one of the best performances ever.

After those three months on the road with Chaka Khan, I worked pretty consistently for the most part. Still, it wasn't easy. The first priority upon returning to Los Angeles from a tour, was making phone calls to everyone in town, including singers, instrumentalists/musicians, and producers, letting them know that I was back and ready to work. Sometimes, this would be a point of contention, as the singers who stayed in town and already had their working, established vocal sections did not always want to disturb the "groove" by changing it up with other singers, even if they knew and had previously worked with them. Sometimes, it would take months before work calls would start to come in regularly. Whenever I would inquire about work, the answer would often be, "I didn't call you for work because I thought you were still on the road." It was frustrating, but this was the politics of the day.

Some session singers even resented the singers who would come in and do both sessions and tours. Informally, it would be suggested that you should choose. Either be available and on-call for sessions, or just be on the road. Loving both sessions and tours and wanting to maintain my status with the unions for my health insurance, I didn't want to choose, nor could I afford to do so. Quietly and conscientiously, I maintained as many relationships as possible to keep my name in the hat for both. Many times, I succeeded. Sometimes, I did not. Most times, I never worried about it, always believing there was enough work for everyone. Whatever projects that were meant for me, were received. Just maintain the flow, like poetry in motion.

STRIVE – THRIVE – TRANSCEND
CHAPTER FOUR

B eing the over-achiever type, I strove to be the best at every-thing. Even as a child attending Catholic School, at one time I wanted to be a nun, which to me meant I would be perfect. For me, transcending my circumstances was the obvious goal. My life was already filled with striving. From striving for acceptance to striving to sing the music of my choice, to striving to get consistent work in the music industry. I was ready to thrive, to exhale. Transcending was a final step, a future prospect blowing in the wind, and I welcomed the challenge. Thriving, however, was within my reach, as I could feel the day was soon upon me. I would arrive at the "thriving station" by following my heart, as it has always kept me aligned with my purpose on this planet, which I recognized as simply singing, and brought me into the music business at a successful level.

My life was proving to be more challenging than I could ever imagine. Of all the things that I had lived through while poet-ically moving through this musician's life, this time there was nothing poetic about it. I was living in my car. I would recognize this while driving around Santa Monica and Venice Beach, see-ing hundreds of people sleeping on sidewalks, storefront door-ways, and parks, this time with the knowledge of what it felt like to be displaced with nowhere to go. "Displaced" was a huge word for me and an all too familiar state of being.

When I really thought about it, displacement was what I had always felt most of my life, even as a child in Memphis. I was never homeless. as we lived in the same house, built by my paternal grandparents, for my entire childhood. But, I never felt a connection or belonging to Memphis, always being the one who stood out or was different. Well, I was an artist in a non-artist environment, which was different. To some people, different meant "special," insinuating that being different was "cool." But, in my parents' eyes, "being different" was a flaw. Eventually, I would realize that this attitude was their way of protecting me. By "fitting in" and not calling any attention to myself, created a safety valve, the only means they could see for me to sustain. While they would spend the time and money taking me to private lessons in piano, organ, and voice, they would constantly belittle my choices of what styles of music were important or the clothes I'd want to wear. They would even ridicule my free-spirited behavior. Most often, it was my mother. My father was quiet about these things most of the time. Regardless, this was the household that molded me and where I first honed my skills as a singer.

THE LITTLE PRINCESS

My godparents actually nicknamed me "the little princess" shortly after I was born. I was told that it was because of the way I held my body upright and lifted my legs as a newborn, which was much too early for any baby to be able to do. For some reason, in their eyes, this translated into some kind of royal or unusually mature gesture. Many things seemed to come to me at an early age. I started reading at the age of four, climbing up into my godfather's lap, helping him with the Sunday newspaper crossword puzzle. I even started first grade a year early, at age five.

As for music, the story was told to me by my Godmother that at Christmas time, when I was two years old, I would crawl up and stand in her chair in her living room and stare out of the window at all the Christmas lights decorating the houses in the neighborhood and describe the colors of the lights through singing the carol "O Holy Night."

My version would go:

OH, HOLY NIGHT
I SEE RED LIGHTS AND GREEN LIGHTS
AND BLUE LIGHTS AND ORANGE LIGHTS
IT IS THE NIGHT THAT THE SAVIOR IS BORN.

Thus began my singing career. At the age of four, I sang "The Lord's Prayer" for my kindergarten graduation. At age seven, I sang "O Lord Most Holy" for my second-grade teacher's wedding. She was this sweet, short, white woman with red hair and large calves. She got married at this huge, cathedral-looking Episcopal Church in downtown Memphis. It was there that her organist, Robert Kirkham, met my parents and offered to teach me privately once I reached the age of ten. Later, Mr. Kirkham would start the Pastiche Opera Company, where I became a member beginning at age 11 and continued until high school. In the opera company, my first role was as a chorus member in our performances of Orff's "Carmina Burana" and Bizet's "Carmen," where my stand-out part was singing the high C ("Your price is love") in "The Toreador Song." At age thirteen, I was awarded the leading role in Puccini's "Madame Butterfly."

In the meantime, my performance career included doing recitals at various churches, performing arias, spirituals, and some musical theater pieces. Once, there was an NAACP event in downtown Memphis, honoring prominent civil rights activist Roy Wilkins. I was the featured soloist on the program, singing conservative gospel arrangements of "Precious Lord" and "If I Could Help Somebody." I believe I was around nine years old at the time. At the age of twelve, I competed and won first place in the Mid-South Talent Revue, singing "Summertime" from Gershwin's "Porgy and Bess." That garnered me a picture in *The Commercial Appeal* newspaper. Ernest Withers, famed for his many iconic photos of Martin Luther King, was the photographer, as I was the only African-American or person of color competing.

At this point, the music that resonated from my mouth was all things classical. Not once had I ever really ventured outside of this genre. It was all that I knew. I imagined that it must have been quite a sight to behold, perhaps even an enigma, for people to witness this little black kid singing operatically. There weren't even any white children around as my counterpart. As my rebellious, pre-teen years began, I dropped the opera company and decided to finally venture into other music genres, this time with gospel. I joined other members of the young adult choir at my church who also wanted to sing traditional gospel music, which was quite revolutionary for our conservative, hymns-only church. My mother, along with every other adult church member, responded with a resounding NO. "Singing that gospel music sets us black folk back two hundred years!" they said.

Boldly, the young adult choir at Metropolitan Baptist Church sang a gospel song one Sunday morning, which included rocking side to side and clapping. I was the featured soloist. I believe the title of this song was "If You Just Hold Out." There was an uncomfortable silence in the church, as the entire congregation was in shock. That evening, my mother received several phone calls from members of the church, reprimanding her for allowing me to display such radical behavior. That ended my attempt to sing gospel in that church or anywhere else, as I retreated quietly with no argument. I was always told that I did not have the vocal capabilities to sing anything but classical music anyway. While on some level I dismissed this judgement, these kinds of damaging statements became part of a painful, subconscious story about the limits of my talent that would be echoed in college by my voice teacher, Mattiwilda Dobbs, at Howard University regarding jazz. "Why would you want to lower yourself to sing jazz?" she would ask me. The trifecta of Blues/Gospel/Jazz are the foundational components of all contemporary music. As a young person studying the history of these genres in undergraduate school in 1980, I could not understand why some black people were so opposed to these styles of music. As I became an adult, the negative sociological implication made here on campus became apparent as America was in the throes of integration. Many Black people were striving to assimilate into this newly mixed society as quietly and non-confrontationally as possible. Anything too Afrocentric was seen as a threat to white acceptance, according to my parent's generation. I guess it was all part of the indoctrination into this newly integrated society.

The conflict showed up in my clothing choices. My mother would constantly ask, "Why can't you dress like your friends? Look at them." This was her attempt to shame me into changing into something more conservative. It never worked, but the implication that something was "wrong" with me weighed heavily on my psyche. Wearing my hair in braids and cornrows was also looked down upon, as I was told that no one would hire me to work anywhere "looking like that." Again, this fear-based doctrine of not being accepted into white society took precedence.

I was this passive, weird black child who grew up in a conservative, "anthems and hymns only" Black Baptist church, who studied and sang classical music since age ten, and at twelve was a member of an all-white opera company in the late '70s in the Deep South. Some might have considered me a prodigy, though that term was never used to describe me at the time. I'm sure my parents, relatives, and friends meant no harm in how they treated me. However, regardless of the intention, it just didn't feel positive and definitely not nurturing. There is no one to blame here and I take full responsibility for these feelings. It was simply a sign that Memphis would not be my home place and that my dreams and pursuits would be realized elsewhere. Striving to be heard, to just "be," was an understatement for me in that environment.

BACK TO LIFE, BACK TO REALITY - 2015 PRESENT

Now, let's talk about the "Spa."

The Korean spa is a place where people go to rest, relax, sleep, get esthetician treatments, and last of all, a hot shower, sauna, and/or steam. Sometimes, parents bring their kids as an event. This appears to be an aspect of the Korean culture, while most Americans consider going to a spa to be a vacation away from their kids (smile). As an American, I lean toward the latter, as it does get a bit noisy at times. Generally, the spa is a utopia for someone like myself who enjoys solitude, needs a hot shower, a bathroom, and a warm place to sleep. The perfect situation would be to have a spa for parents with kids separate from a spa for singles and couples without kids. That way, everyone's needs would be met.

So, this particular Korean spa works this way. If I go before 4 a.m., I have to leave by 11 a.m. or else pay an overnight fee ($10) in addition to the day fee, which is $20. If I stay after 11 a.m., I pay for the second day fee. If I wait until 4 a.m., I can stay until 4 a.m. the next day for the one-day rate. I elected to park at the 7-Eleven nearby and sleep in my car until the 4 a.m. hour and then check in to stay the entire 24-hour period. My usual schedule was now: sleep, then go into the 7-Eleven for my snacks for the day. That way, I didn't have to purchase meals at the restaurant inside of the spa. As a vegan, my choices are very limited there. The spa has four floors. On the lower floor, which is for women only, no shoes are allowed anywhere and no clothing is allowed in the wet spa/sauna area. A locker is assigned to you upon entering, where you are also given a wristband/waterproof key to store your belongings. The floor above is for men only. I assume the same rules apply there regarding clothing and storage of personal items. The middle floor, "jjimjilbang," is the co-ed floor where everyone wears the shorts and T-shirts that are given upon entrance to the facility. They also provide towels, which are available as needed. Robes and quilts are also offered, so you can just lounge around in the nude on your floor, or in your robe or shorts-and-T-shirt uniform. Also, on the co-ed floor are several types of saunas. There's a cold sauna (like a huge refrigerator), a Himalayan Sea Salt sauna, a clay sauna, a jade sauna, and an igloo-shaped sauna that is incredibly hot. Everything is guaranteed to make you detox and sweat out every impurity. On the top floor, there is a roof patio with sofas and lawn chairs, fire pits, and flat-screen televisions (sound is muted). It is decorated with plants and water displays. This is the perfect place for any human being needing to reboot on this planet these days. It is pure bliss.

No one asks questions, as the environment is generally introspective. Most people come to recharge, some come in a group, some work on their computers, some teens come and detox from a night of drinking, others come as a dating excursion, girlfriend gathering, or mani-pedi party. For me, this was my place to shower, go to the bathroom, brush my teeth, rest, soak, steam, relax, and read. These simple things are taken for granted until one finds themselves without them. As a frequent visitor, I became familiar with the other regulars who frequented the spa. Occasionally acknowledging each other with a nod or smile, sometimes we would sit and talk briefly about our day, nothing too heady.

Every now and then, there would be some women who came in to spend the night who were clearly mentally disturbed. Sometimes they would be asked to leave. A couple of times, single women with a child would come, obviously just needing a place to rest and shower for the night. While this was not a hotel, nor was it to be used as such, there was an unspoken policy that allowed people to check into the spa for 24-hour periods, only to leave, wait a few hours, then check right back in. It was a civilized way of handling an uncivilized situation.

For out-of-town visitors or people with long air travel layovers, this was a great place to unwind. For a homeless person like myself, it was a godsend to have a place to shower, rest, and to be treated with such civility. Armed with my snacks and my iPad, I would lay on the heated jade floor, play Words With Friends, then write in my journal, eventually falling asleep until noon. Sometimes, it was difficult to wake up, as my body and spirit were often tired. Sleeping in my car definitely took its toll on my physical condition, including my voice. Often, I decided to get coffee, which is not a healthy choice, but it really warded off the hunger.

Being naked around all these women of every age group and walk of life became a source of empowerment for me. This experience alone has been priceless as my self-deprecating, negative body image began to melt away and soon acceptance set in. What a huge, welcome shift it was to finally realize that not everything is contingent on being a certain size or shape. We come in all forms and varieties and there is beauty in everyone. Every single body is different, as some have scars from surgeries, implants, mastectomies, and injuries, hairy armpits and vaginas, hair loss, tattoos, piercings, discolorations, and birthmarks. In the end, there is beauty in all of it. The women who walk around trying to cover themselves stick out like sore thumbs, obviously self-conscious, now seemingly silly. Admittedly, I felt my puckers and cellulite crevices were cringe-inspiring. However, after regularly being in this communal environment, I embraced the beauty in my own physical body and its perfect imperfections. It really spoke loudly from the inside out through a stance, or a walk, or strut, as I witnessed women walking around nude, in their own truth. What was the most striking, was how they appeared to "feel" about themselves. You could see it. For me, this was transformative.

For almost a year, I continued coming to the spa pretty regularly, seeing those familiar faces. We continued our dance, rarely striking up any deep conversations, but sometimes acknowledging each other in passing with a nod or a smile. Seeing women with dark, facial bruises, painful circles under their eyes, women with their babies and small children in tow, was a semi-normal occurrence. However, in this spa, everyone was equal. Everyone walked around with the same robe, towels, shorts and top that are given upon entrance. There are no questions asked. We all get to come here in peace, to take care of ourselves. When entering that hot tub and immersing in that water, every woman of every race, culture, religion, age, let out a resounding "ah" as every wrinkle left their faces, every muscle relaxed, as they closed their eyes and exhaled the weight of their lives, released it out into the atmosphere and allowed the remnants of that frenetic energy to vanish into thin air. No one could deny that healing.

This spa is maintained extremely well, as the staff is constantly cleaning due to the high volume of people that steadily flow in and out all the time. The rules are that you must shower in between the steam/dry sauna and the hot/cold/warm tubs, so you are always self-cleaning. Soon, I realized this continuous washing as a metaphor for my life. Then, the idea struck me: What if everyone who needed help re-establishing their lives had a chance to just stop, rest, reboot, take care of themselves, then be given some tools to help re-acclimate themselves back into society, within a reasonable timeline? From that moment on, I decided to utilize my time at the spa to write a proposal that would encompass these ideas, with the spa being the central healing component.

Sitting at the round table in the women's area, I finally struck up a conversation with a couple of women who frequented the spa. One of them was entering a new career, giving up her previous small business. Transition. Yes, we were the same. I didn't go into complete detail, but I did tell her that I sing for a living. It was kind of nice to know that someone else had made a similar choice, to switch careers and start anew at the midstream of life. She admitted to living at the spa. However, I didn't get the chance to reciprocate by telling my story because we were interrupted by another woman, who also visited the spa often. She was a beautiful, elderly woman with a vibrant sparkle in her eyes. Somehow, we got into a conversation about yoga. She was a kundalini enthusiast, anthropologist, and all-around medicine woman. Our conversation was always stimulating, as she truly was a Renaissance woman.

Later that same night, the Americans in the room wanted to watch the Grammy Awards on TV rather than the regularly scheduled Korean soap operas that constantly played on the flat-screen television in the women's area until midnight. As we watched the awards show, one of the women decided to share that she'd also had her own business, which went under. When she asked what I did, I hesitated. Always reticent to tell people that I sing for a living, I went ahead and revealed my vocation, a backing vocalist for Chaka Khan, as we all sat there watching the Grammys. For some reason, it was embarrassing. My concern was that they would wonder why I would be sitting here, possibly living at this spa. It was an odd feeling and an awkward position to be in, as I had personally known, worked with, or had some intimate connection to almost every artist on the show. She didn't really react one way or another. Clearly, my ego was speaking loudly, creating all kinds of stories about a preconceived reaction. This was my insecurity about my position in life right now. My concern about what people would think of me regularly being here in this spa was rooted in pure ego. I was worrying what others thought, worrying once more about the "how." How am I going to get out of this position? Looking at myself in the mirror, I often wondered, "How did I get here? What would my father say?" I remembered that he once stated, "I never thought I would have a child going off, trying to become a star." He was not happy with me then.

It soon became apparent that in order to survive this time in my life, I had to learn not be concerned about what others thought of me. Instead, I had to be clear on who I was and my purpose, and to let go of the "how" (Joseph Campbell).

At the end of the day, taking a long, hard look at my circumstances, I had to admit the truth. Yes, things were challenging, but somehow, through it all, in this homelessness, I was thriving.

This lesson in homelessness, was part of my transcendence.

PAST LIFE: STRIVING - 1988

I mentioned earlier how I would first, envision what kind of apartment would be suitable, then just like magic, it would appear. This is what happened with my second home in Los Angeles, which was in the specific area of Sherman Oaks, California, located in the San Fernando Valley. In 1982, while looking at apartments in New York City on the Upper West Side, I came across this lovely one-bedroom apartment with a fireplace and a spiral staircase that led up to the loft-style bedroom. It was $1,300 a month, which was quite pricey at the time. There was no way I could afford such a place, but from that moment on, the beauty of the layout of that place stayed in my mind.

Fast forward to 1987. As a working musician in L.A., I decided that my next apartment had to have a spiral staircase, a fireplace, and be under $1,000 a month. Many of my friends lived in the San Fernando Valley, commonly known as "The Valley." So, I decided to look around at places in the Sherman Oaks area, south of Ventura Boulevard, at the bottom of the mountain that leads you back into Los Angeles. There was a "For Rent" sign out front of this lovely, modern-looking building. On a whim, I decided to stop in, with no appointment made, and investigate. There was a management office on the premises at this time, which answered after I buzzed the intercom. "I am responding to your sign out front. Do you have any one-bedroom apartments available?" I inquired. "Yes, there is a one-bedroom plus loft available on the third floor," said a soft-spoken gentleman. Loft? Really? Inside my body, I was screaming with anticipation. In a calm, unassuming voice, I asked, "Is it possible to see it now?" He replied, "Of course. This building is relatively new, and there aren't many tenants right now. The apartment is empty. Just let me buzz you in and I'll get the keys." I entered the building to a small but well-appointed lobby, all decorated with oversized vases, plants, and mirrored walls. I was in love with the feel of the entire place. Everything was pristine and brand new. The manager was a pleasant man with a lovely smile. With keys in hand, he extended his arm, directing me towards the elevator. We went up to the third floor, then took the short walk to apartment number 304. When he opened the door to the apartment, there it was: The spiral staircase that led to a loft area that was large enough for a queen-sized bed and furniture, right in front of me. The apartment also had a separate bedroom, which was a bonus as far as I was concerned. There, in the corner of the living room, was a gas fireplace. OK, I should have specifically asked for a wood-burning fireplace, but hey, this is Los Angeles. I guess wood-burning fireplaces aren't as popular on the West Coast.

Now, for the clincher. I asked, "So how much is this apartment?" His answer stunned me to my core: "It's $995 a month." Before he could blink an eye, I quickly responded, "I'll take it!" For the next year, I was living my dream, in my dreamy apartment.

After touring for three months with Chaka Khan, I came back to L.A. to face the usual lull in work calls. However, this particular lull felt as if it lasted forever as it took its toll on my finances. I was almost three months behind in my car payments, which meant that car repossession was imminent. My rent was late, with no work in sight. I was constantly staring at the phone, praying for it to ring. Finally, I got a call from Paula, a high school friend who was living in Queens, N.Y., at the time.

I explained to Paula that Chaka had no more gigs lined up and that sessions were sketchy, as I had been constantly calling people to let them know of my return and was waiting by the phone for an answer on some work. At this point, I had a little over $350, which would pay one month of my car note, but then left no money for food or gas. Listening to my dilemma, Paula suggested what I thought at the time was an unusual thing. She suggested that I take my cash and get a plane ticket to New York City and stay with her and her husband for a while. She said that I needed a "change of scenery," a break away from the tyranny of the phone (this was 1988, before cellphones were popular, by the way, so leaving home was a true break away from the phone). Regardless of how unusual the suggestion, this offer sounded heavenly to me. I was mentally and emotionally exhausted from constantly waiting for the phone to ring with offers of work and focusing on how to maintain income in between tours, and it had started to get the best of me. I booked my flight immediately and was off to the Big Apple.

When I arrived at her home in Queens, Paula gave me $40, saying this was some "spending change" to get around Manhattan. Happily, accepting my "spending change," I made calls to a few friends that lived in N.Y.C., and made plans to do some visiting. Then, the magic happened with no solicitation.

One of my friends asked if I was available to do a recording session while I was there. Of course! It never occurred to me to seek work while I was there. The session was to do backing vocals for jazz guitarist/singer Jonathan Butler. This made my trip even more worthwhile. The very thing that I was seeking in LA, found me in New York City. Work.

After about a week and a half, I returned to Los Angeles, a little more relaxed, knowing that a paycheck was coming within thirty days, the allotted time that recording sessions paid union singers, from the Jonathan Butler session. Still basking in the afterglow of the sequence of events that took me from stress and worry about finances in LA, to "taking chances" by going to New York, then getting work, I decided not to worry anymore about what would happen next. It was at this time that I received the phone call that would change the trajectory of my career.

ELTON JOHN

Finally, a few weeks after my return to Los Angeles, a few more sessions started to trickle in. I received a call to do a demo for songwriter, Jeff Klaven, who was the former drummer the '80s heavy metal group Krokus. Demo sessions for songwriters paid immediately most times, and ranged from $100 to $600, depending on how many tracks you sang – or really, how well you negotiated your status. My fee was around $500 for this project. It was on this session that I realized my potential as a rock singer. This was a dream of mine since high school, when my first boyfriend introduced me to Judas Priest, Iron Maiden, and the group that made its most lasting impression on me, Mother's Finest. While I'd always hoped but never quite believed I could really pull off the sound, I was forced to do so on this session. The process in the studio resembled the scene in the Tina Turner bio-pic "What's Love Got To Do With It" where Ike Turner is trying to convince a young Annie Mae Bullock to "sing rougher!" Jeff pushed and pushed my performance away from the blues/ R&B sensibility to a pure rock sound, until my true voice emerged. The song was called "Who's Your Baby," and when it was all done, a rock singer was born. I loved the new sound of my voice and was amazed at the grittiness I was able to achieve after honing such a sweet sound all these years. It felt like home, my calling. From that moment on, with a newfound confidence, my focus became writing, singing, and surrounding myself with all things rock as I continued to define my signature sound, my artistry.

The next call received was to do a session for R&B recording artist Jeffrey Osborne. As a kid in Memphis, I was a huge fan of his work as the lead singer with a group called LTD and became an even bigger fan when he later attained huge success as a solo artist. I hadn't seen him since the Anita Baker debacle and was really looking forward to finally singing with Portia Griffin and Joey Diggs, his main backing vocalists. Twice, auditions were held to replace the third singer in Jeffrey's trio, whose name I cannot recall. However, each time that I auditioned for the gig, the third singer would always return. Finally, this was my opportunity to work with these awesome singers.

The recording studio was at Jeffrey's home. Arriving right on time, I was received like an old friend. We caught up on each other's lives and careers and had some laughs, talking about that fateful night Anita Baker forbade us to see his show. He and his crew had heard that we were fired and thought that it was because of our attendance. "No hard feelings," I explained. "We never really thought it was because of our attendance to your show anyway." Jeffrey then asked me what I wanted to do at this point in my career. This was when I expressed my desire to be a rock singer and that that was my first love. "It would be great to get a gig in that rock realm, to get a feel for that side of the industry," I revealed. We went on to finish the recording, "One Love," the title cut for Jeffrey's new album. It was a really great session with a dynamic group of singers who were as fun to hang out with as they were to work with.

This next sequence of events was told to me later.

Ironically, that very next morning, a gentleman by the name of Bruce Roberts, who wrote Jeffrey's hit "You Should Be Mine" aka "The Whoo Whoo Song," came to Jeffrey's house to present him with another composition. While he was there, Bruce mentioned that his friend Elton John was preparing to go on the road again after a two-year break. Elton was looking for backing vocalists for his tour and was inquiring about singers. Jeffrey suggested my name, emphasizing that at his recording session the night before, I'd mentioned that I was looking for a rock gig.

A month or so later, I received a call from Davey Johnstone, Elton's musical director, asking that I come to his home in the Hollywood Hills to meet with him about possible work with Elton. He asked that I bring a head shot, a cassette tape of my voice/music, and a resume. Not giving much thought to this, I prepared to go. As a singer in this industry, I'd been to numerous auditions and meetings with managers and musical directors, formally and informally. Sometimes they led to work, most times not, but they were definitely a connection to a larger network. Not giving much thought to what I would wear or how it would reflect my personality, I wore a red catsuit with a wide black leather belt, a floor-length black coat and black boots. I simply wore what was comfortable and made me feel like my true self, never trying in any way to impress or entice. Davey Johnstone told me later that what I wore really stuck out in his mind. He said that I looked like a superhero. Whatever I wore, I'm sure it read, "Oh, she's a singer."

Once I arrived, Davey introduced me to his wife and kids,

then we headed to the sitting room, where we had a nice conversation. I can't recall any details other than him asking me some basic questions about my life and my experiences as a singer on the road. He did not play my tape. It was a simple short and sweet conversation. I didn't think much of the interview one way or the other. He walked me to my Nissan 300ZX and I sped off, feeling that he was a nice guy with a nice house and a nice family.

About another month or so later, I received a call from Constant Communications, the Los Angeles Office of Elton John, asking about my availability to do a benefit concert with Elton for his charity Athletes and Entertainers for Kids With AIDS. Rehearsals would be at The Complex rehearsal studios in West Los Angeles. Of course, I agreed to do it. The event took place at the Century Plaza Hotel in Century City, and Charlie Sheen was the host.

Just about everyone in the band was brand new. Jonathan Moffett was on drums, Romeo Williams was on bass, Guy Babylon was on keyboards, and of course, MD Davey Johnstone was on guitar. Fred Mandel, the second keyboard player, was the only band member who had previously worked with Elton John prior to this performance. The singers were Marlena Jeter, Alex Brown, and myself. Rehearsals were easy and thorough. The music for the show, which consisted of cassette tapes of all of Elton's albums, was FedExed overnight. As a group, the three of us got together at Marlena's house and went over all the music before going to rehearsal with the band. Once we got to rehearsal, we were ready for anything. This was called true preparation. This was where the level of musicianship was revealed. Every band member came into that rehearsal just as we did, already prepared in the event Elton may want to change anything musically. You must know the music in order to change or enhance it. We were all ready.

It was a star-studded event, as anyone would expect an Elton

John event to be. I would later learn that he loves a good party and really knows how to put one on. The room was glowing with superstar athletes, entertainers and actors. Everything went off without a hitch musically. The show was amazing – so amazing that we were asked to meet with Elton later that following week for a congratulatory dinner at the Le Dome Restaurant in Beverly Hills.

After dinner, the head of Elton John's London office announced that Elton was preparing to go on the road for a year and that they had prepared contracts for everyone who had performed on this charity event, in the hope that we would consider going on the road as Elton's band. Then it happened. As the gentleman stood at the head of the dinner table making this announcement, his assistants passed out individual contracts, each personally addressed with our name on it. Amazing! We all were given plenty of time to consult legal counsel before signing the contracts, and we all signed on. And just like that, in the blink of an eye, I was on the road with Elton John for the next year – which would eventually turn into six years.

[Me, Elton, Marlena, & Mortonette]

Touring with Elton encompassed all of the things that you would imagine and perhaps had seen on television. It started out with a photo shoot for all publicity, media packages and tour programs. When I look at movies like "Rock Star" with Mark Wahlberg or writer/director Cameron Crowe's "Almost Famous," I smile. So much of what happened in those movies remind me of my tour life with Elton John: the photo shoots, celebrity parties, interactions with fans. Everything that we did, everywhere we went was always done first class, and always with an entourage, which I learned the hard way was important.

It is amazing how many crazy people there are who spend an incredible amount of time and cash to follow music icons around the globe, not always with the best intentions. Of course, there are some awesome fans out there, who reach out to connect with the band and Elton out of pure love and respect for the music. The difficulty is in telling them apart. There have been some fans claiming to be rich heirs who have hosted exclusive rendezvous with the band. I went to one such dinner in N.Y.C. It was lovely but odd. None of the other band members showed up. I was warned by management that it could be a hoax. I figured it would, at the very least, just be dinner with some fans. Whether they were rich or not didn't matter to me. But, admittedly, after arriving there in Greenwich Village at this quaint Italian restaurant, it did feel scary. It was opened exclusively for us. The people there were a bit eccentric, different and kind. Luckily, odd as it was, nothing bad happened. It was just dinner, but the experience warned me of the possibility of things not always happening as expected.

We stayed at the most luxurious hotels all over the world. Every show on the tour was sold out. Concerts in London, New York, and Los Angeles were guaranteed to be star-studded, with celebrities hanging out backstage, watching us perform from the side fills of the stage. Sometimes, they would come up and join us for a song or two. Whoopi Goldberg came up and sang "Jumping Jack Flash" at Madison Square Garden in New York, while Brian May from Queen played "Show Must Go On." Others like Sylvester Stallone, George Michael, and Mick Jagger, to name only a few, just came to hang out.

The most fun would happen when there were other rock bands in town performing, because we would always get together for a party. It was awesome meeting other musicians on the road. Everyone was incredibly talented and happy to be out traveling, touring, and doing what they loved. Quickly, we made friends with singers like John James and Jenny Douglas; Dollette MacDonald, who was out with the Eagles' Don Henley; and many others. Money was no object, as we could ask for just about anything and it would be granted. Once, we were in Denver, staying at the same hotel as George Michael's band. We asked if we could have a joint party after our shows. The road managers got together and booked the top floor of the hotel just for us. This included an open bar. It was awesome.

My colleagues Mortonette Jenkins, who joined Elton's band in 1989, and Marlena Jeter both had boyfriends who came out to visit them while on the road. These occurrences frequently left me to my own devices, so I spent a lot of time alone. Several times, Elton, his road manager and the crew would come into a restaurant near our hotel and I'd be there dining alone. Sometimes, he'd invite me over to join them. Every time, he'd pick up my tab. Many times, I was asked to come hang out and go clubbing. I recall once we were in London. Elton, his valet Teamer Washington, and other friends were going to a place called Brown's and asked me to tag along. Sure, I agreed. I was the only girl in the group (wink wink). Elton was the designated driver in his Bentley. We piled in as though the Bentley was a clown car at the circus. It was hilarious. Everyone was sitting everywhere, on top of everyone. It felt like high school and I loved it. We arrived and as we walked through the club, I overheard someone whisper, "Is that Grace Jones?", referring to me. Ha! What a laugh we all had. What fun. We danced all night.

In Perth, Australia, I ran into the French tennis star Yannick Noah at a restaurant. Being a huge tennis fan, I walked over to his table and invited him to our show. When I returned to the hotel and mentioned to Elton, another huge tennis fan, that I had seen Yannick Noah, he said, "Invite the whole team!" So, I contacted Mr. Noah and invited the entire French tennis team to the concert. Everyone agreed that they were a beautiful bunch of guys.

Of course, as with any tour, some kind of drama or strange occurrence inevitably took place. Once in Melbourne, Australia, we were playing the Tennis Center, which is an outdoor venue. When we hit the stage to begin our concert that night, the bright stage lights attracted swarms of locusts, which began to land on our bodies as we started the show. It was straight out of a Hitchcockian horror movie. There were thousands of locusts everywhere. We were told later that there was a locust infestation that particular year. When those things landed on my body, it felt like a slap, for they were quite heavy to be insects. After the third song, Elton opened his mouth to sing and a locust flew right into his mouth. That was it! Concert over. He left the stage and gladly, we left right behind him. It was the headlines of the newspaper the next day, "Elton John Concert Halted, Due to Locust Epidemic," or something like that. They had to spray the Center to get rid of the locusts. What a nightmare! The following night, though, we were able to return and perform the show in its entirety.

Some occurrences were much more personal. Several people have asked me, "What happens if you get sick on tour?" Generally, the artist pays for any issues that happen to a band member or singer when on the road. There is insurance for these matters, taken out by the artist for tours. Getting hoarse or developing a sore throat can happen, not to mention colds, allergies, and stomach ailments. Getting treatment entails contacting the hotel's front desk and asking for a doctor, who comes to your hotel room with the black bag and stethoscope, just as it's portrayed on television. The doctor's fees are charged to the road manager's room or billed directly to the road manager, as he is the authority and banker on the road. All prescriptions are brought to your room, paid for by the tour. Rarely does one ever leave the hotel for a doctor's visit.

Once, in Hong Kong, I sprained my ankle on the tennis court and showed up at the gig that night on crutches. "What the fuck happened to you?" was Elton's response when he saw me at the show that night. I explained how running for a volley and stepping on a sea of tennis balls initiated the sprain. He made a joke about it, and that was it. Two members of the crew had to carry me on and off the stage that night. The three of us did the entire show on barstools. I believe Marlena and Mortonette were happy about that, though, as our feet sighed relief.

Another particular occurrence began in Germany, where I contracted tonsillitis. Before leaving the country, the illness had moved into my left eye and was diagnosed as conjunctivitis. I was treated accordingly. However, my eye was not improving. By the time we arrived in Switzerland, it had gotten worse and my eyes became ultra-sensitive to all light, including traffic lights at night. I wore sunglasses on stage, as even those stage lights caused excruciating pain. The other two singers wore sunglasses also to maintain a more uniform look. I woke up in Lausanne, Switzerland, the next day, with the worst headache and a black spot in the middle of my vision. I called Mortonette to come to my room immediately, as she was an authority on health and had supreme intuitive power. She came in and started assessing me, saying it appeared that my optic nerve was in trouble.

Immediately, she started to massage the pressure points in my toes and hands that would alleviate this pressure on my optic nerve, then she attempted to contact the road manager. He was not answering his phone, so she called Doug, our assistant road manager, who then took me to the Eye Hospital in Lausanne.

All that I can remember is that I needed a shot of steroids directly into my eye to stop the swelling. While that sounds crazy painful, it didn't matter. My head was throbbing so much, a shot couldn't be any worse. They administered the shot directly into my eye. Mortonette and Doug turned their heads. Certainly, it must have been difficult to watch this procedure. It only felt like pressure, to me, not pain, as the doctor stuck in the needle. My eye turned a dark red, almost black as if there was only a bottomless hole there. It looked pretty scary. Then, they dilated my eye. I was to keep my eye dilated until my next doctor's appointment, which was going to have to be in San Sebastián, Spain, the site of our next gig. Every two hours, through the night, I had to wake up and put drops in my eye to maintain the dilation. Doug and Mortonette would call me through the night to ensure that I did not oversleep. The foremost eye doctor in Europe was from Barcelona, so everyone was ecstatic to know that I could possibly get the best care in Spain, suggesting they could fly him into San Sebastián. However, when we arrived, the doctor was out of the country. Evidently, what I had was an ailment called uveitis, not conjunctivitis. This misdiagnosis was why the medicines were not working. In the interim, my illness was getting worse. The uveia – the pigmented part of my eye – was inflamed and threatening to sever my optic nerve, which would cause permanent blindness.

Unbeknownst to me at the time, though I was told later, the band held a meeting to decide my fate. Drummer Jonathan Moffett had explained to the band that his wife had the same illness and that it did leave her partially blind in one eye. It was decided to take me off the road and place me in the care of doctors in London. My eye was still to be consistently dilated, so my vision was sparse. I was flown to London and placed in the Mayfair Hotel, with a personal driver. Every day, my limo picked me up and took me to this doctor's office in London. Every evening, someone from Elton's office scooped me up from my hotel and took me out to dinner. I do not remember the doctor's name, nor do I know if I ever knew his name. He was an elderly, serious man who tended to my eye and that was it. No small talk. On huge doses of steroids, this time by mouth, I explained to the doctor that I could still sing and wanted to immediately return to my gig. He said it was not possible to leave until he was certain my eye was stable. It was about a week, near the end of my stay in London, before the doctor finally admitted that my vision had been in peril and the situation had been quite serious. Evidently, it was his practice to never tell a patient anything negative until he confirmed all facts. I never knew the seriousness of my illness until they were convinced I would fully recover. I appreciated that.

My first gig back was a video recording done in Verona, Italy, in 1989. If you looked closely, you could see that my eye was still a deep, dark red. Later, I would hear that that particular strain of tonsillitis hit several members of Elton's crew as well. One member had to have an emergency tonsillectomy, and another had issues with the tonsillitis moving into his nasal cavities, requiring an emergency hospital visit. Everyone survived, but at this point it seemed we all looked forward to the end of this strenuous tour.

It was nearing the Christmas holiday and Elton, being the generous one, always mailed us awesome gifts and personally signed Christmas cards. Regardless of where I was, my gift was sent to me. Most times, Christmas was spent in Memphis. For a couple of Christmases, I received this huge woven wooden basket from Whole Foods with all kinds of gourmet goodies. Once January arrived, it was time to hit the road again, usually to Australia and New Zealand. Overall, for almost six years, we would do the U.S. tour in the fall, the Australian tour in winter, and the European tour in the spring and summer. Then, it would start over again, the same schedule, year after year. These were busy times. These were thriving times. I could actually allot time for personal vacations, flying to the south of France once for a week-long stay in Nice, driving up and down the coast from Monaco to San Tropez. Another vacation was driving up the California coast to Pebble Beach, then on to Napa to visit wineries and hang out with friends in San Francisco. My most fun vacation was driving to Santa Fe, New Mexico, renting a chalet at Rancho Encantada, buying all the accoutrements to take skiing lessons on the Santa Fe Basin, and going horseback riding up in the mountains in all of that snow. It was beautiful. I went on all of these vacations alone, which would get lonely, but still, I enjoyed every minute. Finally, I was thriving.

PURPOSE

CHAPTER FIVE

spent many days and nights in my den as a child, jumping off the arm of the sofa, landing my choreographed pose, singing and dancing for my imagined audience, then doing my interview with Johnny Carson or Sammy Davis Jr., who had variety shows on television at the time. Enamored and in awe of the fact that Mr. Davis could sing, dance, and act, it became my goal to also become a "triple threat." I had already studied music and dance since the age of six, done musical theater, had opera company experience in my preteens and teenage years, and had been a member of the Thespian League, winning first place trophies in acting at the city and state tournaments throughout high school. However, receiving a scholarship to Howard University in vocal music was the determining factor that singularly aligned my pursuits to music. From that point on, acting and dance took a back seat. Even though I did study acting and dance at Howard U., my main focus was perfecting the gift that stood out the most, my voice.

HOWARD UNIVERSITY

At the beginning of my first semester, there was an opportunity to work in Las Vegas with Kirk Stewart, a Howard University professor and former jazz pianist for Billy Holiday, Sarah Vaughan, and Della Reese. I didn't go. I was so enamored with being away from Memphis and being a part of Howard University's campus life, I couldn't imagine postponing even one semester.

My time spent at Howard was mixed, as I felt caught between two worlds. First, my vocal training was strictly classical, which was fine as I was accustomed to this. However, the desire to master other styles of music was strong, but so was my lack of confidence when it came to singing them. At the time, the department of music at Howard was very conservatory in their approach, as it was heavily classical, though they also had a Jazz Studies degree, which catered to instrumentalists only. There was no jazz vocal teacher in the department at the time.

Howard University was a Mecca of Black excellence, attracting world-renowned black artists who would visit and perform or speak there regularly. It would not be unusual to see people like the Nation of Islam's Minister Louis Farrakhan, singer/pianist Nina Simone, actress Ruby Dee or her actor husband Ossie Davis, and jazz vocal great Betty Carter walking around the main campus, which we affectionately called "the yard."

The first jazz performance that I ever attended was a Betty Carter concert at Howard University's Crampton Auditorium. Some friends of mine were chosen to be her opening act, so I tagged along as their pseudo-wardrobe mistress, just to attend the show. During the concert, I stood in the wings watching their performance. Afterward, Ms. Carter appeared with her assistant, preparing to walk on stage. She was like a lion, fighting to be released from a cage, as she jumped up and down, rolling back her shoulders and flailing her arms as if to loosen up her body, pacing the floor in anticipation, revving up her energy. When they called out her name, she hit the stage like a comet. She was pure energy. She was on fire. Matched with her vocals and scatting prowess, she owned that stage like nothing I'd ever seen before. You could not take your eyes off of her. She was like a shooting star! It was in that moment when I realized, this is what I wanted to do. Own my audience.

Since jazz was the only other genre available to study, I decided to pursue it. Vocally, jazz would also be an easy introduction into something other than classical music, and it was familiar to me since it was the only music played in my house growing up. While there was no jazz vocal teacher to mentor me, I decided to take the instrumentalist approach, learning to scat by ear, listening and replicating various instrumental solos. I went ahead to pursue and receive a minor in Jazz Studies, which meant studying Jazz History, Jazz Piano, and Improvisation. However, my Jazz Piano professor, John Malichi, former pianist for Sarah Vaughan, would have me sing for him as he played instead of really teaching me anything on piano during my private lessons. One could say that my jazz vocal study was rather unorthodox. Singing around on campus and in practice rooms, jamming with fellow musicians, somehow garnered me the attention of Mr. Fred Irby, the director of the Howard University Jazz Ensemble. He asked me to sing lead on a HUJE recording titled "Loving You Is Ecstasy," written by my classmate, bassist Carroll Dashiell. It was my first solo recording of any genre. Needless to say, I was excited to do it. Mr. Irby submitted the song to Downbeat Magazine, which garnered me a Best New Jazz Vocalist Award. Howard University's radio station, WHUR, put my song in rotation, and it played all over the D.C., Maryland, and Virginia area. Soon, I was asked to perform around campus, culminating with the HU Jazz Ensemble opening up for Dizzy Gillespie at Fort DuPont Park in Washington, D.C. However, I never boasted about this achievement, as my vocal teacher, a former Metropolitan Opera star, Mattiwilda Dobbs, was not amused. My work with the ensemble did not affect my classical voice lessons, so it never affected my grades, but Ms. Mattiwilda Dobbs made it abundantly clear that jazz singing was, in her opinion, "beneath" me.

Still trying to convince me of what she felt was my purpose, Ms. Dobbs invited me to accompany her to a concert by foremost soprano Leontyne Price at the Kennedy Center, which was an incredible opportunity. I was honored to attend, as Leontyne Price was by far the most iconic opera star to ever grace any stage. To accompany my teacher, who was her predecessor from the Met, was a truly historical moment for me. While I still was not convinced that classical music was my true calling, hearing Ms. Price perform was mesmerizing. She received five encores that evening and after the concert, Ms. Dobbs took me backstage to meet her. It was like meeting royalty. Ms. Price was grand, so much larger than life in her persona. There were few words spoken, as our meeting was short, but certainly this experience left an indelible mark, questioning my purpose even more, as I wasn't certain I could "own my audience" or even possess the voice to be an opera or jazz star. To be like Leontyne Price seemed an unreachable goal. I thanked my teacher, then went about my way.

I continued to be the good student, joining sororities and music fraternities for women, and really trying to blend into college society. Yet, I still felt the stigma of being different, which was the residual effect of an upbringing that prevented me from really enjoying any kind of success. I just closed my eyes and sang at every opportunity, ignoring the responses.

As graduation was fast approaching, the assistant Dean of Fine Arts asked if I would be interested in attending a summer music festival camp in Lenox, Massachusetts, called Tanglewood.

It was a prestigious classical music program, taught by world-class classical musicians and teachers. Phyllis Curtain, a professor at Yale University, was the voice clinician-in-residence and I would be under her tutelage. But, it was expensive to attend, and the thought of continuing more classical education was a turn-off at this point. Immediately, I turned down the Assistant Dean's offer to apply. He nevertheless continued to needle me about it, saying how beneficial it would be, etc., then he counter-offered with a scholarship, which meant it would be completely free for me to attend Tanglewood. Knowing this was something special and that he had used his connections to get me the opportunity, I reluctantly accepted his offer.

TANGLEWOOD MUSIC FESTIVAL

Attending the Tanglewood Festival Summer Program, was by far one of the most rewarding experiences I'd ever had. It was my first experience rooming with a person of another ethnicity, as my roommate was a white girl from Atlanta. She had never had an interaction with a black person before. We were each other's first experience, and it was a good one. She was an instrumentalist, so I only saw her at bedtime. There was an honor system at the camp, so there were no locks on the doors anywhere. It worked, as there was not one incident the entire summer. The rooms resembled college dormitories, sparsely furnished with two twin beds, desks, and chairs. Our daily class schedule resembled a vocal workshop, led by Phyllis Curtain. Each student came prepared with several arias to perform in the event you were called upon. Ms. Curtain would randomly call a singer to come forward to sing. Afterward, she would offer critique and suggestions on how to improve one's performance through her vocal performance techniques, which proved invaluable. Among the students who were members of my class were fellow

Howard University classmate Glenn Nixon, Korliss Uecker from
South Dakota, Rebecca Gumbel (niece of TV journalist Bryant
Gumbel), and Marquita Lister, a student from Boston University
whom I felt was the second coming of Leontyne Price. Her voice
was phenomenal. I often wondered how Phyllis Curtain could
possibly make Marquita sound any more perfect, but she did.
Her vocal techniques were invaluable.

In the vocal program, I was one of four African-Americans
chosen in a program of maybe 15 students. For the first time, I
got an opportunity to hear others in my age group sing classical
music. For the first time, I could hear what my teacher heard
in my voice. Perhaps, I did possess the skills to really sing this
music. I had always been told I did, but never really took the
comments seriously. Phyllis Curtain was an awesome teacher,
and her vocal analogies relating to technique were easy to comprehend. I incorporated a lot of her ideas into my own teaching
vocabulary.

Tanglewood, which was in the Berkshire mountains
of Massachusetts, was also the summer home of the Boston
Symphony Orchestra and its celebrated conductor, Seiji Ozawa,
which meant that they rehearsed there. That summer, the composer in-residence was renowned composer Luciano Berio
from Italy. Composition students came from all over the world
to study with him. Luca Francesconi, one of the composition
students from Milano, Italy, was one of my new friends made at
Tanglewood. One evening, he invited me to a dinner for the composition students at Seiji Ozawa's Tanglewood Residence. The
special guest was Luciano Berio. When I look back at these days,
it is amazing that I had that kind of access to these awesome
international icons. My memory of that night, was of Mr. Ozawa
making pasta with a crazy amount of garlic and Mr. Berio, with
his thick Italian accent, just laughing hysterically. There was
so much garlic in that pasta, my mouth literally burned. It was

a great night filled with red wine, garlicky pasta, and lots of laughs.

At the end of the Tanglewood summer program, Luca and the other composers in the program decided to make a trip to New York City, since this was their first visit to the United States. New York City? I jumped at the opportunity to tag along, having never been there myself. They all graciously allowed me to join them. So, there we were, in two rented cars, both packed with all of my stuff from my dormitory. It was crowded, and it was fun.

NEW YORK CITY - FALL 1982

New York City in the 1980s was no joke. It was the height of the crack cocaine epidemic in the U.S., and most major American cities were in economic turmoil. New York felt the brunt of both of these events, as the city was out of money to maintain its infrastructure and drugs were making most neighborhoods dangerous to dwell in. However, there I was, hanging out with a crew of Italians, sleeping on the floor of their friend's apartment on Riverside Drive on the Upper West Side.

After one week, they prepared to return to Italy and I had nowhere to go. Making that phone call to Memphis, I told my parents that I was in N.Y.C. and wanted to remain. They were livid, demanding that I return home, saying, "We will buy you a plane ticket to Memphis and that's it. We will not send you money to remain in New York." Determined to be independent, and hellbent on pursuing my purpose, which was singing in some form, I refused to return to Memphis. My parents found a woman who was related to their neighbor who lived in the house diagonally across the street from them. This woman lived in an apartment in the heart of Harlem on 122nd Street at Lenox Avenue. She agreed to allow me to live with her in her one-bedroom apartment where I would sleep on the sofa in the living room. That became my first residence in New York City.

Now, this woman I lived with in Harlem, whose name I can't recall today, never allowed me to have a key to her home. I was only able to leave and return to the apartment whenever she did, which was around 7:30 or 8 in the morning and returning around 6 or 7 at night. My life under these conditions didn't last longer than a month or so, because of one particular incident.

It all started one evening, after I'd been out all day looking for work. I returned at the agreed upon time, but when I knocked on the door, she did not answer. I sat out on the stoop, awaiting her arrival. While waiting, the neighborhood thugs walked past me several times, eyeing me as they passed by. I was dressed in knee socks, penny loafers and a skirt, sticking out like a preppy sore thumb. They knew I did not belong there. Agitated with the woman's seeming disappearance and nervous for my safety, I knocked on the door for the fourth or fifth time. Suddenly a gentleman I'd never seen before answered the door and walked right past me without speaking. I continued into the house, into the living room. There she was, coming out of the bedroom. With a slight smirk on her face, she made a statement under her breath alluding to the fact that she'd had "company." It was obvious that she was inside the apartment with her "company" the entire time, leaving me outside on the stoop.

That was it. Grabbing my purse, I sat on the sofa and scrambled around for my address book. Finally, I found it and scanned through each page, looking for someone to call to help me find another place to live in the city. I came across an old phone number of a guy that I had met while at Howard University, whose name was Billy Toles. He was a Howard alum who had taught a clinic on the record industry, as he worked in sales and marketing for Capitol Records in Manhattan. At the end of the clinic, he offered further mentorship in the music industry, should any of us ever choose to come to New York, and gave everyone his phone number, saying, "call me any time." This was my only option. I hoped he would have a solution to my living situation, as he was the only person that I knew in New York City.

The next morning, after the woman left the apartment, as usual, I left at the same time. Once she was out of sight, having continued down the street towards the D train subway entrance, I walked to the corner to the nearest phone booth, which was located on Lenox Avenue and 122nd Street, right in front of a funeral home. Just as I opened the collapsible doors of the phone booth, a hearse pulled up in front of me. As I called Billy, the attendants got out of the hearse, went around the back of the vehicle and opened the doors, pulling out a stretcher with what appeared to be a dead body. There was a tag on the toe that was sticking out from under the blanket that completely covered the remainder of the frame. This was a sign. That visual of death represented the reality of my surroundings, which were killing me. It was time to leave.

Billy answered and I began my speech, reminding him of how we met, and explaining that I was out on the streets of New York at 122nd and Lenox with nowhere to go. Within ten minutes, he came right over in his car, picked me up, and brought me back to his house at 128th Street and St. Nicholas Terrace. He gave me keys to his home immediately and said that I could live with him. It was a lucky gift, as he was a good guy, very upstanding and trustworthy with no agenda. Finally, I had a home, a real home in N.Y.C. I continued to live in his apartment in Harlem for about six months. Things were looking up. My subway stop was on Harlem's well-known 125th Street, near the world-famous Apollo Theater, though I would walk down to the 127th Street entrance, closest to my home. It was an express stop, so I could get to midtown at Columbus Circle and 59th Street in less than five minutes, which was great. Otherwise, the neighborhood was hell, as there was a constant layer of broken glass for the length of the block along 127th Street, all broken drug vials from crack cocaine use, which crunched loudly under my feet as I walked up the hill to my new home. And while there was a bodega (small grocery store) in the middle of the block on the north side of the street, it was scarcely stocked with groceries.

One day, I decided to go into the bodega to buy a few groceries, which would be all that I could afford to live off of since I never asked Billy for food unless he offered, which was rare. My grocery list consisted of a small 99-cent brick of cream cheese, a small package of crackers, and a bag of Jolly Time popcorn kernels to make homemade popcorn. I walked into the small store and noticed that there was hardly anything on the shelves. I inquired about my items one at a time. "Do you have any cream cheese?" The guy behind the counter looked at me oddly and angrily. He answered, "We don't have no cream cheese!" I thought that was odd. Then, I asked again, "Well, do you have any crackers?" Again, he answered, this time a little more agitatedly, moving his face a little closer toward me, "We don't have no crackers!" Hmmm, OK, now it all slowly started to sink in. This was not really a bodega or grocery store. This was a front of some kind, probably to sell drugs. With my heart in my throat, I tried to hide any reaction, and quietly turned and walked out of the store, never to return. Luckily, they didn't follow me, nor did they ever bother me, as I had to walk past that bodega every day to get home and to the subway. Walking in any other direction like, say, through the park across the street from my apartment building, was not an option as everyone in the neighborhood knew that it was too dangerous and that you ran the risk of getting mugged, raped, or robbed. The entire area was a depressing sight, as the homeless would gather around garbage cans and set fires in them to keep warm over on St. Nicholas Avenue. There was one neighborhood dude who greeted me each morning as I walked to the subway station, while peeing over the side of his porch into his front yard. It was rough and scary, but I was here in New York City pursuing my dream.

Having had zero experience in looking for a real job, I re-enacted what I saw on television, by getting up each morning, dressing up in my dress, stockings, and heels as if going to work, getting on the subway to midtown Manhattan, then landing at Chock Full O' Nuts Coffee Shop for a cup of coffee, a muffin, and a New York Times newspaper, sitting at the counter looking at the Want Ads. I decided that looking for a permanent job was best, so my Want Ad search focused solely on permanent job agencies, which meant permanent secretarial work. I would mark my findings of these agencies in the newspaper with a pen, then go to the nearest pay phone to call and make appointments, which I would attend throughout the day. Horrible at typing, I never got a single job. After walking the sidewalks of New York City in high heels, looking as if I were going to work, I walked into Saks Fifth Avenue on Fifth Avenue, and went up to the Human Resources Department. The director was a black woman, who offered me an application. By the end of that same day I had my first real job, selling handbags part time. However, that job didn't last very long, as I could not use the cash register efficiently. One of my customers, specifically a German woman, came in to buy several handbags. I kept mixing up "charge-send" with "charge-keep," forcing me to re-enter the purchase over and over, which completely agitated the customer. They fired me soon after that mishap. Eventually, I found a job in Woodside, Queens, at G. Schirmer Music Publishing House, mailing out orders for music instruction books.

I was still focused on singing. The Blue Note in Greenwich Village was the popular spot to hear jazz at that time. On one particular night, Sarah Vaughan was performing. Having no money to buy a ticket, I stood outside on a cold winter's night, hoping somehow that I'd catch someone's eye, and that they would have pity on me and help me get in. It didn't work, so I "put my tail between my legs" and slowly walked back to the D train station on West Fourth Street and headed back to Harlem.

One day, an old Howard U. friend called me from Los Angeles. It was Wayne Linsey. He called with a singing opportunity, to be the featured singer with jazz trumpet player Tom Browne, who had couple of hit R&B/jazz records including his first hit, "Funkin' For Jamaica." I was familiar with his music and jumped at this opportunity. Wayne put me in touch with Tom's personal manager, Jimmy Boyd, who also managed singer/guitarist George Benson. I telephoned Jimmy Boyd and made an appointment to come to his home, further up in Harlem, to discuss touring with Tom Browne.

When I arrived and walked into Mr. Boyd's house, I was shocked to see roaches crawling up the walls of his apartment. Mr. Boyd directed me to a chair on the other side of the living room. As I walked past the doorway to his kitchen, there was a mouse crawling around on the burners of the stove. His grandkids, two elementary-aged boys, were playing in the living room, totally oblivious to what I deemed a roach infestation. I kept my purse in my lap and sat nervously, looking around my feet, as I could see a roach crawling toward me on the carpet. Jimmy offered me the job as featured singer for Tom Browne on the recommendation of my friend Wayne, so there was no audition. He told me the gig paid $400 per week, which was significantly more than my minimum-wage job at G. Schirmer. I quit my day job and accepted my first professional gig, my first tour.

Around this time, Billy had received a call from one of his Howard University classmates, singer Marva Hicks, inquiring if he knew anyone who could sublet her apartment on the Upper West Side. She was on the road with Lena Horne at the time and would not be returning to New York for almost a year. Meanwhile, the current renter was causing some problems, according to the doorman of her building, and she needed someone to take over right away. The rent for her studio apartment was $398 per month. How incredibly synchronistic, as the rent was almost the amount of my weekly salary. In those days, that amount of rent was incredibly low. Most studio apartments were double that amount, however, Marva had been in that apartment for more than five years and the rent would remain low until she moved out. I quickly agreed to sublet her apartment for the remainder of her tour. It was the first time I had ever lived alone.

The Upper West Side neighborhood was a popular area of Manhattan. My apartment was on West 86th Street between Columbus Avenue and Central Park West. The building had a 24-hour doorman, which made it feel safe. Things couldn't have been better. There was just one hitch: The apartment was incredibly small. I was on the third floor and as soon as you got off the elevator, walked down the hall to the apartment and entered the front door, you were in the kitchen. Behind the door was a cabinet and stove top which consisted of four burners located on top of a small, three-foot-high refrigerator. There was an oven to the right of the refrigerator and zero counter space. The room had a sleeper sofa the size of a love seat and a small television on a table. There was a floor lamp next to the sofa. The sofa let out into a full-sized bed, I believe, but it was almost the entire width of the living room. The bathroom had a full-sized tub, which was great and a rare find in New York City apartments. In fact, the bathroom was almost the size of the living room. There was only one window. Hungry and not really having money for food, I continued my diet of cream cheese and crackers. Luckily, Marva left chamomile tea bags, flour, and sugar, so I splurged and went to the market and bought Nestle's Toll House morsels and made batches of chocolate chip cookies, which I ate for weeks.

I was dating one of the bartenders at Mikell's, a local

nightclub up on West 97th Street. My first night at the apartment, I asked if he would come over and spend the night. We slept for what seemed like forever. I awakened several times to go to the bathroom. The apartment was so dark, you could hardly see your hand in front of you. After the third time, I decided to check the clock. It was an old clock with hands, not a digital one, that said 3:18. I thought, "God, it's only 3 a.m.?" I looked out of the window. It was always the same scene, which was the building next door with a window to someone else's apartment. Their light was always on, in what appeared to be a hallway, displaying an old grandfather clock. This time, I decided to open the window. I stuck my head out, as there was no screen, turned and looked straight up. The sky was blue! It was day time! We got our clothes on and went outside. It was after 3 o'clock in the afternoon. From that day on, I would leave my apartment every day whether I had places to go or not, just to avoid the constant darkness. It was suffocating.

TOM BROWNE

Coincidentally, I had previously sung Tom Browne's "Funkin' For Jamaica" for an event at Howard U in my sophomore year. Never in my wildest dreams did I ever imagine that I'd actually be working with the artist himself. One of my first gigs with Tom was at the Blue Note in Greenwich Village. Yes, the very Blue Note where I had stood outside, hoping to get in to see Sarah Vaughan. He was scheduled to perform there for two nights. The first night's show was awesome. However, on the second night, Tom didn't show up, due to a financial disagreement with his manager. At the last minute, the club brought in trumpeter Woody Shaw with pianist Kurt Lietsy and saxophonist Sonny Fortune. They had me sing a few jazz standards. I had no idea who they were or the caliber of jazz royalty I was working with until later. As a result of my work with Kurt and Sonny, I was also asked to perform on a small gig with jazz icon, Dr. Billy Taylor. These gigs rarely paid any money, but the experience of working with these jazz greats was priceless. However, my immaturity and ignorance forced me to dismiss this opportunity in favor of choosing to hang out with friends at a weekend party somewhere in a rented house in Connecticut. It would be the first and last time I would make such a choice, compromising my work.

Tom Browne also played bigger venues, including the Beacon Theater on the Upper West Side. Most of our tour stops were at clubs and jazz festivals with some theater venues, opening up for jazz greats like Herbie Hancock and Pieces Of A Dream, and sometimes R&B artists the Gap Band, New Edition, and Atlantic Starr, to name a few. Being the only girl in the band lent itself to some special treatment. I never had to share my hotel room, and the guys were like big brothers, or so I imagined, having never had a brother.

Again, just like in the movie "Almost Famous," fans would often want to take us to their homes and offer us free drugs, just to hang out. This happened to me once with a fan after a gig somewhere down South, possibly Tennessee. This fan acted as a chauffeur, driving a mini-van, which in those days looked like a miniature RV. He was a vibrant, heavy-set black dude, really nice, who offered a tour of the city, which included endearing me with free cocaine and weed. I participated in this just for the fun and excitement of the "road experience." The fan was so high on drugs that as I got out of the van, he slammed his thumb in the door of the car, which was completely shut, never realizing it until he tried to walk away.

I definitely took my share of drugs, specifically cocaine and weed. But, for some reason, I was never really a fan of those drugs, especially not cocaine, nor was I an addictive personality. I also hated cigarettes. Luckily, my drug experimentation days were very short-lived. My thing was trysts. Being on the road and returning to the same cities and, many times, to the same venues made it easy to retain relationships with guys with whom I connected with whenever I got in town. It was all in fun, never anything serious, and in that sense I was a true "road dog."

Tom Browne's career was on the downward slope at this point. His wife wanted him to leave the music business, as his touring was becoming inconsistent and she wanted to start a family. Before his life as a recording artist, Tom was a commercial airline pilot. Whenever it was possible, Tom would rent a small plane and fly us to the gigs to maintain his flying hours. Some of the band members were reticent to get on board with him at the helm. But, for some reason, even though the band did not, I trusted that he knew what he was doing. On longer flights, he would have a co-pilot. These were my first experiences flying in a Cessna or a six-seater plane. I thought it was exciting. However, there was one occasion when the flying privately in bad weather, just like another scene from "Almost Famous," became my real-life nightmare.

We were flying from somewhere down South (I believe it was Atlanta), on our way to Cleveland, Ohio. It was a day flight, but the skies were a bit ominous and dark. About an hour into the flight, we hit a rainstorm with high winds, thunder and lightning. The plane bounced around like a plastic bag in the wind and it was frightening. Tom and the co-pilot kept their cool, which helped me to stay calm. The guys were completely silent, like zombies, stiff as boards in their seats, obviously terrified. Tom told the co-pilot, "We need to land somewhere until this storm dies down." They got on the radio, asking for the nearest airfield to land. My recollection is that initially, they did not receive a response. Then, without using his cockpit monitor, Tom visually spotted what appeared to be a runway below. His concern was that it was a military base, which meant that landing there without prior radio communication could incur possible retaliation or weapons drawn as we could be perceived as a threat. Now, the hairs on the back of my neck began to stand up. Then, Tom made the ultimate statement, "We better hurry and make a decision, we are running out of gas." At that point, I joined my brothers in zombie mode, sitting still and quiet with, I'm certain, a blank stare. He radioed in the specifics on our location, then asked permission to land. This time, he got a response and as we prepared to land, I closed my eyes and said my prayers. When I opened them, the wheels of the plane touched the ground, landing safely in all of that rain. An elderly white gentleman came out onto the runway, helped us out of the plane and directed us to the small, one-room terminal. The building was empty, so we sprawled out in the sitting area. It appeared to be a small aircraft terminal for private planes, located in the middle of nowhere, as it looked as if we were in an enchanted forest of greenery. I believe we were somewhere in North Carolina. It was a relatively modern room, sparsely decorated with floor-to-ceiling windows, tufted '60s styled seats, and ottomans. We were there for a few hours, everyone warm and safe. As the storm ended, we got back on the refueled plane and continued our flight to Cleveland, arriving there safely with not a cloud in the sky.

After about a year of touring with Tom Browne, his wife's persistence in pressuring him to leave the music business eventually won him over. Seeing this coming, I had already applied for graduate school at Juilliard in New York City and the Eastman School Of Music in Rochester, N.Y. I was accepted into the Eastman's Master's degree program in Music (Voice). I contacted my former teacher from Howard, Mattiwilda Dobbs, and told her of my acceptance. As a gift, she sent me tickets to see soprano Kathleen Battle sing in the Mozart opera "Cosi Fan Tutte" at The Met in New York City – a gift that, I'm certain, was also meant as an encouraging hint. I attended the performance in my regular preppy attire, as I did not own much other than

the clothes I wore on stage with Tom Browne. My tickets were
near the front of the theater, in the center aisle, among a slew of
fashionably attired white patrons, all dressed in formal evening
wear. Once again, I stuck out like a sore thumb. Even before intermission, my patience waned as I was completely bored out of
my mind. The thought of remaining until the end of this opera
was unimaginable. When intermission finally arrived, I went to
the ladies' room, then continued out the door. I couldn't stomach
the thought of returning, even though I knew my teacher would
be unamused by my attitude. It was then that I realized, I do not
like opera. I love recitals, but opera and musical theater were not
my thing. I called and thanked Ms. Dobbs for the tickets and told
her that I preferred doing recitals to opera. Her response was,
"Well, who do you think would come to see you? That's why you
have to do opera." Oh, my God. That meant I'd have to be an opera star to get a recital gig. That was disheartening. I graciously
acknowledged her response, then said my goodbyes.

I went ahead with my back-up plan and attended Eastman in
1983. My teacher was another former Metropolitan Opera star,
tenor Seth McCoy, whom I had read about in Ebony Magazine
as a child. Mr. McCoy had been a mailman for twenty-two years
before deciding to audition for The Met. The rest is history, as
they say. I was one of about nine African-Americans in the entire
college. This was another enlightening experience, attending a
college that was exceedingly rich in resources for its students. It
was like living at a well-appointed bed and breakfast, as opposed
to going to Howard, which was more like a hotel franchise. Not
bad, just different. The dormitory felt like an old English-style
castle, as it was a stone structure. We went into the commercial
kitchen and made our own breakfast in the morning. Dinner
was served buffet-style and you could go back for seconds, which
was new for me, totally different from the cafeteria-style meals
at Howard University. It was lovely.

The students who were in the vocal music program with me were completely dedicated. When I went by their dorm rooms at night, Leontyne Price or some other opera singer's records would be playing. Meanwhile, I was blasting Toto and Chaka Khan, which should have been an indication that the shelf life of my being an Eastman master's candidate would be short.

Before the end of the semester, one of my dorm mates knocked on my door, alerting me that I had a call. The telephones were located in the middle of the hall and shared by everyone on my floor. I walked down the hall to the enclosure where the house phone was located. "Hello?" It was Tom Browne. He said, "Hey, I need you to go on the road with me. We are leaving in a month. Will you do it?" I tried to convince him that I was in school and wanted to finish up my master's degree. Then he said, "Why are you doing that? You don't need a degree to sing, you need to just sing."

He was right. Even more, I knew I didn't want to be an opera singer. What did I want to be? A jazz singer? I could not answer any of those questions at the time but knew for certain that it was time to leave. I was wasting my time at Eastman, and while I enjoyed the camaraderie amongst my fellow singer friends, I went ahead and made an appointment with the Head Master of the School and submitted my resignation from Eastman.

Before the Fall semester ended, I was back on the road with Tom Browne. Ironically, one of my Alpha Kappa Alpha Sorority line sisters, Kim Singleton, had moved to New York City to work as an electrical engineer for Con Edison, the electric power company for New York City. She was looking for a roommate. We were a perfect match since I was gone most nights and she was at work all day. We found a one-bedroom loft-styled apartment on 33 Gold Street at Fulton Street in the Wall Street district, just a couple of blocks away from the newly built South Street Seaport. However, by the next summer, Browne was flailing again, trying to decide between staying or quitting the business. I had already launched my second back-up plan, which was an application and acceptance into the Master in Arts Administration degree program at New York University's School of Education, Nursing, and Arts Professions (SENAP). I hoped that this degree would give me some information on the business end of music. But, after completing my first eighteen hours of that Fall 1984 semester, I realized that this program was for non-profit businesses only. There was no music business degree at the time. Not knowing what to do, or how to fulfill the next steps toward my true purpose, I was lost.

Looking back on those days, I can clearly see how I was the perfect candidate to fall right into background singing. Not only did I have the skills, it was a way to sing for a living without having to hold down a regular job. And it would give me the time and experience to figure out who I was as an artist.

MY PURPOSE - 2014

Being a career background singer (or session/tour singer) was never my intention. I never even knew this career existed until I moved to Los Angeles. As I stated before, it takes a certain skill set to do this job. With vocal skills in technique and improvisation, along with a natural ear, which entails being able to listen and execute in exacting detail, makes singers like myself perfect for singing background. You have to be a jack of all trades. That was the job. You also have to be well-versed in a number of music genres, which is easy for session singers since they can hear and mimic sound in detail. However, being able to sing all of these musical styles can become problematic, as the issue becomes not knowing who you truly are as an artist when it comes to expressing yourself on your own. What is your real voice, when you can do so many other vocal styles well? What speaks to your heart?

Is this sound what you think people want to hear from you? Or only what's currently popular? These were not easy questions to answer. It took a while, but I finally accepted that I could sing classical and jazz well enough to have a career, but did either of these genres speak to my heart?

In 1986, while on the road with Anita Baker, I was approached by Scott Folks, then the A&R executive from Elektra Records, about a possible recording contract. He also approached my bandmates, saxophonist Gerald Albright and keyboardist Bobby Lyle. He asked me, "Why should I choose to sign you to Elektra over someone else?" As soon as he said it, I wondered that myself. I couldn't say that my voice was better than anyone else's or that it had anything special to offer in that R&B/jazz music genre. Truthfully, I could do it and it would have been an easy sell for me, a black woman to sing in this style. The marketing strategy was already in place, and the market was already saturated with these types of recording artists for the major record labels to exploit. I would have fit right in with everyone else's expecta-tions, and certainly, I could mimic an R&B/jazz singer, which is exactly what I'd be doing because, in my heart and soul, I knew that was not me. That was not my true voice. While both Gerald and Bobby got record deal offers, I did not receive any offers and was never approached again. I thought that even Scott Folks recognized that R&B/jazz was not my true voice.

Finding my sound through that recording session with Jeff Klaven was monumental. Still, I had to be more specific about my purpose. At that time, it was the '80s and the glam rock/hair bands ruled. While I loved some of them – like Motley Crüe, Def Leppard and Whitesnake – they didn't wholly reflect my style either. I searched and searched for "my sound," my musical dop-pelgänger, and came to the conclusion that the music would have to be composed by me. As for marketing? That was the other one-hundred-and-fifty-thousand-dollar question. What was my look? What was my persona? What artist did my music sound like? Who was my demographic? No answers. So, I concentrated on writing what was in my heart. But when it came to producing the recording, my collaborating producer's influence would over-shadow and take over my musical persona. Even trying to explain what I wanted musically seemed futile. The producers did not understand, or perhaps my explanations were unclear. Either way, it was frustrating. Soon, I realized that what I was proposing to do musically had not been achieved yet. Actually, it would be another decade before the fashion and music genre that I was actually composing in – alternative rock – would even be created. I was ahead of my time, which is just as bad as being behind the times. So, my focus returned to maintaining a backing vocal gig to make money to pay the bills. My development as a unique solo artist kept getting postponed. I would go on the road and make money, only to return home with nothing musically recorded or written that represented me. Soon touring became a double-edged sword.

This time, in 2014, I return to L.A. more confident and more knowledgeable about my music and persona. However, now the question becomes, how do I get my music out to the masses to be heard, in a way that also generates income and allows me to be self-sustaining? In this new music business, it is all about knowing your brand and being savvy with social media to get a following, developing communities to sell product. Writing one's own music is also the last frontier where an artist can make money. It was never in record sales, as the labels have always made up to 90 percent of the royalties earned from record sales since the beginning. Now music is a means to selling other prod-ucts. It is 99 cents per download, so no one is making big money royalties from that, just giving away music. My next venture is to get heard by singing my own music live somewhere and then develop a following at a venue would create a fan base and new customers to buy merchandise and music, profits from which would go directly to the musician –me. No middle man or label. More than anything, artists like myself need to be empowered to understand their validity, their artistic necessity to human life. Artists are healers and this should not be taken lightly.

However, soon it will be revealed that the upcoming events in my life were a setup, exposing an even higher purpose that had been enacted, but not fully realized. Like the episodes of ABC's hit tv show, Scandal, methodically, the pieces of my purpose in life evolved. Soon, I would understand the reason for everything that I was going through. It all began at Hollywood's Lucky Strike Live and at the Whisky A Go Go on the Sunset Strip. More on this later.

Me and Elton

"SLEEPING WITH THE PAST" - ELTON JOHN - RELEASED IN 1989

At this point in my life, my spiritual interests moved into a more science of mind/ Buddhist-centered belief. With the blessing of Rev. Cecil L. "Chip" Murray of First A. M. E. Church, whom I confided in as a member at the time, I decided to check out Rev. Michael Beckwith at Agape Church of Religious Science, by attending a service one Sunday in Santa Monica.

It was as if I'd landed on the moon and was experiencing the rituals and religious protocol of extra-terrestrials, as my first impression noted this place was quite different from anything I had ever experienced. The music was different and the people were different, as I witnessed them participating in their cere-monial rites and original melodies, all of one accord. Michael Beckwith spoke, or as I interpreted it, channeled the spirit, and I was speechless. Immediately, scrounging through my purse for a pen and any piece of paper, check stub, or Post It to write down the main points of his sermon, I was mesmerized. He spoke about how we as human beings live in a state of either striving or thriving, but few of us aspire to transcend. From that moment on, he had me. This belief system, based on the teachings of Ernest Holmes, resonated with me instantly. Soon after hearing this message, I joined Agape, and these teachings would be the template of my spiritual life, which directly affected everything that I did as a singer/artist.

My work schedule had me traveling constantly and hustling for recording sessions whenever I was in town, so committing to choir rehearsals at a church was no longer an option for me. Plus, it was clear that while I could sing gospel music, I was not a gospel singer. At this point in my life, I had a very general perception of my artistic identity. My main focus at this time was Elton John and how best to do my job. He loved touring, as we were on the road approximately 90 percent of the time during my six-year stint with him. I had little time or energy left to really concentrate on my solo career. Nevertheless, it was a glorious, worry-free time where I owed money to no one, my savings was in the six figures, and I was only responsible for myself. Everything on Elton's tours was done in first-class fashion as I traveled the world, residing in five-star hotels, going to celebrity parties, doing photo shoots, garnering positive newspaper reviews, and even flying via private jet. It was a great way to spend my twenties.

There were other advantages to working with Elton. Back in L.A. or N.Y., producers would also call to hire "Elton's singers" as a vocal section for major producers such as Don Was and for recording artists like Joe Cocker and Ofra Haza. Other times, I received personal calls to work for producers Glen Ballard, Patrick Leonard, and Arif Mardin, who hired me to sing on a recording for Bette Miller. Work was consistent and frequent. As I said, there wasn't much time available to do anything else really, as his tour schedule consumed much of my life. I was happy and paid. But I also knew there was one thing being neglected amongst all of this celebrity: Me.

Being hired to do that song demo for drummer/songwriter Jeff Klaven was confirmation that I needed to write my own songs. I asked Jeff if we could write some songs together for my project and he agreed to do so. We recorded a couple more tunes at his studio. Initially, I solicited Jeff's help as a producer and co-writer, thinking his experience in the rock world superseded anything I had in mind. They were great rock songs. However, in my heart, I felt they did not really represent me as an artist. I did not know how to express what was needed musically to reflect who I was as an artist. This was a valuable lesson. In order for me to be successful in this relationship, I had to be clear on who I was and what I brought to the partnership. I had to know my role and voice it. Sounds like a marriage, doesn't it? Finding the right producer and songwriting partner is a challenging yet necessary journey. It is a nurtured relationship that hopefully leads into a marriage of creative ideas and, like a marriage, it has to be the right fit.

So, I started writing music for myself, by myself, while back on the road with Elton John. On my time off in between tours, Elton's musical director Davey Johnstone and keyboard player Guy Babylon asked me to do a recording session at Guy's house. It was a song for Davey. I, in turn, asked if they would record one of my songs, titled, "If You Loved Me," which was an acoustic guitar and vocal tune with Davey playing guitar, as a barter. Later, I booked some time at Capitol Records recording studios in Hollywood and solicited some help from other musician friends, recording three more original compositions. Though I wasn't confident about my production, at least the vibe was more representative of me, so it was a start.

I took advantage of every chance that came up for me to sing live as a solo artist and sang my tunes. The AFTRA union would present showcases in those days with singers like myself, fresh off the road, who were also pursuing solo careers. It was an opportunity to hone some skills in front of an audience as a solo artist. Still, nothing else really happened from doing these gigs. Before long, it was time to hit the road again. It would seem that most of my time was spent singing background. Perhaps I still wasn't spending enough time on my own music. I began to doubt my abilities. Then, the most valuable opportunity revealed itself. I was able to watch Elton John write music.

In 1988, the entire band was flown to Randers, Denmark, to record Elton's next project, which was titled, "Sleeping With The Past." For about a month we resided at Puk Studios, which was a beautiful, state-of-the-art recording facility with lovely living quarters with a spa/pool/ jacuzzi, a pool room, a gourmet kitchen and dining room, all out in the middle of a pig farm. Yes, a pig farm that stunk to high heaven, but it was awesome. The crew lived on the grounds of the studio while we band members lived at the hotel in downtown Randers. We were given BMWs to drive back and forth to the recording studio. We had a personal chef who provided all of our meals throughout the day. Band members worked at different shifts. Every morning around 11 a.m., the three singers drove in to the studio for a traditional English breakfast, (of course, this included a food from my childhood, pork 'n' beans). After breakfast, Elton received the lyrics via email from his writing partner, Bernie Taupin, sat at the piano and started to play. He never second-guessed himself, he always trusted what he created first. As he played through some musical ideas, everything was recorded. He would come up with a basic idea in no time flat, then on to the next song. My lessons learned here: Trust your instincts. Don't second-guess. Trust your talent. It was one of the most valuable experiences of my life.

There were a series of tea breaks and a lunch break, then the band would record the music. We would record our vocals closer to the end of the day, after everything else had been recorded to track. The evenings were spent going out to a pub, throwing darts, playing pool, swimming, and exercising. It was an awesome environment in which to do nothing but create. It was exquisite. Going to the pubs was also entertaining, as Randers was a huge drinking town. It was the first time that I witnessed some guy bend over and release a fart while another guy lit a match, causing a blue flame to shoot out the back of his ass. Pure comedy.

After the recording was done, we returned to the road. One of the things that Elton and I had in common was our love for tennis. In addition to checking into my hotel room, working out at the gym for an hour and a half to two hours, sightseeing or attending a museum, having a bite to eat, then relaxing and prepping for the show, my routine on the road always included consulting the hotel concierge about hiring a good tennis pro to hit balls with first thing in the morning. Many times, I would see Elton on the tennis courts early. He traveled with his tennis pro. One morning after tennis Elton offered me a ride back to our hotel. I told him that I had been writing music and was feeling unsure of my writing skills, questioning if the material was any good. He offered to have a listen to my songs and give advice. Great, I thought. This would be a deciding moment for me. Either I had the talent to write songs or not, and surely Elton John would know the answer.

What might have been a few weeks seemed like a few fore-vers before I finally heard back from Elton about my songs. We had performed at the opening of the Trump Tower in Atlantic City and one of the executives from Elton's label, MCA Records, was among the guests at the show. Afterward, Elton approached me, saying, "I gave your music to one of the guys at my label. He's here tonight and I want you to meet him." Wow, what a shock. I was elated and anxious.

His name was Richard Palmese, whose position was Executive VP of Marketing and Promotion at the time. Mr. Palmese shook my hand and told me how much he loved my performance that night. Then, he invited me to call and make an appointment to come in and speak with him at his office when we returned to Los Angeles. This was it. The chance that I had been waiting for. With Elton backing me up, I felt I had the best possible chance at a recording contract, this time doing the music that I loved: Rock.

When we returned to Los Angeles, I made the appointment to meet with Mr. Palmese at MCA Records. As I entered his of-fice, he was on the phone, playing "If You Loved Me," the song I'd recorded with Davey. He hung up the phone, then came over to the area where I was directed to sit. A very nice man with a warm persona, slightly rotund, receding hair line, and black horn-rimmed glasses, he welcomed me with a handshake, then sat before me.

He stated that he was just on the phone with Elton, who had told him which songs were his favorites, and the order in which he liked them. He then said, "Well, I thought you would be another Patti LaBelle for us, and had planned to hand you over to our black music division. However, your music is more rock, and should be considered for our rock music division."

Hmmm, duh? I thought to myself. My point of contention. I couldn't make it any clearer that I was a rock singer. Certainly, the genre of my music had been discussed beforehand. Obviously, the music itself also spoke volumes. Why would my music ever be considered anything else? Mr. Palmese said that he would consult the rock division and get back to me. Smiling and somewhat hopeful that, finally, my music would get heard by the right authorities, I shook his hand and walked out of his office.

It would be about a month or so before I would gather the nerve to call back to see what the results of my conversation with Mr. Palmese were. Calling in, I was nervous and reticent. Mr. Palmese came to the phone. "Well, I consulted with my rock division and we just don't know what to do with you at this time," he said. To say I was disappointed was an understatement. Defeated, was more like it. If I couldn't get a record deal with Elton John's help, how could I *ever* get a record deal? I went into a bit of a depression, but never said anything to anyone about the entire experience. Returning to the road with Elton felt different after that. I can't remember what Elton said about it afterward. One thing that does come to mind, was that he did mention going to Chris Blackwell at Island Records, but nothing was spoken to me about this after it was mentioned. I made an inquiry about Island Records to Connie Hillman, head of Constant Communications, Elton's Los Angeles Office. She didn't seem knowledgeable or interested. After that inquiry, I stopped asking. While in London, members of Elton's office approached me, asking if I would be interested in doing house music, which was very popular at the time. I turned it down, feeling that if I started my solo career singing house music, I would be stuck. This genre would have been an easy sell for a black woman with a big voice, and I'm sure it would have been successful. But, if I chose that road, my opportunity to do what I really wanted to do in this business would be thwarted. Being black, female, and singing rock was a hard sell. At this time, the only people of color having some success in the genre were Lenny Kravitz and my friends Living Colour, thanks in part to Mick Jagger. They were black, but they were men. I wanted to be the female version, at the very least. But, the labels simply were not willing to take the chance.

After that disappointing end, Elton John took a break from touring for about a year. I returned to Los Angeles, a little defeated but somewhat hopeful that there must be another way to get my solo career off the ground. The '80s rock music scene was being ushered out as it was the top of the '90s. Soon, the grunge music scene coming out of the Pacific Northwest took over the airwaves like a tsunami. This music, termed alternative rock, was edgy, insightful, with thought-provoking, sometimes with politically motivated lyrics. It was a cultural collaboration, reminiscent of the music of the '70s. It had groove and was heavily influenced by funk, hip-hop and other African American art forms. I felt it confirmed the historical identity of rock music. Elton told me that he saw himself as an R&B singer, which I imagine some people would question. However, I understood his point. He brought soul to his music. This brought to light the truth, that rock music is an African American art form, extending from R&B, performed by people of all walks of life, bred on angst and revolutionary ideas. Most rock musicians of the '70s, especially those from outside of the United States, knew this. White America had labeled rock music as their creation. However, alternative rock proved otherwise.

Many people suggested that I move to London or somewhere in Europe to start a solo career. It was believed that the European public was more open and receptive to new, innovative music than the U.S. audience at the time. While I did understand this, my feeling was that I had not fully pursued my interests here in the U.S. I was still a touring backup singer. Knowing that the rock group Living Colour had started and was supported by the Black Rock Coalition in New York City, I decided to move there and take my chances. My friend Michael Bearden, a former school mate from Howard University and now the former musical director for Michael Jackson, Madonna, and currently for Lady Gaga, offered his place for me to stay while he was on the road. Taking him up on his offer, I moved upstate to Pelham, New York.

One of my friends from my college sorority was also living in N.Y.C. and was considering going into artist management. She offered to help me produce three showcases, which included putting together music press kits, pictures, marketing and promotion. All I had to do was pull together and prep my band. Because of my previous connections with musicians there, I was able to find the "dream team" of rock bands. All of the members were distinctive and well-known. My music director and guitarist was Ronny Drayton (also MD for Nona Hendryx of LaBelle); with Fima Efron (from A Tribe Called Quest) on bass, Nick Moroch (recorded with David Bowie, BeeGees,) on second guitar, and Zach Alford (of the B-52s, later with David Bowie) on drums. Greg Mann from MediaSound Recording Studios was my sound engineer. I switched my diet to vegetarian and started jogging every morning. In the evenings, we rehearsed in Manhattan. I was focused and driven. My friend who was acting as my manager had her sister create and make an outfit for me. It was a pair of black leggings that resembled stockings with garters; a white, long sleeved, cuffed and ruffled Edwardian-style shirt that I left unbuttoned to the center of my chest; a long, red tuxedo tails jacket; and a pair of thigh-high boots. Prince would have worn this outfit.

The band and I performed three shows, one at The Cat Club, another at the Bitter End in Greenwich Village, and one at CBGB's in The Bowery. The shows went well and the Black Rock Coalition was helpful in its support. The labels that were invited came out in numbers. But the word was that they really were looking to sign a white, male rock group like Jesus Jones, which was really hot at the time. At this point, the labels didn't think women in rock could really sell records. This was right before the emergence of the Lilith Fair and the '90s angry white women movement with Melissa Etheridge, Alanis Morrissette, and the host of other female rockers who eventually changed the face of rock music. Again, I was ahead of my time. And once again, I returned to Los Angeles, feeling completely defeated.

I looked for something to blame my defeat on. One of the issues that quickly reared its ugly head was my weight. My inner voice would say, "Your weight was why the record deal didn't happen." Of course, I believed that these feelings were confirmed by the people who were around me at the time. Soon enough, I would realize that I had created the entire scenario.

Elton was still on break at this time, so I decided to devote every ounce of time and energy to losing weight. I joined a weight loss clinic and upped my exercise and tennis regimen. In the end, I lost 65 pounds, and in 1992, I returned to tour with Elton John, feeling more fit and more confident. At this point, Gianni Versace was creating the staging and our costumes. We were wearing black, sadomasochistic-looking outfits with strapped, black boots with four-inch heels. "Painful" was an understate-ment when talking about dancing in those heels onstage for a two-and-a-half-hour show. Our house slippers were at the bottom of the stage every night. Regardless, we did our jobs. Performing in my new, leaner body, wearing Versace, boosted my self-esteem and my belief that finally my weight problem had been conquered and that now, everything was in alignment for me to receive what I had long hoped for and dreamed of: becoming a solo recording artist.

Elton John prepped to do another AIDS charity event, this time at the Universal Amphitheater in Los Angeles. I was chosen be part of a skit, doing an excerpt from "The Rocky Horror Picture Show," a campy, theatrical presentation that included choreography. While I was a pretty good dancer, musical theater was not my thing. There I was, feeling totally out of place, on stage with comic actress Kathy Najimy, who had recently secured fame for her role in the Whoopi Goldberg film "Sister Act." I knew Elton must have set up this role for my visibility, so I did the best that I could. At the same time, there was talk of a movie on the life of Tina Turner, whom we'd met at Elton's birthday party in Paris. The discussion was that I was being considered to play Tina Turner. When I heard this news, I could not really comprehend it. Acting was a vocation I had not considered since college, as it was "out of the box," eons away from snagging a solo artist record deal, which was as far as my tunnel vision could see. I didn't stake much energy in these conversations, as they sounded so far-fetched. In the end, the film producers decided to cast an actress, Angela Bassett, and use Tina's actual voice, rather than a singer. The rest is now history, as "What's Love Got To Do With It" became a box-office smash.

As members of Elton's band for the AIDS Charity event that year, we backed up Tammy Wynette, Clint Black, and my favorite singer, Terence Trent D'Arby. Sheryl Crow was also one of the many guest artists on the bill. Before achieving stardom as a solo artist, Sheryl had been a tour/session singer with Michael

Jackson and would sometimes suggest me for session work from time to time, which was truly appreciated. In rehearsal for the charity event, she came over to me, stage left. We hugged and exchanged courtesies, as it had been years since we'd seen each other. Then, she asked, "Hey, I heard you had a record deal. What are you doing here?" I couldn't really answer other than simply saying, "No, it didn't happen." That was a defining moment for me. I was so embarrassed. Obviously, someone had been talking about my MCA Records meeting in the industry, though I had no idea who. This exchange with Sheryl made me feel like an utter failure, as I just wanted to hide under a rock. All of my self-esteem went out of the window, and from that point on, I was ready to quit everything. I was ready to end my backing vocalist career and really try to move into solo artistry, but still had no idea how. I was 32 years old, with some savings, some cool clothes and other objects to my name, but nothing significant to show for all the many years in terms of a musical body of work as an artist on my own right. I began to question what I was doing with my life at this point. I had no music and no real personal life, as my new slimmer body did not bring in the record deal or love relationship I'd dreamed of for so long. It was as if I'd found my purpose, my bliss, then success was snatched away from me. What could all of this mean? I am a singer. I am a songwriter. I can't get a record deal, though I'm supposed to be fulfilling my purpose. What do I do now?

My sixth year with Elton was routine. The three of us singers were now being hired as a trio to do backing vocals on recordings with artists like Israeli pop singer Ofra Haza for producer Don Was, and for English rock and soul star Joe Cocker. Two years after the one where I saw Sheryl Crow, Elton did another benefit concert for his Athletes and Entertainers for AIDS Foundation, held once again at the Universal Amphitheater. This time, the theme was excerpts from "West Side Story," which included a knockout performance by Barbara Streisand of the song "Somewhere." Later, there was a recording under the same "West Side Story" theme but using different artists. The net proceeds from this recording went directly to benefit AIDS victims.

At the show Elton performed "I Feel Pretty," which was frolicking fun to perform with him on stage. However, Little Richard did the recording, and we were called to back him up. He was absolutely hilarious, definitely a larger-than-life character of a man. He constantly boasted, just as he'd done on television, of his success as the "greatest rock and roll singer in the world." Then, he tempered it with self-inflicted jokes on how huge his head was. He would jokingly say, "I know you're looking at me because my head is too big for my body." It was funny and it was true. He does have a big-ass head! But his heart, soul, and voice are even bigger.

David Paich was the producer for this record project. He asked if I could return and do a session, singing the lead and background vocals on "Somewhere" for Aretha Franklin to follow, as she would be doing the recording from her home in Detroit. Of course, I agreed, so we scheduled another session for me. As always in this job, I came in and did the recording session, approaching the lead vocal with some nuances that I felt Aretha would naturally use, in addition to my own interpretation. It worked, as David contacted me later after the demo was submitted, to say that Aretha loved it. All that was left to do was to fine tune the backing vocals, since it was decided they would use me to sing all of them, this time with Aretha's lead.

CONTRACT NEGOTIATIONS 101

Even though there are regulations in place regarding the use of union singers and musicians, sometimes there were occurrences that called for some smoothing over, as the AFTRA scale was higher than the instrumentalist musicians and singers rates with the American Federation of Musicians (AFM). Instead of creating any disharmony, there were ways to resolve a sticky issue whenever a producer questioned the contract amount billed to the record label.

Once, I was owed a sizable amount of cash because I was the contractor, as well as doing solo/duo scale, which was the highest AFTRA scale. Also, I stacked nine tracks of music, three tracks per part, plus the song was more than three minutes and thirty seconds in length, which meant the final total would be doubled, so it was a few thousand dollars. Most singers with my vitae would have charged double scale. However, I was never comfortable with insisting on such, and thought that single union scale was fair. My union rep constructed a reasonable solution. I filled out a contract for the producer, charging the scale fees per hour or per track, whichever was the highest amount. However, I would neglect to include the doubled amount, as the AFTRA contracts stated at the time that for all songs that were over three minutes and thirty seconds in length, the total amount would be doubled. At this point, the majority of songs released were well over this time length. This was great for union members but producers would find it a point of contention when it came to paying out of their budget. So, I left the doubled amount out of my equation, that way the pay would appear to be half of the quoted fee. However, after that contract was submitted and the record was released, listing the song as being over three minutes and thirty seconds long, then the union had the right to go in and bill the record company for the remaining balance of my money, which was the other half of the singer's union contracted fee. I would simply have to wait until the record was released to get my remaining balance. About a month or so later, I received the first check, and in approximately two months after the record was released, I received the other half of my earnings.

PRESENT DAY - 2015

There was a guy at Mel's Diner that always came in during those wee, 4 a.m. hours. He was a regular customer like myself. So, we would strike up a conversation from time to time. He talked about his upbringing and his possibilities of playing professional golf. "I was in the top ten as a teenager and could have gone pro. But, my coach said that I was too focused on girls," he explained. He ended up being a salesman and appeared to be quite happy with his life.

Many times, especially when life was uneasy and work was slow, I would ask myself the question, "Why continue pursuing something as challenging as singing after so many letdowns?" Unlike the gentleman at Mel's Diner, it never occurred to me to ever focus on or consider anything else while I was studying to be a singer. I love men, but rarely did I ever have a committed relationship and never would any man stand in the way of my career. Music always came first. It defined me. For a long time, I thought that my blind dedication to my craft meant something was wrong with me, as did some family and friends. My life was always all about my work, which can be a lonely existence.

Because of my successful career as a backing vocalist, at the top of my game basically, one might think that my goals have been fulfilled and that that would make me happy. But no. While there have definitely been glorious moments of excitement, success, and pure fun on the road and in the recording studio, again, that remaining goal of being a solo artist seemed to elude me.

Right now, the music business is in a transient state. Major labels are being forced to merge to stay afloat. They're not spending money to build artists anymore, but instead are manufacturing pop stars under a singular, sure-fire formula that guarantees a certain amount of return for their investment. Actually, everyone wants to be a star and few aspire to be an artist.

So, why would I want to pursue a career in this music

environment at this point in my life? My only answer is that an artist recognizes him/herself to be just that, an artist. That's all one knows to be. This is my purpose. I am an artist. I am a singer. It chose me. I am a witness to the healing affect singing has on others as it heals me simultaneously. This voice is a gift and through this gift, is how my purpose in this life on the planet is fulfilled. It is not a choice in exchange for fame or money, though these things are part of the compensation. Even if singing were only a 20-thousand-dollar-a-year career, my pursuit would be the same. One of the lessons learned this time around, living in Los Angeles again, is that even as my purpose evolves, singing started this journey. My voice is the foundation that supports it all.

Looking back on my life and seeing how things fell in place synchronistically, affording me this experience in music, is what has kept me going, taking chances, and moving forward. I feel it is my responsibility to continue to take these chances, pursuing this solo career regardless of age or the conditions of the music business. These amazing coincidences keep coming and continue to confirm my every move, letting me know that, yes, I am in alignment with the Universe. This is not a mistake. Keep moving forward.

So. yes, still after a full, successful career doing recording sessions and touring as a backing vocalist, ten years as a college professor, and raising a child, here I am back in Los Angeles again, 13 years later, for the third time, still pursuing my dreams. Still possessing the vocal capabilities and the physical prowess to perform on stage with the energy, drive, and determination to truly focus. I felt it was "do it now or never."

PRESENT DAY PERFORMANCE TIME

It's Monday night at the Crescent Hotel, and as usual, the Cookies are performing. As I walk on to the patio, just across from the

bar, I see a familiar face. It's Jonathan Moffett, former drummer
of The Jacksons, George Michael, and Elton John. We got the gig
with Elton at the same time. We embrace as it has been almost
twenty years since we've seen each other. He is such a lovely guy,
still sweet, quiet and gentlemanly, exquisitely dressed, still obviously meticulous about his appearance. We begin our conversation, catching up on what has happened in our lives since the
Elton John days. He asks me if I'm still doing my rock thing. "Of
course!" I answer, as I'm glad he remembers this. He says, "You
know there is this serious rock jam going on over at the Lucky
Strike in Hollywood. They only use musicians with a résumé and
you would be great for that venue. You should meet me there
and check it out. I can introduce you to the guys that run it. The
jam is on Wednesday nights." Now, this opportunity sounds like
music to my ears, as I've been wondering where the rock gigs
were. This would be an opportunity to sing, work out my solo
rock on stage performance, connect with other rockers. "It's free
though. There's no money in it, but it's a cool networking spot,"
Jonathan intimates. "I'm fine with that! So, when are you going?"
I ask. Jonathan says he'll be going this coming Wednesday. Cool.
There is no cover, I just have to park.

So, Wednesday comes around and I head over to the Lucky
Strike, a rock-and-roll bowling alley on Highland Avenue. It's a
cool venue. Large open space. The sound is conducive to heavy
rock music and there are people bowling in the back of the room.
Only in Hollywood.

I find Jonathan and he quickly takes me backstage to meet
the guys. Chuck Wright, bassist for '80s rock icons Quiet Riot,
runs this Jam Night along with Adam Mandel. It is quick and
efficient, though it is crazy crowded backstage with musicians
going on and off stage, guitar techs managing instruments, singers sitting in the wings waiting to go on. The crowd is loud and
excited. The word is they don't rehearse. Everyone is given songs

to sing and everyone plays them verbatim, like the original recording, in that same key. For that level of musicianship, this
works. The bands sound amazing. There is a lot of personnel, as
they change players on just about every song. Adam asks me to
email him my information/résumé and he would email me the
specifics.

I'm excited at the possibility of doing this. Looking on the
stage, I know and/or recognize musicians who play with some
of my favorite rock bands. This would be an awesome way to
connect into the rock world and into the new music business,
as most of them were younger than me.

I go home and email Adam and Chuck my short bio.
Afterward, I get an email from Adam with a huge list of songs
to choose from, to sing. Many of the songs are known, but I don't
know the lyrics. I choose three songs, mostly Jimi Hendryx tunes.
The majority of their list consists of '80s tunes. Well, the time
had arrived, I needed to learn some music. I choose "Voodoo
Child" by Jimi Hendryx. Almost immediately, Adam emails me
back with my scheduled performance date.

So, Wednesday night rolls around. I have no idea how this is
gonna work out, as now reality sets in that no rehearsal means
trusting we all are of one accord with entrances and endings to
the song. Also, what about monitors? There won't be any time to
make adjustments in front of a crowd. I personally hate when
some artists do a sound check during a performance. I know
sometimes you have to, in order to do your job, but it's distracting
for everyone. Anyway, just before I get on stage, Adam introduces
me to Paulie Z, the announcer for the show, who then asks me
who I've toured with so that he can mention it in his introduction. Then Chuck comes up and says, "I got Doug Pinnick to play
bass for you." My response is, "Cool." However, I am so focused on
remembering my lyrics, it doesn't register who Doug Pinnick is. I
get on stage and bam! It starts. I don't remember much after the

first few notes. I can't hear myself, as the monitors are too low. Singers generally have a difficult time hearing, especially with rockers blaring loudly on stage. The energy is crazy. The crowd is 100 percent with me, so I just get carried into the momentum of it all. The musicians on stage, they are killer. It is an incredibly high-strung feeling, like jumping out of a plane, free falling, screaming all the way! I love it.

When I get off stage and go out into the audience to meet some friends and get a drink, people start coming up to me to congratulate me on my performance. It's exhilarating. My friend Neal comes up and gives me a congratulatory hug. Then he says, "Damn, girl, you had Doug Pinnick playing with you! That was awesome." Then it hits me. Doug Pinnick was the lead singer and bass player for Kings X, one of my favorite rock groups from the ' 90s. Wow. That blows my mind. Now, this is the arena I have always longed to be in. This is a defining moment for me. Somehow, I've got to turn this into income and musically find my place here. These are the musicians of like mind that I wish to surround myself with. This is the beginning of a long-standing relationship with other alternative rock musicians that directly affects my performance life forever. This is in alignment with my purpose. All I could say to the universe is "thank you" and then, "Just show me, how does it get better than this?"

AMIDST ADVERSITY
CHAPTER SIX

In our society, an artist is a celebrity who is worshipped like royalty. Like royalty, artists wear a crown, adorned with all of the trappings of wealth, power, and sometimes burdensome responsibility. Truthfully, that bejeweled crown can feel more like a crown of thorns, and yet it is still a crown nonetheless.

The vast majority of society has no idea what an artist is or what it takes to maintain such a life in an environment that treats you differently, installs a false sense of security, enhances stories or outright lies about your life in the media where you are constantly misunderstood. For some, handling the trappings of fame at any level can be challenging, resulting in drug addiction, body dysmorphia-related illnesses, or just sheer depression and low self-esteem from trying to please everyone. Still, most artists maintain a razor-sharp focus on their craft, turning a blind eye to the minutiae. At the end of the day, artists are driven to perform regardless of the income or issues that come with the lifestyle. It is our DNA.

Where artists are seen as eccentric, flighty, or free-spirited, most times we are managing our vulnerabilities and, acknowledging the weight of being in constant touch with our feelings, as every move is dictated by the heart. Artists are channelers of the spirit that accesses our life experiences and turns them into art that is revealed through our instruments. This is powerful. This is what people who become fans connect with, sometimes obsessively so, as they weave their emotions about these celebrities into their own personal lives. Connecting to the art and the artists assists them in accessing their own feelings, which is healing, but can also be dangerous when there is an unhealthy balance between reality and imagination.

In essence, artists are healers who are sensitive, sometimes evasive, and oftentimes self-reflective, which can be difficult for others to live with. Many times, their mates are also fans who may sacrifice their careers and wellbeing to take care of the artist, sometimes with the best of intentions, sometimes not. As stated earlier in the book, the life of an artist is lonely and can contribute to one making questionable decisions regarding personal relationships. My personal experience witnessing what shall be called a "pseudo-Yoko Ono-type" relationship is a fond memory. This is not an insult to Yoko Ono and John Lennon at all. It is used only in the literal sense.

ARTISTS AND THEIR MATES

This particular artist had been seeing this person for quite some time. Everyone around the artist was in agreement that the intentions of this "mate" were questionable. However, the artist would do nothing without the consent or advice of their mate, which was not always good. It appeared the artist allowed their mate to control many aspects of their life, which was disturbing to watch. On one of our U.S. tours, this "mate" decided it was time to accompany the artist on the road, this time insisting on joining the band as a second guitar player. The only issue was, this person could not play guitar at all! Of course, the suggestion was insane. Only an egomaniac would have the audacity to accompany an artist of this stature on a world-class stage, and play before thousands of fans, thinking their abilities were worthy, at the expense of jeopardizing a major concert. Crazy! But, the lonely artist wanted to maintain the peace and the relationship, and so it was done. However, there was one stipulation. Unbeknownst to the "mate," the artist had the sound to the mate's guitar turned off in the house/concert venue, which meant the audience could not hear a sound from the second guitar. They could only see the "mate" jumping and dancing around on stage with the guitar strapped around him, seriously making faces, totally strumming a guitar but with no sound coming from it. Fucking brilliant. The only people privy to the horrific noise coming from this mate's instrument were the musicians on stage who stood near the mate's monitor, which was avoided on stage like the plague. One night after the show, unbeknownst to the mate, the band got together on one of the tour buses and played back a recording of the show with the mate's guitar added to the stage mix. My God, it was hilarious. The sound was as if a toddler were strumming a toy guitar with their feet. To this day, I don't believe the mate ever knew the guitar was never heard by the public.

Rarely do we find mates of one accord with our nature. Of course, there are a few lucky ones who marry their soul mates, twin flames, or other half. Otherwise, it can be a lonely existence and many times a tumultuous life.

The melodious sound that is made and profound messages artists share with the world, comes straight from the mouth of God. Yet, it comes at a heavy price, trying to balance this non-worldly state of being with the physical and mental world and its vices and mind-altering drugs, which reminds me of my personal experience with such drugs.

DRUG TEST

While I am no stranger to marijuana and am an avid supporter of it, neither weed nor any other drug has ever totally captured my spirit to the point of choosing to use it incessantly. I am not an addictive personality. Having been around artists who are users who have had a difficult time releasing their addictions, I decided to do an experiment. I wanted to know what was so mesmerizing about smoking cocaine, that one would sacrifice their lives and the lives of their loved ones for it.

On this particular night, a singer friend of mine invited me over to her home. It was a "girl hang," as her roommate had been through some drama and we decided to support her with conversation, listening, and a number of tequila shots. In my drunken state, I decided to call and check in with an artist I'd worked with. In the background, I could hear through the phone, the artist had guests. After a short exchange, the artist invited us over to join them. So, my singer friend and I hopped into my car and we headed over to the party. Her roommate decided to remain at home.

When we arrived, the house was darkly lit with warm lights and candles on counters, window sills, tables, in every corner of the room. Everyone was drunk as they also had been doing tequila shots. They were singing along with the loud music being played on the boom box, which is what we called a portable CD player at the time. After exchanging hugs and kisses with everyone, we were ushered to the living room floor where we sat around a low, Moroccan-styled table. In the center of it was a large pipe, resembling a hookah. Apparently, we got there just in time, for the next level of the party smoking /free-basing cocaine, was about to begin. Quickly sobering up, I made the conscious decision to try it, as I was wondering how it would affect me. Amidst the sounds of Joni Mitchell music playing in the background, I took my first hit off the pipe. BAM! In a blink of an eye, my spirit left my body and suddenly, I was hovering overhead in total separation, suspended above the table. Not certain if I was breathing, the feeling was zombie-like. I could not move.

For a moment, things got a little frightening as I was not certain if I could return to my body. What felt like forever probably only lasted a few minutes, but it was the longest minutes of my life. My prayer at that moment was that if I could return to my body, I promised never to do this drug again. Eventually, the high wore off and I felt normal again. However, the artist suggested we go to another house to join another party already in swing. At this point, I decided to commit to making this a night to remember, all in the name of rock and roll. After all, this is the music business and this hang tonight would only solidify my status as a true rocker with even more road stories to tell.

I offered my car as transport for the three of us, but felt too inebriated to drive, so I asked my singer friend to drive my car. Inebriated herself, she drove us to the party in second gear of my manual drive vehicle, all the way. As we arrived, everyone had left except for the host. After a short stay, we left, deciding to return to the artist's home. We all piled in to my small Nissan 300ZX, this time with me behind the wheel. Earlier that week, I had purchased movie popcorn from the cinema and had wasted some of it on the floor of the backseat. The artist saw the kernels on the floor of the car and said, "Wow! Look at all of those rocks," referring to the popcorn kernels, thinking they were cocaine rocks. "That's popcorn!" I answered. The artist shrugged and simply looked puzzled. As we pulled up to the front of the house, the artist announced, "Hey, I've got another rock, come on in and let's party." It was at this point that I realized, this night would never be over in the eyes of those who love the drug and this was not me. Both my singer friend and I said our goodbyes and we headed back over to her home, where we both crashed for the night.

That experience taught me how that first high is what is always being chased. Understanding its allure, I never tried nor did I ever have the desire to ever try smoking/free-basing again. It simply was not worth injuring my health. Not my thing.

While drugs can be physiologically addictive, emotionally, when one is overwhelmed with life's complications, choosing to desensitize or anesthetize can be an appealing, seemingly viable option. Hence, a couple of vodka cocktails or glasses of dry, red wine were my choices. I always felt that some artists who got caught up and/or addicted don't realize that the purity of their spirit is not conducive to the adverse effects alcohol and other control substances create, because they are free spirits who should not be controlled. This, combined with the sub-conscious programming that happens from being surrounded by a competitive, non-artist culture, can wreak havoc on the lives of artists who are simply trying to live their dream.

Another issue that comes to mind is how significantly relationships change. Even your relatives and friends treat you differently. Rarely would any non-musician friend or relative call me up just to say, "Hey, didn't want anything, just checking in to see how you are," or "what's up?" or talk about what's happening in their lives. During the years on tour, I visited Memphis for the holidays. The first thing on my agenda was to borrow my parents' car, go out and visit people and reconnect with friends and relatives. It was rare that my schedule would allow for such things. I was able to maintain connection with a couple of my friends from high school. But, there were times when some of my relatives would not even answer the phone or return calls. Sometimes, they would schedule visits, only to cancel or simply not show up at all. Once, a cousin of mine who did show up decided to accompany me to another cousin's house for a visit. When we pulled into the driveway, parked and walked up and rang the doorbell, she would not answer the door, nor would she answer the phone as we returned to the car and called from our cell, watching her look out the front window from her living room. There were hard feelings, but that ended my attempt to stay in touch. After a while I realized, just like that scene in the

Julia Roberts movie "My Best Friends' Wedding," where she looks back and realizes that she is running after the guy but no one "is running after her." The only time I would ever hear from anyone would be for tickets or backstage passes to a show they heard I may be in town for. If things were slow and work was infrequent or they heard I may be struggling or financially tight, these same people would be the first to criticize, reciting their mantra, "So, why don't you get a real job?"

As a teenager, being a musician led me to believe that the only reason anyone really liked me was because I could sing. Otherwise, they would have nothing to do with me. This belief played itself out in my life in a negative way, which I will discuss later.

When everything is in place – meaning, when I am loving the music I am making and being able to take care of the basic needs of food, clothing, and shelter – there is nothing better. The cultural experiences, world traveling, band relationships, the love for creating music, and improvising, all make up a life that is rich and nourishing to the soul. On tour and in recording sessions, doing a great job and being recognized and appreciated, is the sweetest reward. Being around people who understand the idiosyncrasies of being an artist and have respect for my talent, makes me feel loved and accepted for being me. As stated earlier, acceptance is a necessary state of being in the life of an artist, for everyone, really. Soon, I would realize that acceptance is key to everything.

On the other hand, living amidst adverse conditions, meaning when things are off-center or unbalanced, can be downright miserable. This includes enduring the constant criticism of friends and relatives, not getting paid enough money to eat or pay rent, not getting enough calls for work, doing "work for hire" music projects that are crappy but doing them for the money, or getting asked to do work as a favor in a belittling way. This is

when that voice screamed from my subconscious, with words
authored by parents and a society who never understood artists,
saying, "When are you gonna get a real job? You should have
known you can't make a living doing music!" Regardless of all
the work and accolades, doubt inevitably set in. Second-guessing
the choices I'd made in my life would become a constant and
soon I would find myself reasoning whether I should find some
other vocation to "fall back on."

MY TURN – 1993

The most transformative thing of all happened near the end of
1993. It was my turn. I was pregnant!

While on the road with Elton John, I had a day off while we
were in Lexington, Kentucky, so I decided to fly to N.Y.C. to visit
my friends Sandra St. Victor and Peter Lord from the group The
Family Stand. Sandra knew of an ob-gyn who would open his
office privately, as Sunday would be my arrival day, to administer an ultrasound exam to make sure all was well. We arrived
around midday to his office in Mt. Vernon, New York. The doctor was a very lovely, soft-spoken black man. He turned on the
lights and escorted me to the exam room while Sandra remained
seated in the waiting area. Nervous and excited at the same time,
awaiting the verdict as the doctor spread the gel on my stomach
and moved the scope around, I could hardly lie still. Then, he
finally said, "Ah, there's the heart beat!" Wow, I was nauseous,
happy, and five weeks pregnant.

I returned to Kentucky to the tour but decided not to say
anything for the standard three months that doctors always
suggest, to ensure everything was OK. During this time, my
heightened paranoia to be healthy for the baby got the best of
me. My concern was about the strenuousness of my vegan diet,
travel, and work routine. I wasn't certain if this was good.

Once, in Germany, there was an episode where the smoke machines used on stage to create that mysterious ambiance caused me to have a full-blown asthma attack. I ran off stage to the side fills in the middle of the show. Kai, Elton's limo driver who was also a doctor, happened to be back stage. Quickly, he came to assist me as I was wheezing heavily. After examining me, he administered a shot of theophylline for the asthma. Worried that this medication may hurt the baby, I had to tell him of my pregnancy. Luckily, all was well. Luckily, Kai knew how to keep a good secret.

At the end of my third gestational month, we were in Orlando, Florida, where I found an ob-gyn to administer my final "road" exam. Everything was great. From that point, we traveled to Tel Aviv, Israel, where there was heightened security and the temperatures were over 100 degrees Fahrenheit. Regardless, I maintained my workout schedule, not jogging, but playing tennis in 103-degree heat. Crazy, I know, but I love the game. Once they got the security measures intact, the outdoor concert was a great success. I made the front page of the newspaper in Tel Aviv, with Elton kissing me on the lips, as he often did during our introduction on stage. This front page came to my attention as I had hired a driver to take me on a tour of Jerusalem. As I walked through the lobby of the hotel on my way to meet the driver, I noticed people pointing, staring, and whispering. The concierge alerted me, showing me a copy of the morning newspaper. There, on the front page, was my slight tummy and growing breasts, revealing my pregnant state. Initially, no one on tour noticed until after this particular concert, then the drummer loudly inquired as to why my breasts were getting so big. It was time to tell the news.

It didn't appear that anyone was ecstatic about this pregnancy except me. The overall response was indifference. The guys only wanted to know who the father was, as they all knew there was no consistent boyfriend that they knew of and I had not slept with any of them. Since none of the band members appeared to be genuinely happy about it, I decided to keep to myself from that point on, as an effort to steer clear of all negative energy that was not in alignment with my pregnancy. As far as Elton was concerned, he seemed happy. However, my feeling was that he thought this pregnancy meant that I had decided not to pursue a solo career. He saw me as a person who would place my baby first, before my career. He was right.

My best friend, Kim Edwards-Brown, was my only source of comfort and support at this time. She was back home in Los Angeles, going through a divorce. For both of us, it was perfect timing, as she offered to come out on the road to take a break

My best friend Kim Edwards-Brown

from her situation and spend time with me as she felt I needed the support. She was right. Our tour had about seven days in Paris. Kim came over and stayed in my hotel room with me. This would be one of the most unselfish revelations of true friendship I would ever know. We did the tourist thing, visiting the Louvre and other Parisian main attractions, talking and laughing. Those supportive days in Paris during that time were the most treasured moments of my life. Kim was also there in the birthing room when my daughter was born. She was a true friend. Approximately a year and a half after our time together in Paris, Kim Edwards-Brown passed away from brain cancer.

At the end of the 1993 tour with Elton John, I had to find a place to live. In the interim, I stayed at the parents of my friend Lisa (backing singer from my Chaka Khan tour days) in Newberry Park, outside of Thousand Oaks, California. My concern at this point was whether to remain in Los Angeles with a child. I always thought I'd raise my daughter in a more child-friendly environment, away from the constraints of "Hollywood," even though the "Hollywood life" was my job. Indecision influenced me to dismiss buying a house. Instead, I rented a lovely home up in Topanga, a hippy-dippy village up in the mountains near the ocean between Santa Monica and Malibu. Life would be simple and quiet, as I nested up in what looked like a treehouse on the side of a mountain.

Soon after my move into my new home, my baby girl was born two months before her due date. My water broke during my Bradley method (a grassroots alternative to the Lamaze method) childbirth class. My friend Kim Edwards-Brown was my birthing coach. We drove over to my friend Brian's house to get a change of sweatpants and drop off my car before heading to Cedars-Sinai Hospital in Beverly Hills, where I was scheduled to give birth. After lying upside down in a double-reclined position to slow the birthing and save what water was left, my daughter was born 23 hours later. It was a totally natural, no-drugs childbirth. She was three pounds, twelve ounces.

That next morning, there was a dark orange cloud mixed with billowing black smoke in the air over Beverly Hills. I turned on the television in my hospital room to see breaking news of a huge fire in Topanga. Evidently, the high winds had blown the smoke toward Beverly Hills, which was approximately 20 miles away. As I looked closely, I could clearly recognize that the scene on television was actually just above my house. In addition, I remembered smelling gas leaking before leaving home for my childbirth class. Anxiety started to creep in. What a crazy coincidence. Quickly, the panic dissipated, as all that mattered was my child and myself and we were fine.

About an hour later, I received a call at the hospital from my landlords, who had been told by my neighbors that I was having the baby, though I'm still not certain how my neighbors knew this. They called to assure me that the house was OK and that one of the neighbors behind the house had even stayed and fought the fire from the roof of his home. Crazy. After a few days, Brian, who kept my car while I was in the hospital, picked me up from Cedars Sinai and we drove up to Topanga, where we parked at the bottom of the hill on Topanga Canyon Boulevard and Fernwood Pacific Drive, and walked up Fernwood Pacific Drive one and a half miles to check on my house. There were firemen living on the porches of every residence in Topanga Canyon, protecting the homes. We passed by and waved, and a feeling of calm came over me that, yes, I was protected. When we reached my house, there was a business card placed between the door and the door frame from the fire department that watched over my home. Everything was intact. The grounds across from the houses were black and still smelled of fire, but the houses were saved. That is what mattered most. We walked back down the hill to my car, feeling elated. What an experience of love and community, also physical fitness. Brian kept announcing to the firemen as we walked passed them, "Hey, she just had a baby!"

After approximately two weeks, Brian drove my daughter and I home to Topanga. Soon, I began to wind down, realizing that the impact of touring non-stop for ten years at that point, the pregnancy, the delivery, and the fire had subconsciously taken a toll. I was exhausted. Since my daughter was premature, I was instructed to stay home for the first couple of months. Thankful and relieved, I was more than happy to do so.

I hired a live-in nanny and for the next several months, fell into bliss, caring for my daughter. Not realizing how high strung I had been, traveling all of those years, now doing nothing but being a mom completely agreed with me. But, my peace of mind changed as my savings soon began depleting and going back to work was imminent. Now that I was a mother, the question became "What kind of work?"

I did get a call from The Rolling Stones, asking if I was available to take Cindy Mizelle's place on tour in 1993. She was the third singer of that initial trio that included Lisa Fischer and Bernard Fowler. After much deliberation, I told them I would do it, if I could bring my nanny and newborn on the road. They contacted me again, saying they decided not to fill the spot, which left me with mixed feelings. It was high-paying gig, but my child came first. In the end, they never added a third singer, and for the next twenty years, Lisa Fischer and Bernard Fowler were their only backing vocalists.

TOURING - BABY AND ME - JEFFREY OSBORNE

I settled into my life in Topanga, loving every minute of it. With the assistance of my live-in nanny, I was able to sleep until 10 a.m. and take walks with my baby on Will Rogers Beach. I also hired an interior decorator to assist in making my home into a French/Country themed chalet. My friends often came up to visit and sometimes spend the night. I'd give them a blank check to buy groceries at Mrs. Gooch's (now the Whole Foods Market), since it was prescribed that I stay home with my premature daughter for the first few months.

About five months later, I received a call from Jeffrey Osborne's organization, asking if I would go on the road to Japan to do the Blue Note Club tours in Tokyo, Osaka, and Fukuoka. They agreed that I could bring my daughter and assured me that I could use the nanny services at the hotels since they were quite reliable. Feeling unsure and naturally skeptical, it took a minute, but finally I agreed to do it. This would be my daughter's first trip overseas. I consulted with the pediatrician on what to do on this long trans-Pacific flight. She was five months old but looked younger because she was a smaller premature baby. I got ear drops for her, just in case, formula bottles and a travel-sized breast pump, as I was still breast feeding, had snacks, toys, everything. Everyone on the plane, including the flight attendants, were amazed at how quiet she was. She never cried once during the nearly twelve- hour flight to Japan.

When it came time to go to the gig in Fukuoka, the nanny arrived. A lovely twenty-something woman walked into the hotel room. Just as I prepared to leave, my daughter started to cry. The nanny spoke a little English, enough for me to feel comfortable, as she tried to reassure me that everything was fine. I felt semi-OK about this but went ahead to my gig. When I returned, it was as if my daughter and the nanny had remained in the same stance since I'd left, as my child was still crying at the top of her lungs. I thanked the nanny and took my baby in my arms. This hotel nanny thing was not going to be easy.

The next city was Osaka. We had two nights at this gig. When it was time to leave the hotel, the nanny arrived. She was accompanied by an interpreter, as she spoke no English. She looked as if she was thirteen years old. She picked up my daughter from the bed, not supporting her neck and held her low, near her belly, not close to her heart. I flipped out. No, she could not keep my baby. I bundled up my daughter and took her with me to the club, which was within walking distance of the hotel. It was cold and snowy as I walked briskly to the Blue Note. When I arrived, Jeffrey and the band were already on stage. I walked across the club to the dressing room area to the road manager and told him that things didn't go well with the nanny at the hotel and that he had to watch the baby. Hesitantly, he took my daughter in his arms as I rushed on to the stage. Halfway through the set, I glanced over toward the dressing room and noticed the road manger just standing there alone without my baby. I left the stage and went over to him and asked, "Where is my daughter?" He answered matter-of-factly, "Oh, she's fine. She's in the dressing room." "Alone?" I asked. He looked puzzled as if something was wrong with me. I quickly walked past him and there was my child, swaddled in her blanket, on a small chair, alone in the dressing room. Needless to say, I was furious. "Are you crazy? You can't just leave a baby on the seat alone like that! What if she rolls off?" As I picked my child up in my arms, one of the Japanese tour coordinators walked over and offered to watch the baby so I could finish the show. Finally, some relief.

The last night in Osaka, the hotel sent in a new nanny. She was an older woman who seemed more experienced. She knew how to pick up a baby, supporting her head. I was told later that it was their culture to hold the baby low, close to the belly. However, she held my daughter close to her heart as I instructed. While she didn't speak English very well, we had an agreement of spirits. Also, my child was quiet in her presence, which for me was another indication that everything would be OK. It was the first and only time that I felt comfortable to leave for my gig. In Tokyo, the tour coordinator again came to my aid, taking care

of my child at the club during the gig, so that made things easier. While this experience ended well, it affirmed my belief that
touring with child was not for me.

BAY-AREA BABY

I returned to doing recording sessions and decided to lay off the
live-in nanny to cut down on costs and hire sitters as needed. I
found the most awesome Persian woman and her family through
my friend Sandy (from the Anita Baker tour). She was inexpen-
sive and loved my daughter. A perfect match. Admittedly, I was
a bit overprotective, as sometimes I would drop my daughter
off at the sitter's home and give her the time of my return. Then,
during my recording session, I would excuse myself for an outside run during lunch break, then drive like a bat out of hell to do
a surprise visit to the sitter's house. She would give me a strange
look, but everything would be fine. She never said a word, but I
believe she knew of my concern. Worry was my middle name, as
still I continued to have second thoughts about raising a child
in Los Angeles.

I had a chance meeting with multi-platinum record producer
Narada Michael Walden (producer for Whitney Houston, Mariah
Carey, and Aretha Franklin). His recording studios were up in
the San Francisco Bay Area in a town called San Rafael in Marin
County, just across the Golden Gate Bridge. In 1995, I went up
to the Bay Area to do a session for Narada. He also had me stay
over as his guest in his home. We knew each other, as I had also
dated his brother a couple of times, a few years prior. I decided
that the area would be a lovely, quiet place to raise a child, away
from the inauthenticity and insanity of Hollywood, so I told him
of my plans to move up and asked if he could help me get more
consistent work there. While my plan was to be an in-town session singer, working mainly for him, bad timing once again took

its toll, as he was on the down side of his popularity and work calls were coming in at a slower pace. Instead, Narada turned me on to everyone he knew, including Mike Keller, who had a jingle house turning out commercial work in nearby Sausalito at the time.

Me & Narada Michael Walden

I moved to the beautiful, quaint little town of Mill Valley, California, living walking distance of the town's center, among the towering redwood trees. It was like living in an enchanted forest. I set up two things: 1) a personal trainer at a gym in Corte Madero and 2) I contacted an agency and got a nanny to come during the day to assist with my baby. The woman I hired seemed nice woman, though a little eccentric, and there was something uncomfortable about her. My daughter hated her and would scream whenever she was in her presence. Once, I came home and the nanny was on one end of the sofa and my daughter was on the other end. The nanny said they were having a "Mexican stand-off." This was a sign that this relationship was not ever going to work. Needless to say, this nanny's services were short-lived.

Living in Mill Valley was really lovely, as I befriended other moms who were out on the stroll with their baby carriages. The pediatrician, whose office was in San Rafael, would do house calls, which he did once when my daughter got really sick with a flu. The pharmacy delivered to my front door. It was good, old-fashioned, small town just outside the bustling city of San Francisco. The only setback was my landlord, who was very odd. He lived in Stinson Beach, which was about thirty to forty minutes away from Mill Valley, over some mountainous terrain. He seemed very nervous and high strung. Something in my spirit told me not to trust him, but I went ahead and rented the house. When my friends visited from Los Angeles, they thought my house was haunted. Soon, this would become an issue.

While work was slow in San Francisco, the quality of the work that I did was supreme. When Narada did work, it was always with interesting projects and amazing artists. One of my favorite gigs was with Clarence Clemons, the sax player from Bruce Springsteen's E Street Band. Narada was a lover of great singers and a rocker also, so we connected on the music and our birthdays were a day apart. His birthday is April 23rd and mine is April 22nd. He hooked me up to do a gig at Sweetwater's in downtown Mill Valley. It was a fundraiser to buy new sound equipment for the venue.

I got to the gig, not knowing exactly what I would be singing, only to be told to meet up with a dude named Jerry and his daughter. I arrived, met Jerry, and we went downstairs into the basement of the club. Jerry then introduced me to his daughter and said that we were going to sing backup for him. This was cool, as it just felt like a good, old, small-town kind of gig, getting me acclimated to my new environment. He started teaching me the choruses to the song and his daughter and I decided on our parts. He never sang the entire song, just the choruses. They were easy and as I sang them, they sounded somewhat familiar. We got on the tiny stage to perform and they announced Jerry's name. It's Jerry Harrison, guitarist and keyboardist from the iconic rock group Talking Heads! All I could do was shake my head. Also on stage was Bob Weir from The Grateful Dead. Then, the realization kicked in that I was on stage singing with rock royalty. Damn, that Narada never said a thing.

As time moved onward, my finances started to tighten up uncomfortably. I ended up driving back and forth to Los Angeles now, for recording sessions. This was taxing, but a woman does what a woman has to do. It was equally strenuous on my daughter, as she would get car sick from time to time, which made me feel even more guilty.

I received a call from Elton's offices in Los Angeles, asking my availability to do an Aids Benefit Concert for his foundation. The theme was "excerpts from the Broadway musical 'West Side Story'." As a member of his band, we would back up all of the artists who performed on the program. It was yet another great opportunity to work with a star-studded cast of music's greatest icons, ranging from Tammy Wynette to Barbra Streisand. It was also great timing, since my rent was about to be late. I informed my landlord that I had a gig in Los Angeles and I'd be able to pay my rent in full when I returned.

The gig was spectacular. The next evening after my gig, I picked up my daughter from her godparents' house and drove back home to Mill Valley, arriving around two in the morning. Everything in my neighborhood down inside the forest was still, as all that could be heard were the waterfalls in the distance and the rolling stream that was on my next-door neighbors' property. While this was a very safe neighborhood, it was still a bit unnerving, coming into an empty, quiet house at that time of night. My only concern was possibly walking up on raccoons.

I got safely inside of my house and locked the door, only to hear a sudden knocking at the door. Mortified by the thought of who this could possibly be at this hour, I looked out of the side window. It was my landlord. I open the door and he rushed in. "Where is my rent?" he demanded. I explained to him that I had just returned from working in Los Angeles and that I had to make a deposit first thing in the morning. He insisted that I write a check immediately, so I quickly got out my checkbook and started writing. He took the check, turned, and left. The next morning, I got to the bank as it opened, deposited my check and asked the teller to please put his check through, as it was not certain if there were any holds placed as a bank procedure. It was a large sum, so customarily, they held a portion of it. However, she assured me that this check would go through with no holds attached, which was all that mattered.

While nothing illegal had taken place, no threats or eviction notices, and my rent was paid in full. However, from that point on, the damage had been done to my relationship with this landlord, as I was never again comfortable in that house. Since I had no idea exactly what time I would arrive home that night, it was unnerving to know that my landlord was parked somewhere where I could not see him, watching and waiting through the wee hours of the morning for my return. That was crazy. Soon after that event, other odd happenings occurred. I came home one night and my front door was wide open. I didn't get out of my car but stayed with my daughter in the back seat and called the police. They arrived quickly and searched the house. There was nothing there, nothing missing. Another occurrence was when the electricity mysteriously went off, then an hour or so later, came back on. The ghosts of "home issues past" had returned for another visit. Now, I was terrified, as I was alone in this town now with child. There was no friend there to comfort me. I contacted a girlfriend of mine in Los Angeles who was a psychic and knew other magical practices. I solicited some advice on what to do. She informed me that the spirits told her that something bad had happened in that house and that an entity lived in the shag carpeting in the living room. Something in my heart agreed with everything she said. She told me that she would send me some oils to place on the windows and doorways for protection. I received the box of oils in the mail within days. At this point, I was placing toys in front of my front door, to make noise, alerting me should someone enter without knocking. Needless to say, I wasn't sleeping. Also, I was in the midst of trying to get my daughter to sleep alone in her crib. Having been told by the pediatrician to let her "cry it out," I placed her in her crib. She screamed and cried for hours. I felt guilty and horrible. After several hours, she finally quieted down. I went tipping into her bedroom only to find her with eyes closed but standing up in her crib like a miniature zombie, as she would not lie down. I picked her up in my arms and took her to my bedroom and laid her next to me. That's when I decided to never leave her alone in her crib again. The house won. I just needed an exit strategy.

NARADA MICHAEL WALDEN

Narada decided to do an all-star, ten-day tour of Japan. He asked me to sing lead on two of his songs, "Baby Come To Me" by Regina Bell and "Freeway Of Love," which he also wrote and produced for Aretha Franklin. The rest of my work included backing vocals for the other artists on the tour: Tevin Campbell, Patti Austin, Shanice, and Mickey Thomas from Jefferson Starship. It paid well and I saw it as an opportunity to move out of my house in Mill Valley once and for all. This also meant leaving my daughter for the first time. I was grateful for work that was substantial enough to finance this move, yet heartbroken that I was considering going back on my word, an agreement I made with myself. I did not want to leave her for any length of time. This tour was my best option, after my previous experience of using the hotel nannies. I contacted my daughter's godparents and my Persian babysitter in Los Angeles. Everyone was in place to take care of my child for those ten days.

I drove my daughter down to Los Angeles to her godparents' home before the last rehearsal. While everything went smoothly, I knew that this moving-around life was becoming too much for both of us. The thought that, hopefully, this would be the last time, was all that my mind and heart could carry at this point. Narada gave me the name of a trusted moving company to which I could give the keys to my home and they would pack, move, and store my entire house while I was away at rehearsal. This worked out perfectly, as this last rehearsal would be a long one as we prepped for the tour.

This Japanese tour was massive, as it was a star-studded band, with keyboardist Joe Zawinul and the original members of Weather Report opening the show. We all traveled together. The band included Greg Phillinganes and Frank Martin on piano, Sheila E. and Alex Acuña on percussion, Alphonse Johnson and T.M. Stevens on bass, Kirk Whalum on saxophone, and Patti Austin, Shanice Wilson, and Tevin Campbell on lead vocals. Of course, Narada on drums. Nikita Germaine, Tony Linsey, and I performed backing vocals. We sang leads on all the hit songs that Narada had produced, including Aretha Franklin's duet with Wham's George Michael, "I Knew You Were Waiting," and his hit songs he did with Whitney Houston, including "I Wanna Dance With Somebody," just to name a few. It was an incredible show and we sold out at the Nippon Budokan in Tokyo and other arenas. What an awesome tour!

This successful tour ended the day after my birthday, which

was also Narada's birthday, and I awaited my most awesome gift, seeing my daughter. Her godparents were supposed to bring her to the airport and meet me in the baggage claim area. Impatiently, I looked around until finally I spotted my daughter in her godmother's arms. As I walked toward them, my daughter was not smiling. In fact, she was wincing, as if she was afraid. I took her in my arms and she placed her little hands on my shoulder, pulling back and looking at my face. I could clearly see in her eyes that she did not recognize me at all. There was an uncomfortable silence as she just stared at me. I looked in her eyes, trying to remain calm, though deep down inside, I was shocked and almost tearful. After a few seconds, she slowly relaxed her arms, moved closer, then rested her head on my shoulder. Finally, she remembered me. To me, this was the sign that I could never leave her for a long period again. It was a horrific experience for me to see my baby react this way. Swiftly, these touring days would be coming to an end.

ZERO ... AND THE HEALING BEGINS – PRESENT DAY – 2016

On one of my Wi Spa trips, I decided to eat in their restaurant, which is rare since their vegan options are extremely limited. My choices were shrimp fried rice without the shrimp or veggie hot stone bibimbap minus the egg. So, I sat there eating and out of nowhere came a familiar face. It was Chaka Khan's sister and former manager, Tammy McCrary. She was just as surprised to see me as I was to see her. We hugged and she told me that she was there to meet some girlfriends for a book club. She invited me to join them and, of course, my response was a resounding yes!

We caught up on our lives and she told me about her new business venture, which is an online artist academy called artistologyacademy.com. It sounded incredible. The main principles of teaching artists about branding and other business aspects of the music industry are centered around a philosophy from the book "Zero Limits" by Joe Vitale, one of the stars of the movie "The Secret." His book is based on his meeting with Hawaiian therapist Dr. Ihaleakala Hew Len, who expanded on a belief system called Ho'Oponopono. This concept explains that one should take 100 percent responsibility for everything good and not good that happens in their life and explains how to focus on living in a space he calls "zero limits" where one's entire movement and existence from moment to moment is dictated directly from the Divine. No planning, just purely living in the moment. Lastly, the concept acknowledges the negative subconscious programs that dictate the lives of human beings. Dr. Len corrects this through what he calls "cleaning," or speaking energetically the words "I love you," "I'm sorry, please forgive me," and "thank you." Every experience you have and every person you come in contact with happens for a reason. There are no coincidences, so it's all good. The concept sounded very intriguing so I quickly accepted the offer to join these ladies and hear more about this book.

As if a light went off in her head, Tammy said, "You're a teacher! Would you be interested in teaching an online music course for my academy?" Now this was really incredible, as I had been trying to get an online course launched for two years now, since meeting up with my friend in the Bay Area. I told Tammy that I had already written a curriculum and it was just awaiting the video components. Wow! It's finally happening!

I met with Tammy and her friends. It was a lovely and short introduction, as they all had spa appointments for massages and other services. No one seemed at all interested in talking about any book, let alone this one, so Tammy and I continued to converse. She emailed the PDF of the book to me and I couldn't wait to read it! That night, before closing my eyes, I lay there on the heated jade floor of the spa and began reading from my iPad. From that moment on, I decided to apply the concept of "cleaning." The results were amazing. Here's an example of zero limits when I applied it.

After paying for my spa passes, purchasing food, paying for the gym, and paying to get my car out of repossession, I ran out of money. Of all days, it was the day before my birthday. I had been invited out for a drink on the night of my birthday, but had no cash or plans for food, dinner, or anything else. I thought I'd better just park at my spot in front of Cafe Gratitude and save my gas to have enough to get to Nobu in Malibu for my birthday drink. I pulled into my parking space, climbed over and reclined my passenger seat all the way back, got my quilt, sweater, and jacket, and prepared to sleep. Then I got this overwhelming feeling of sadness. I started to cry. I started to wail. Was I feeling sorry for myself? It was almost midnight, the witching hour of my birth. Look at me. What had I accomplished? Did I progress? Regress? I just started saying prayers. Prayers of thanksgiving for my life, my great health, the strides in my career. I knew that I had moved forward, but living in my car had started to take its toll on my mental state. That depression was starting to rear its ugly head again. I knew rationally that everything would be OK. But, I also knew I was exhausted, hungry, and just mentally drained. Being that it was my birthday only made the feelings worse. The harder I cried, the more I prayed, asking God, "What's the right thing to do now?"

Then it hit me: *There is nothing I can do. I give up, I let go, I'm on zero, I don't know what else to do!* I cried myself to sleep. Needless to say, it was not a restful sleep and it was short. At 6 a.m., I drove over to Starbucks. It was my birthday. Suddenly, an email notification popped up on my phone. It was from Starbucks, saying, "Happy Birthday! Today, you have received a free beverage of your choice!" Yay! I get a free tall decaf soy latte. I went to wash

up in the bathroom, then realized I really needed a shower to
go out with friends today, so I texted my friends in Encino and
asked if I could just come over and take a shower. They said yes,
so after getting my free latte, I drove to the San Fernando Valley.

While I was there, my friends informed me that I could also
wash a load of clothes and watch my favorite television show,
"Scandal." Cool! They had recorded it and I could catch up on
last week's episode. Thankful, I relaxed and watched TV, got
cleaned up, and put my clothes in the washer. Then I checked my
emails and my text messages. I had received a joyful text from
my friend Jen weeks ago and just couldn't respond at the time.
I decided to sit and write her a full explanation of what's been
going on in my life. She wrote back and said that she wanted to
do something for my birthday. What she did then was nothing
short of miraculous. Jen gave me a three-night stay through
AirBnB. Wow, a bed! I would get to sleep in a bed in a room by
myself for three nights! Oh my God! Not only that, she sent me
$100 through PayPal for food and gas. Tonight, on my birthday
night, I knew I would be in my own bed. That meant a lot. After
I finished my laundry, I prepared to go to the gym but received a
call from the woman from AirBnB, asking me to pick up the key
to the house right away, so I postponed my gym appointment
with the trainer to get the key.

The AirBnB property was located in West Los Angeles. As
I pulled into a parking space in front of the building address,
there was a 1970s minivan parked on the street with a teenage
guy washing the windows. As I walked past the van on my way
to the apartment, I could smell marijuana. Of course, a 1970s
minivan would smell like weed. It's straight out of a TV situation
comedy. Anyway, I got to the door and the house, which actually
was an apartment, is a bit messy as if she was not expecting anyone. She directed me to my room, which was actually a loft, so
it was open to the entire living room downstairs, which meant

no doors and no privacy. Also, there were kids' toys everywhere and a dog. My first thoughts were that this would not be a quiet stay, since my sleep space was privy to everything that went on in the living room and kitchen. Plus, there was just something strange about the entire situation. The woman excused herself to do something upstairs. I immediately took a video and pics of the space and sent them to Jen. Not really knowing what to expect, my instincts were telling me that this may not be a good place to stay with strangers. Then, I heard music. The teenager who was outside cleaning the "weed" van came in and started playing music on his phone. Not a big deal, but I knew that my living space was open to this noise. I look again and notice, the living room has a twin bed set up. Obviously, this has been converted into a sleeping area for a child. OK, it was time for me to leave. I called Jen and explained the situation. After some back and forth with the AirBnB management, she was able to change the reservation with zero financial penalties.

So, now the plan was to check in late at a home in Pasadena. I knew Jen was trying to get me near my beloved water, but I was just ecstatic at the prospect of sleeping in a real bed. At this point, it was after 3 p.m., too early to head toward Malibu for my drinks. Jen hadn't sent the money for food and gas, so I just stayed parked in West L.A. for a while. As I was sitting in my car, a call came in from my friend Bridgette Bryant, wishing me a happy birthday. Bridgette then asked me, "What are you doing for your birthday?" I told her about the drinks later and that I had nothing else planned. Then the miracle. She said, "Then I am taking you out to dinner right now for your birthday. We will go to our favorite vegan spot, Sun Cafe in Studio City!" I could not believe my ears. I was in that moment going to get food. I don't really know how to describe how I felt. I was so tired from lack of sleep. My eyes were still tight and red from crying. Eye drops were useless. I felt a reverence around me. I knew that I was literally being carried by God. Each and every moment as I lay in the passenger seat of my car, I just prayed, thank you to the God in me that had sustained me through adversity and blessed me with loving friends who extended themselves for my birthday. Then, I apologized to the God (my birth name, Natalie) in me for being so stressed out about my circumstances, and not trusting that everything would be OK. Then, I told myself, "I love you so much" for taking care of my health and wellbeing and moving forward in faith in spite of the challenging times. I would cry, then cry out "I love you, I forgive you, thank you. I still believe. I know it's going to be OK," over and over until I finally went to sleep. So, to see the power of the Divine working on my behalf before my very eyes, supplying my food and shelter, I felt humbled and in awe, and most of all pure gratitude.

So, now it was time to drive to Studio City to meet Bridgette for dinner. I got a call from her saying she's running late, so I pulled over once again after I get closer to the restaurant. Then, I got another surprise phone call, this time from Rickey Minor. He's an old friend who is an extraordinary bass player and well-known musical director currently for the ABC television show" American Idol" and many other shows, and former music director for "The Tonight Show with Jay Leno." I rarely speak to Rickey but had just run into him in Hollywood when I was on my way to sing at Lucky Strike a few weeks prior. Rickey called to say Happy Birthday and that he'd like to meet up with me to discuss a business proposal. He requested that I bring with me a list of ten things I want to accomplish immediately, in five years, and in ten years. This was an unusual request, but I agreed to do it. That was easy, since I write incessantly about my goals and dreams all the time. By the time I finished my conversation, it was time to continue on to Sun Cafe for dinner with Bridgette, then on to Nobu Malibu for drinks with Neal. What an awesome birthday it turned out to be.

Later that evening, I arrived in Pasadena at the AirBnB home

MEMOIRS OF A BACKUP DIVA

of Margo, a lovely Asian woman who met me outside and handed me the garage door opener for my car. That was an extra added gift, indoor parking, so I didn't have to worry about street parking regulations. My room was well appointed, neat, and very quiet. Needless to say, I slept like a baby.

That next morning, Margo and I had the most stimulating conversations about our common interests, yoga and the healing qualities in music. Now, I wanted to cry because I knew that I was placed here to listen, learn, and remember. Those next three days were pure heaven. I slept, worked on music, and watched Netflix. I even got up at 4 a.m. and went to kundalini yoga with Margo. Afterward, she took me out for coffee and a bagel for my birthday. This was a birthday I will never forget. From this moment on, my new mantra was, live at zero, where every moment is dictated by spirit. Zero limits. Zero!

ANOTHER ZERO LIMITS EVENT

I took my last $20 and went to the Korean spa and brought snacks. That night, I received a call from Tammy, Chaka's sister, asking me to vocal coach her child along with another little boy for a performance they had coming up the following Sunday. This was awesome unanticipated income. We agreed to schedule the lesson for Wednesday afternoon at 5:30 p.m. However, the following day, she texted me with a cancellation, asking to reschedule for Thursday, which was still doable for me. So, on Wednesday evening, I was able to get a discounted pass to the spa, which left me money for food and $5 for gas. The guy at the service station thought I was nuts for asking for such a minimal amount with gas being over $4 per gallon. This meant I was only purchasing a little over a gallon of gas, which didn't go very far in a sprawling city such as Los Angeles. I could see it in his face.

Plus, he kept repeating, "So, you just want $5?" "Yep, that's it!" I responded.

I slept well that night at the spa, then got up and out by 11 a.m. to go work out with my personal trainer. Later that day, I would be going to teach vocal lessons to Tammy's son and his friend at 5:30 p.m. Just as I pulled out of the parking lot of the spa, I received a text from Tammy saying, "Sorry, I'm going to have to cancel our lesson today." Crap! I texted her back, informing her that the last-minute cancellation incurred a $25 cancellation fee. She agreed to the payment, but in the meantime, I had to do what I never wanted to do. I had to call my mother and ask her if she could give me gas money and food. I could not figure any other way to remedy this situation. I had to eat and I had less than a quarter of a tank of gas. My mother informed me that she could not help. So, instead of stressing about this, I continued driving toward LaBrea Avenue where I would turn south towards Inglewood to get to the gym when suddenly, I got another text, this time from my trainer: "No work out today." No! Those workouts were life savers, de-stressers for me. When I got to LaBrea Avenue, I couldn't make a left turn anyway, due to road construction. Taking a last-minute lane switch to get over and make a right onto LaBrea, I decided to go to Starbucks in Hollywood on LaBrea and Sunset, to hang out there and figure out what my next steps should be.

I made the right turn onto LaBrea, not even going one block before looking to my right. Just as I was about to turn my head, I noticed a woman getting out of her car in the parking lot of a restaurant called Republique. It was Stephanie Jeffries, whom I had recently met through my friend Sandy Simmons-Williams. I rolled down my passenger window, catching her off guard, and called out her name. Surprised, Stephanie answered, "Hey, what are you doing?" I gave a short explanation of my day, then the miracle occurred. She said, "Park your car and I'll take you out for lunch." Stunned at the offer and wondering where to park and with what money, as I didn't even have cash for the parking meter, of course, the universe provided a parking space for me directly in front of the restaurant. As I parked in my God-given space, before I could get out of my car, Stephanie came to my meter and popped in her credit card. *Voilà*, lunch! We had a delicious lunch, with leftover salad for me to take away, and talked about life, family, career for two hours. It was such a lovely way to spend an afternoon. Soon, it was time to leave, as rush hour was fast approaching and there were no parked cars allowed on LaBrea Avenue at this time. I hugged and thanked Stephanie for a lovely lunch, then hopped into my car. Just as I was about to drive off, Stephanie pulled along the driver's side of my car and hollered out her passenger window. "Hey, Need some gas?"

I tell ya, those days after reading that book, "Zero Limits," totally changed the trajectory of my life.

ACCEPTANCE
CHAPTER SEVEN

I was skimming through my news feed on Facebook one day and came across this story on the 12 steps of Karma. The one that stuck out for me was Acceptance. It stated that you cannot change your life until you can accept where you are right now. Somewhat familiar with this philosophy, as Chandler from Mel's Diner had expressed this virtue to me before, for some reason it resonated with my spirit differently this particular day. At this point, I had been homeless for almost two years. My focus was always on getting work, making goals for more work, leaving messages and emails, making lists on whom to contact regarding work. It was a constant imbalance, having no place to reboot, to sleep consistently, or re-energize. I was always about securing the future, now realizing that meant totally ignoring the present. But, in my mind, I thought I was constantly living in the present, having made decisions that only dealt with what came before me in that moment. This would not be true. While only dealing with what was happening in that moment, my moment would be spent listing goals for tomorrow. The fact is, if the sentence starts out saying "I'm gonna ...," then that's setting up the future.

It was as if I never wholly accepted my life as a homeless person. Who would? Soon, this definition of acceptance would begin to sink into my consciousness. Rather than fighting my instabilities, worrying about the future, I decided to be more efficient in accepting my life as it is, only focusing on the present. Whenever I examined my present life, in that moment, I realized that everything was really ok. My health was good, I had food, a place to sleep that was covered from the outdoor elements and reasonably safe, and my voice was still vibrant and I could make my living singing. In that moment, I was happy. That's all that should really matter because, that's all I have. The book "The Art Of Happiness" by The Dalai Lama, now made more sense. Having read it years ago, and understanding it in theory, now my life was becoming a clear example of his concepts. Only being concerned about how other people viewed my circumstances, would I fall out of happiness. It was an old behavior that now, I was ready to break. Living under the belief system of my parents weighed heavily on me, as it was my understanding that living under these homeless circumstances, one would be ridiculed and looked down upon, revealing "something is wrong with me." I didn't know nor had I ever heard of anyone close to me being homeless. Possibly, this is why it never occurred to me to apply for aid or general relief as in, food stamps, or consult other agencies for assistance. I ignored the fact that things were ever that bad, but they were. Sometimes solicited or unsolicited, friends would help by giving me cash or treating me to a meal. But, most times things were always on the edge of nothing, meaning there would be no money for food, or I would drive around on very little gas, waiting to the very last minute before calling anyone for help. Many times, I was embarrassed to even ask for help. At this point, my mother did not know that I was sleeping in my car, as I was certain, she assumed I was at a friend's home. Keeping her head in the sand, she never asked questions and I never offered any information on my whereabouts. Regardless, it was always an issue if I ever asked her for help. Most times, regardless of my circumstances, her answer was no.

I remember not having one dollar in my wallet and a friend happened to call that day. As I drove around, we talked for a while. Finally, I admitted that I had not even money for a candy bar and had not eaten all day. She told me to go to a food bank. In my mind, I had envisioned that she may offer to send a couple of dollars via PayPal. If it were me, having $5 in my bank account and knowing that my friend had nothing and hadn't eaten, nothing would stop me from Pay-Palling them at least $2. My feelings were hurt, but being the passive person that I was, I said nothing.

On the other hand, I had friends who were a lifeline. However, I rarely contacted them for help. Most times, I would just hunker down, say prayers, and try to sleep off the hunger. The lowest point was allowing, then eventually asking, my now-20-year-old daughter for money. She would gladly offer $20, sometimes $100. It would really tear me up inside, but I had nothing. The only saving grace in this turbulence was that I knew that the lifestyle I was able to provide her was a good one. She attended private schools up through fourth grade. Her public-school education was great in Cambridge, MA. She had traveled and spent quality time in Japan, several islands in the Caribbean, Paris, and Amsterdam by the time she was 8 years old. She studied music and ballet every year of her life, ending up at Alvin Ailey. We lived in beautiful homes in lovely neighborhoods from Topanga to upstate New York to Mill Valley, CA. I knew from my past experience, that these challenging times would also pass, as I still felt confident that financial security would return to my life. However, soon I learned, there was a high price to pay for only looking at the positive side of things. Not accepting my present circumstances was wreaking havoc on my life. Being in this cycle, constantly placed me in a state of action, which probably sounds like a good thing. I would later realize it had an opposite effect.

ALMOST SETTLED - 1995

I returned to Los Angeles from a successful ten-day tour in Japan with some of the music industry's top musicians and Grammy award-winning artists, to staying briefly at my friends, the Anderson's home with my daughter. After a couple of months, I voluntarily returned my car to the dealership since work was slow. It was a thought that I should consider finishing graduate school and start teaching college. So, I kept my things in storage in San Francisco and flew home to Memphis, to study for the Graduate Record Exam (GRE). I was there for three months. My head simply was not engaged, but I pushed through. After taking the exam, my scores were mediocre at best. It would be in my best interest to take it again to get a better score and expand my chances for a better choice of graduate programs. In my spare time, I read "The Celestine Prophecy" books and started doing the exercises in the attached workbook. Being in Memphis was not conducive to my artist lifestyle. My mother placed my daughter in day care at a facility owned by her friend and fellow retired school teacher, Irma Foster. It was around the corner from her home, which was convenient. At least, my child was in good hands.

After three months, my friend Paula, whom I'd spent that time in Queens, New York, called and said, "You can't stay in Memphis, that place isn't for you." She and her husband had separated at the time and Gary was looking for someone to rent out his place while he taught some classes at Clark College in Atlanta. "Why don't you move into Gary's apartment for three months while he's teaching in Atlanta?" So, it was agreed. My daughter and I flew back to L.A. and lived in Studio City, CA, for three months.

It was a little challenging, but I got enough session work to pay the meager amount of rent Gary charged me to stay in his apartment. In the meantime, I decided to get copies of my resume to start looking for a job, any job. So, I put my daughter in the stroller and walked the streets of Studio City for miles, in search of work, while also taking her to the park as well. Having no car at this point, I strolled down Ventura Boulevard near Laurel Canyon Boulevard. Right at the corner was a Kinko's, so I decided to inquire about possible work there. The clerk at the desk smiled pleasantly, asking if he could assist me. I inquired about any positions available and offered a copy of my resume for his review. The clerk looked at my resume and laughed. He asked, "Why are you looking for work here?" I pointed down to my child in the stroller and said, "I don't want to go on the road any more. Surely there must be something I could do." The answer was a blank stare "no," so I simply thanked him and strolled on out of the store. My next stop was Color Me Mine, which was a make-your-own pottery store. My daughter and I actually went there, bought and painted pottery as a present to her godparents one Christmas. Again, I was met with the same looks, the same attitudes. Evidently, it was just unimaginable that a person with my résumé would be considered as a candidate to work at such establishments. I never knew that getting a regular job would be so hard. By the end of three months, my finances were in dire straits as it was nearing Christmas 1995.

Out of the blue, a call came from Jeffrey Osborne's office, asking my availability to do a gig New Year's Eve in Washington, D.C. Yes, of course I was free to do the gig, but the question was, who would take care of my daughter? My friends in New York City had been in contact with me since my daughter's birth, begging me to come to N.Y.C. so they could meet and possibly babysit. They had not seen her and were hoping something could be arranged in my travel that would bring me to the city. I asked

Jeffrey's office if they could fly me in to New York so I could drop off my daughter, then put me on a train to D.C. for the gig. They were hesitant to agree and slow to respond. As everything was left suspended in mid-air, synchronicity intervened once again. Chaka Khan's office called out of the blue, inquiring if I was available to do New Year's Eve at the Beacon Theater in New York City. That was the answer needed. The bonus, in addition to having sitters for my daughter, she paid the most money for the gig. So, we were flown to New York City. Chaka's Tour Manager was Simone Morrison, an awesome force of a Afro-Caribbean woman from London. She fell in love with my daughter and between her and my friend Felicia Collins (former guitarist for Al Jarreau and then-current guitarist for CBS' "Late Night With David Letterman"), my child was looked after during the sound check and show. We rocked that New Year's Eve show, co-headlining with The Ohio Players, one of my favorite groups that I grew up listening to in Memphis.

After that show, my friends convinced me to stay on the East Coast for a while. Chaka was touring somewhat regularly but mostly on weekends. However, my issue was leaving my daughter. I just didn't want to do this again. Chaka suggested that I meet her friend Sarah to watch my child while we were away doing weekend gigs. This worked out OK, as my daughter was getting older and she loved Sarah. So, I decided to accept my life as a touring mom, as the path of least resistance revealed itself and things started to fall into place. We stayed on the East Coast, living with my friend Carla in New Jersey, then later with my old friend Sandra St. Victor in Brooklyn. Sarah was always around to watch Vaughn when we did gigs on weekends in the states. Whenever we did television shows like "The Rosie O'Donnell Show" in N.Y.C., my daughter would come with me and Simone would watch her while we were on the set. If we toured for periods longer than a weekend. I would fly her to my mother's house in Memphis. This schedule was OK, since She was only 2 years old at this point and had not entered school.

While in N.Y.C., I landed a part-time teaching gig at The New School For Social Research in their Continuing Education Department. The money was not good, but it would be my first college level teaching experience. More and more, I would put into the universe that a college job would be great, as I didn't want to leave my child. This last experience escalated my concern.

Once, while in Memphis after a gig with Chaka, I was called me for another last-minute gig. The initial decision was to bring my daughter with me. But, the night before we were to leave, she got sick with the flu, vomiting and developing a fever. I knew then she would not be well enough for the plane trip. When my mother put her in her car seat to take me to the airport, she thought she was going with me. Once we arrived at the gate, I had to explain to her that she couldn't go because she was too ill. She was devastated but instead of throwing a childish tantrum, tears rolled down her face as she was completely silent. When I went to kiss her goodbye, she silently turned her head. She would not look me in the eyes. It was a grown-up response that hurt me to my core. I got on that plane in tears. At this point, I felt the scars of this lifestyle were forming. Something had to change. While I knew that as a single parent, it would be great for my child to have another adult in her life, especially a grandmother, which is something I never had, it was still difficult to leave her though she was in safe hands. These memories still weigh heavy on my spirit even to this day.

The next tour with Chaka was a bus tour that ironically, stopped through Memphis. My mother invited the entire band and crew over for dinner. A couple of my friends from high school came over. It was fun as people in the neighborhood who were out for their evening stroll, were caught off guard by the huge tour bus parked in the cove in front of my mother's home. We had my favorite meal at the time, which was turkey, dressing and collard greens. My mother's best friend, assisted her in preparing the meal. It was a great time. The best part of all was that I told my daughter that she could come on the bus with me and finish the tour with me and go back to New York with me. She was head-over-heels elated. I always hoped this would make up for that morning I had to leave her.

SIGN NUMBER TWO

Traveling on tour buses is by far my favorite way to travel. It is a home away from home. We always had great fun on Chaka's bus tours.

These buses are equipped with a refrigerator, microwave, coffee pot, hot water kettle, Wi-Fi and flat-screen TV, and twelve bunk beds with interior lights for reading, stacked in threes in the mid-section of the bus. The back end of the bus is the artist's suite, which consists of a full bathroom with tub and shower, and a full bedroom with queen-size bed. You have your snacks and food, and your choice of movies. I loved lounging around in sweats or in my onesie. The bathroom was clean; the agreement was that if you had to poop, then we would stop at a rest stop for their facilities. We would check into a hotel for showers. It was a leisurely way to travel where we could go at our own pace. My daughter loved it.

When we got to Chicago, we stopped to eat at a restaurant, then walked down Michigan Avenue to where the bus was parked. My child was happy, as it was hot and sunny and we were all rested and fed and just enjoying being outside. Suddenly, she decided to run down the sidewalk. At first, it seemed fun, then I looked ahead and noticed that she was approaching the entrance to a garage parking lot, where cars were exiting from underground. There would be no way for drivers to see her as they came out of that lot, as she was under three feet tall. I ran down the street as quickly as possible to catch her before she got to the entrance. Just when I caught her, I made one misstep and bam! I sprained my ankle. My bandmates helped me the rest of the way, and onto the bus. When we arrived at the hotel, they brought out a wheelchair to assist me to my room. I did the show that night on crutches. As fun as it was to have my daughter on tour with me, it also came with some liabilities. This was sign number two that a change was coming soon.

Back in New York, now staying in Brooklyn with my friend Sandra St. Victor and her teenage daughter, I decided to look for an apartment of my own. At first, the consideration was her area, which was the Park Slope neighborhood. The area was fast becoming a popular choice for seemingly everyone on the planet at the time, as rental rates began to skyrocket. Around this time, I watched the movie "Baby Boom" with Diane Keaton, who plays an advertising executive who, after the death of a relative, is willed guardianship of a small child, making her an instant single mom and then decides to leave the hustle of the Big Apple for a quiet, rural life. This movie influenced me to look for a house in the country, away from everything urban in N.Y.C. I just wanted the simple life. I was already speaking my desires to the universe, telling it, "I don't have to tour any more, I just want to live somewhere up in the country and work in a General Store," reflecting my need more and more each day to just get away and make this shift. A friend suggested I check out Rhinebeck, New York, located off the Hudson River up in Dutchess County, which was three counties north of New York City. It was about a two-hour drive away and could be reached via Amtrak. I took the train up to the Rhinecliff/Kingston station, then taxied into downtown Rhinebeck. It was a beautiful, quaint little picturesque village, with shops that were filled with trinkets and such, like the Hogwarts Village in the Harry Potter movies, straight out of an old New England picture book. As I walked down the main thoroughfare, I happened upon a real estate office that had listings of house rentals in the window, so I decided to check out the pricing.

Battistoni Realty was the place and I believe it was Ms. Battistoni that assisted me. We looked through a book show-ing pictures of houses for rent in the area, and there it was: A lovely, white, wood-framed farm house on seventy-two acres of land, with two ponds on the property. There was a General Store down the road. The price was $950 per month, which was the lowest rent I had ever paid since first living in L.A. during the Natalie Cole days. I agreed to rent it. My new home was in Clinton Corners, New York, on a route, as there was no house address. Loved it! Now, all I needed was a car of some kind, as I was now in the country. The smallest parcel of land on my street was five acres, but most people had at least twenty acres. My landlords lived on twenty-two acres, just down the road. On my property, there was a small guest house rented by an elderly white gentleman. He was a lovely guy, whom I recall liked to pick the blackberries off the bushes around the house. We all got along well.

Shortly after moving into the farmhouse, I was contacted by a woman named Jan Shapiro, who at that time was Interim Chair of the Voice Department at Berklee College of Music in Boston. She was given my name, as there was a possible part-time posi-tion available in the voice department. Chaka was about to do the VH-1 "Hard Rock Live" television show in N.Y.C., so I invited Ms. Shapiro come down to the city to the taping of the show. Afterward, she offered me the job. Happily, I accepted, as finally this was my chance to get off the road for good. Following the path of least resistance had paid off in getting me exactly what I asked for. My daughter was approaching 4 years old and attend-ing a preschool in Millbrook, the closest large town to Clinton

Corners. Now, the time had come to develop a strategy for getting to Boston from upstate New York, and to figure out how to care for my daughter as well.

The commute was tricky in that it entailed driving thirty minutes to Poughkeepsie, New York, to catch the train to Manhattan, which was then a 100-minute ride. Then, catch a bus or train to Boston. Eventually I found a ten-year-old Honda Accord that cost $400. I purchased the car and drove it to Boston twice a week with daughter in tow. I dropped my daughter off at Bright Horizons daycare in Brighton, Massachusetts, not far from Berklee College, then pick her up in the evenings. My boss, Jan Shapiro, also offered her home in Newton, Massachusetts, for me and my child to stay in town on my work days. Later, my Berklee student Ruby Amanfu cared for my daughter at Berklee's dormitory while I worked the next day. The following semester, Nura, my student from Luxembourg, bartered free voice lessons in return for taking care of my child in her home in Somerville, Massachusetts, while I taught at Berklee during the day. Everything was beginning to work out. In the summer, after teaching at Berklee's Five-Week Program, I decided to look for tour work to increase my income since the part-time teacher's pay wasn't enough to fully sustain me. This meant leaving my daughter in Memphis with my mother. Sequestering her in Memphis in the summers only made it feel more like a vacation visit, which eased my mind a bit when it came to leaving her.

One day after classes, I decided to take an impromptu bus ride down Massachusetts Avenue from Boston's Back Bay area, where Berklee College of Music was located, across the Charles River to Harvard Square in Cambridge to get the feel of the area. At the end of the bus line, I got out and walked around the village, eyeing shops and other cute little tucked away places along the cobblestoned paths. I walked for about twenty minutes down lovely, historic Brattle Street, passing the original houses of the

Tories that settled in this country in the 1700s, to an area of
Cambridge called Huron Village. It was love at first sight. It
felt like home. There was something appealing about how the
architecture mixed the historic with the modern. If I did decide
to move to Massachusetts permanently, this would be the place.

My first introduction to the voice department at Berklee
was fraught with both acceptance and ridicule, topped off with
a couple of tablespoons of jealousy. It was not quite a recipe for
disaster, but it did create some controversy, which initially re-
sulted in a lot of non-communication. There were not too many
friendly faces.

In the beginning, there were few professors like myself, who
were conservatory trained and worked in the commercial music
business. We had no idea what we had to offer, being placed in an
environment such as Berklee, or exactly how to regurgitate what
we had learned and experienced as professionals in the music
industry to share with students. It was quite an exciting time, as
we were the authors of a new curriculum, creating and writing
as we learned how to teach. Initially, we were met with some
resistance from professors who had been employed at Berklee
in the voice department for years, some whom had not moved
up in their ranks and were quite discontent. It was understandable, but not easy for the newcomers. Many times, I would be
questioned on my knowledge of basic classical technique and
repertoire. Unbeknownst to them, my conservatory training and
background as a member of an opera company before entering
college thoroughly prepared me. This knowledge caught many of
them off guard. However, once the word got around the department that I was legit, they left me alone.

Also, there was a fear among some of the old guard professors that teachers with my vitae would be so popular that we
would steal students away from their rosters, which meant taking money out of their pockets. Again, this was understandable.

But, because of the growing popularity of the voice department, which increased rapidly in size within my first three semesters, there were plenty of students and work hours for everyone. As time went on, these teachers began to let down their guards and protective masks and started to communicate more. Eventually, everybody got along just fine.

Initially, I was concerned with how to approach teaching contemporary vocal lessons, as my entire music education was strictly classical. Everything else, I "learned in the street," so to speak. After I gave her a mock voice lesson, Jan Shapiro, Chairman of the Voice Department, assured me that everything would be fine; she felt that with my education along with my experience, intuitive knowledge, and ear, I knew what to do. She had total trust in my abilities. It was the genius of Jan Shapiro to hire professional working singers in the music business who also had college degrees for the department. We had the collegiate vocabulary and contemporary music experience. This combination was a rare and priceless commodity, that was key to the establishment of this new contemporary music education model. All that was left was to develop a pedagogy, and Berklee was the perfect platform. This was empowering.

Meanwhile, back in Clinton Corners, New York, life in the country was just fine. I jogged the country roads, mowed my huge yard with an old-fashioned, motorless lawn mower (what we used to call a push mower in Tennessee, where I grew up). That first year was beautiful, as it was the life I had envisioned up to a point. My daughter and I had quality time together. If she got ill, I took her with me to Boston to work, making her a pallet to lay underneath the piano in my office, as I taught voice lessons. Her world was filled with music.

Soon, my 10-year-old Honda had to be replaced. When my landlord performed a free oil change one day, he informed me that the car was totally rusted underneath. He would not charge me and suggested I get another car before the engine fell out. I asked my mother to assist me and for the first time, she actually gave me the cash to purchase a 9-year-old Jeep Wrangler. It was in good condition, except it still had a carburetor, which I soon found could be a bit problematic. Regardless, the car got me back and forth on the Massachusetts Turnpike to Boston from Clinton Corners, which was what mattered most.

Meanwhile, as my daughter got older, I noticed she needed to be around her peers more. This became an issue, as the community in Clinton Corners was very culturally segregated, meaning most families kept to themselves. The parks were barren. I would inquire with parents at the pre-school in Millbrook about the cultural environment of this area. "Most kids only play with their relatives" is what I was told, so my daughter was rarely invited out on play dates. Sometimes, the owners of the General Store, whose daughter was around the same age, would bring her in to work and she and my daughter would play around the store. One other time, there was a family who did extend an invitation for a play date. My daughter cried and cried when it was time to leave, which was an indication that she really needed to be around kids more. This country life was becoming too claustrophobic and isolating. On weekends, my solution was to drive two hours down to Manhattan. I'd park over on West 83rd and Amsterdam and go to the Children's Museum, then to the Diana Ross playground at 81st and Central Park West where my daughter would play all day, then end the day at Cafe Lalo's for a Belgian waffle before getting in the car and heading back upstate.

The following Thanksgiving, I had people up to the house for dinner, including a couple of students from Berklee who were from Australia. That Monday after the holiday, exhausted, I got up at 3 a.m. to drive to Boston. This time, I left my daughter at home with my sister and brother in-law, who were visiting for the holiday. It was cold and damp, around 40 degrees Fahrenheit, as I headed north on the Taconic Parkway. Once I got to Columbia County, the last county in New York State before crossing the Massachusetts state line, the weather was much colder and there was snow on the ground. Suddenly, my car lost control and started to skid. I'd hit black ice and went into a spin. Knowing not to use the brakes in this situation, I just froze as the car spun out of control for what seemed forever. I could see to my right that there was a drop down a steep embankment, so, I decided to hit the brakes to try to swerve the car toward the middle of the road away from the drop and into a snow bank. I touched the brakes and the car spun out in more circles, then finally swerved straight toward the snow embankment on my left, as I'd hoped. But, hitting that embankment was like hitting a concrete wall. My car flipped over the snow bank onto its side. I was left dangling sideways by my seatbelt. The rear window, behind where my daughter would normally be seated, was blown out. I was shaken up but OK. It took a minute, but after wiggling and maneuvering my body in this sideways position, I managed to release myself from the seatbelt. My first thought was to just stay in the car. It was dark, freezing, and I was in the middle of nowhere. Then, it occurred to me that the car could possibly be leaking fuel, which meant it could catch fire. So, I tried to open my car door to climb out. After trying several times, I could not lift the door at that angle. Just as my panic escalated, a man appeared, seemingly out of nowhere. He climbed up the side of my car and was able to open my car door, helping me to get out. As I got into his warm car, the engine still running, he asked if I was all right. I said yes. Within minutes, the highway patrol stopped by. Another synchronistic moment. They took me to a nearby diner and told me to just stay there until they flipped my car back on its tires and towed it to the nearest repair shop, which was in Redhook, New York. Then they would come get me.

I thanked them and went inside for a cup of coffee, then made the phone call to my house to tell my sister what happened and asked her to alert my job. When I got to the repair shop, I was told that my car only needed fluids restored, there was a tear in the hard top and the window was blown out. Otherwise, it was driveable.

Though it could have been worse, this entire incident upset me to the point that I couldn't drive over 40 miles an hour on the freeway. Every road looked like black ice to me. I was completely freaked out, especially knowing that my child's life was spared because she didn't accompany me that morning as usual. I couldn't stomach the thought of driving my child in that car in the winter months again, so I decided to find someone to care for her who could get her to preschool and keep her at home.

Using students as sitters worked for me at Berklee, so I decided to drive over to Vassar College in Poughkeepsie, New York, to solicit some help. I went to the student activities desk and met a young woman named Ebony, who ran the front desk. I gave her a flyer and asked if it could be posted there. The requirements were that the sitter had to have a car and be willing to drive thirty minutes to my home, spend the night at my home, drop my daughter off to school, and pick her up from preschool. I would have dinner prepared for both of them on Monday and Wednesday nights. Ebony replied, "I have a car. I am available to do this job." So, Ebony became my new nanny. She was a sweet, soft-spoken girl from Detroit. At Vassar, she was studying pre-med to continue to medical school to become a doctor. She was a great nanny: dependable, and trustworthy, and my daughter liked her. We continued our friendship for the next twenty years, through her completion of medical school and through her residency. Today, she is an emergency room doctor at a hospital in Austin, Texas, and we are still good friends.

Though things soon went back to a normal routine, I was

never comfortable driving on the highways to Boston from upstate New York again. At this point, Jan Shapiro had offered me a full-time position at Berklee College of Music, but I decided to turn it down, because the money offered was too low for me to consider moving to Boston full-time. Getting a decent salary to live in town was the only way I would accept the job. My commuting days were over. I decided that it would be best for me to move back to Los Angeles, but this time, I'd put my foot down and only accept work as a session singer. There would be no more touring, as my daughter would now be entering kindergarten.

After spending two years back on the East Coast, living the "Baby Boom" dream up in the country in a farmhouse on seventy-two acres of land, and commuting almost daily to the cradle of New England – Boston, Massachusetts – it was time to head west again. With no one answering my call for help except for Ebony, who came over to assist me in loading some of my furniture onto my twenty-six-foot U-Haul truck, I packed my entire four-bedroom house alone, then unpacked the contents into a storage unit.

My car never drove the same after flipping over on the Taconic Parkway, but I knew it was imperative that I have a car in Los Angeles. Driving across the country was my most cost-efficient option.

At the final hour, on the last furniture haul from the house to the storage facility, I stopped for gas, but mistakenly put regular gasoline into the truck, not realizing it only used diesel fuel. The truck then had to be towed from the gas station at Salt Point Turnpike. It had my last haul of furniture from my house, which included the heaviest items: my sofa, chaise, and my beloved white wrought-iron baby crib. The rental company threatened to charge me an exorbitant fee for my mistake and said it would be at least a week before I could complete my move. Exhausted and short on time, as at this point there were about eight or nine days left before school was to start on the West Coast, I decided to leave my remaining furniture in the U-Haul truck and take off. My friend Felicia Collins gave me her blessings along with the cash to drive across the country, saying, "You can't pay me back, for what I am giving you is priceless. I'm giving you peace of mind." With that, my daughter and I got in my 9-year-old Jeep Wrangler – with the rag tops strapped on with cloth belts and belt buckles – and took what would have normally been a three-to-five-day trip and drove for what ended up being seven days across the United States on Interstate 80. That trip alone is worthy of another book.

PRESENT — 2016

On this night, I was set to sing at the Whisky A Go Go on The Sunset Strip again with Doug Pinnick from the alternative rock group Kings X, one of my favorite groups from the '90s. The next day, I was scheduled to teach a voice lesson to a new student. That coming Saturday and Sunday, I was scheduled to work on a television show, thanks to music director Rickey Minor. I was just given money by friends the day before, so I could eat, buy gas, and sleep at Wi Spa. Finally, things were coming together.

I woke up from a restful sleep, showered, ate my apple and prepped to go work out with my trainer. I had plenty of time until my gig. Just as I was putting on my shoes to leave the spa, the woman from the front desk came downstairs and she asked me if I have a Mini Cooper. I answered "yes." She then told me that my car was being repossessed.

In a panic, as I ran upstairs and outside, I got into "zero limits" mode, envisioning the repo guy in my mind, and telling him sincerely, "I'm sorry, please forgive me for causing you ill feelings because of my non-payments. Honestly, I imagine it can't feel good to take someone's car that way, even if it is your job." Then, I mentally thanked him for alerting me to facing my responsibility and understanding my circumstances, and finally, I sent him love for being a human being, just out here doing his job.

From a distance, I could see his energy was harsh, agitated, and rude. However, when I got to my car, the gentleman was very kind and even apologized to me for putting me through this ordeal. He informed me that I could get my things. I tried to organize and assemble as much as I could, to physically carry it back inside the spa. My entire life was in that car, all of my clothes, shoes. I fought the tears and tried to organize my bags as best as possible, to make them portable. "What's the right thing to do today?" This mantra ran through my brain. After returning to the lobby of the spa, I made calls to my friends, asking for help to just think things through. I'd left messages with the MusicCares organization, which I had intended on contacting for aid before but had put off. I even called my mother, but she didn't answer so I chose not to leave a message. Now, this is zero, truly zero. All I could do was sit there in the lobby of the Spa and feel completely zero.

After a while, I stopped tearing up. Deep down I believed. I believed it was all going to be OK. I started to get hungry and I had to go to the bathroom. Not wanting to check back in to the spa, I just sat there and I prayed, thanking God most of all for this experience because I knew that something this horrendous meant that this was a sign of transcendence. Always asking to learn my lessons in this lifetime so I would not return, as I wanted to be an angel helping people from the other side on my next time on earth, I now prayed that God would show me what I was to learn from this experience. Obviously, there was something to gain here. I then asked God for forgiveness for not seeing this lesson sooner, and I forgive myself for being so hard on me and not allowing me to fail. Then, I say to the Divine, "I love you for everything you have done, for sustaining me this far, for this experience because I know this experience solidifies my launch into another level of success. I love myself for looking people straight in the eye and saying yes, I am who I am, and yes, this is happening to me. I don't feel at all ashamed. Again, I send love to my friends individually and ask forgiveness for stressing them out. Most of all, I send them gratitude for being my friend." Then, like the gentleman sitting across from me here in the lobby of the spa, I laid back, closed my eyes and began to meditate.

At that moment, all I was concerned with was getting to the Whisky to sing that night. I had four bags of clothes with me that were too heavy to walk any distance with, so catching a bus and walking wasn't an option. It crossed my mind to call my friend Nura, since my suitcase was in her storage area at her home. I could take some of these bags there, so I texted her and told her what's happening. Nura was at work in Santa Monica and wouldn't be able to get to me in time for my gig but suggested that I use one of the ride-sharing services, Uber or Lyft, to get around. I texted back letting her know that I have cash on me, but no cash in the bank for Uber or Lyft, as neither service accepts cash payments. Nura offered to set up a Lyft ride for me to get to the Whisky. Thankful, I accepted. Now, I had a plan of some kind.

I continued to be as quiet and still in my mind as I could. Deep down in my spirit, I knew everything was gonna be OK. I tried to continue to meditate, though my mind was just racing. I was in a constant state of "thank you, I'm sorry, please forgive me, I love you" – over and over and over I said these things to myself. At times, I cried, wiping away tears before anyone suspected I was losing it. Then, I finally settled into a peaceful state. Nura texted and asked what time I need the Lyft. I told her that any time around 8 p.m. was good, as I needed to eat something before I go in to sing at the Whisky. The manager of the spa allowed me to leave my things at the front desk while I re-entered the spa to go to the bathroom and purchase chips in the small store located on the women's floor. I returned to the lobby, got my things, then sat in meditation for nine hours (from 11 a.m. to 8 p.m.). The power of meditation is what attracted strength, positivity, and divine assistance to my side that night.

As it got closer to 8 p.m., the Lyft driver was somewhere in the vicinity, but can't find the driveway entrance to the spa. I went out and walked around the corner, and there he was. What a nice guy. Apple jack hat, black horn-rimmed glass, red hair, and thick red beard, kind of like a hipster, Irish Santa Claus. He was so fucking cheerful. He asked about my day, and I told him truthfully just how crazy a day it had been. He then told me that everyone who had gotten into his car that day had stated that they were having a crazy day. I share the details about my car getting repossessed. He expressed his sorrow, then says that he has been through this same thing as well. I felt relieved to know that I was not alone in this experience. He said that it was all going to work out and finally, I smiled. He told me that he is a comedian now, doing stand-up at a club in Manhattan Beach. I asked him how that process works, as I know nothing about what comedians do and how they do it. Is it total improvisation, or prepared? He explained his process. Suddenly, I was feeling better as I was getting further away from my situation. As we approached the front entrance to the Whisky on Sunset, I saw a couple of the guys who are part of the crew. I joked to the driver that when they saw me with all of these bags, they were going to ask if I was moving in. Just as I opened the car door and attempted to step out with the first of my four bags, one of the guys noticed me and rushed to the car to assist. Sure enough, he said to me, "Hey, what are you doing? You moving in?" Right on cue. He helped me with my bags, got me checked in with a badge and drink ticket (man, could I have used a cocktail right then), and carried everything up the stairs to the dressing room. As other members of the crew looked at me with all of this stuff, I told them, "It's a long story."

I was very early, as it was around 8:30 and I was not due to sing until 10:30 p.m. I told everyone, that I was going to grab a bite to eat, and while they suggest that I go to the Rainbow Grill up the street, I was thinking about the new Thai spot because I'm vegan and there would be more food choices there. But, as I walked up the street and in front of the Rainbow, I saw Kevin, the backing vocalist, and others from the Whisky coming out from what I suspected was their dinner. Kevin came up to me with a big welcoming hug and asked how I was. I told him that my car got repossessed. He knew that I'd been living in my car, so he told me that he would see what he could do, assuring me that people love me and that everything was going to be OK. He reminded me, as he had before, that he has been through this, too. It was reassuring and daunting at the same time to hear this. All I knew was that I wanted to just grab a bite to eat then get mentally ready to perform.

There's nothing's on the menu for me to eat at The Rainbow except salad – a bad salad, at that. I was too mentally spent to get up and continue to the Thai restaurant, so I went ahead and ordered the iceberg lettuce salad with canned olives and Italian dressing. Before I knew it, it was time to head back to watch some of the show and get ready to sing.

I hate stress. As a singer, it's my worst enemy, as it wreaks havoc on my voice. The acidity or whatever it is in my throat that makes my voice hoarse, as if I'd just vomited, makes me angry. This was not the night for me to have vocal issues. I was singing with Doug Pinnick, for fuck sakes. I wanted to be at my best for this opportunity. Whatever, I thought, I'm gonna make the most out of it. My attitude, as always, was that the voice I have today is the voice I need for the gig. So, I accept my voice as it is. Hey, I'll use the anger as angst for my performance.

I got through the performances and the feedback was good. Everyone, including Doug, was happy. That's what mattered most. After the performances, Kevin asked if I could stay to the end of the show. I told him of course I could. I still had another pass to go back to the spa, which is where I'd planned on sleeping that night. He offered to take me to the spa after the show. Great. I had a plan.

At the end of the show, the crew broke down the stage. Quickly, the capacity-filled room emptied out. Kevin and Adam, one of the captains who runs the show, asked that I come into another dressing room. Then it happened: Adam informed me that it was called to his attention that I needed help. He then told me that I was loved and that I was part of the "Jam Fam, " the group of performers and crew members associated with the Tuesday night show, "Ultimate Jam Night," and that Maureen, the assistant to Chuck, the other captain of the show, has offered to help me fill out forms for The Recording Academy's MusiCares program and other SAG/AFTRA-related agencies for financial assistance and that I can stay at her home on her sofa while I did this. This was incredible, because Maureen lived close to the places where I was set to work at the end of the week, the voice lesson in Burbank on Thursday, the Saturday rehearsal also in Burbank, and the Sunday television show taping at CBS Radford in Studio City. Then, Adam handed me a fist full of money and said that it was from their T-shirt sales and that I could use this for food and other expenses.

I couldn't stop crying. I felt grateful and utterly helpless. These people were strangers, really. I'd seen them over the years as I'd come in each week either to sing or hang out. I graciously accepted their assistance, then they helped me get my things back down the stairs to Maureen's car. For the moment, I had a place to sleep indoors and not in my car or the public spa. The emotional healing begun through prayer and belief had begun.

ZERO, I TELL YOU

Acceptance, acceptance, acceptance is the mantra. I'm at zero, I'm at zero, I'm at zero was the other half of the mantra. There was literally nothing to be done but to accept my circumstances. It was completely out of my hands, I was no longer in control of my life. My every footstep was solely guided by God. I didn't know these people who offered help when I had nothing. This is when the magic happens, as I have heard these stories on "The Oprah Winfrey Show" and read the biographies of how people triumphed over adversity. It was my turn.

If you had looked into my eyes, my guess is that you would have seen nothing, just a blank stare with nothing behind it. I was barely alive. It was as if someone or something else was animating my body, as my movement was not dictated from my mind. My heart was simply open like a wound. I guess that's how the oxygen of spirit got in to heal me, as I was in a state of pure acceptance. Pure zero, hands up in the air. Now, it was time to listen for instruction from God on what my next move should be. It was paralyzingly empty and spiritually awakening to watch what was happening to my life from inside my body. I was forced into total silence and observation as I watched miracle after miracle shape my life.

SURRENDER

CHAPTER EIGHT

TWO STEPS FORWARD, TWO STEPS BACK

Have you ever felt as if you were not in your body, like you were hovering around your flesh, observing what's going on? Most times, experiences like this occur in my dreams, which makes sense, especially if you believe the spirit can become omnipresent, simultaneously traveling outside the body during that last rim of sleep. However, I've been having these feelings more frequently, even in the waking hours. Months ago, when first noticing these feelings, I thought it was depression or stress because of my unstable situation. Worried that this was an indication that, finally, I was losing my mind, my antidote was to somehow get more sleep or, at least, get a better quality of sleep. Now, after understanding how essential it is to maintain a sense of zero limits, as taught by Dr. Len, I wondered if these feelings of separation of spirit and body were due to living in a zero state. What started out as a sense of uneasiness now became a more accepted feeling. So, I stopped worrying about it. I let go. I surrendered.

Sometimes, acceptance and surrender feel one and the same. Acceptance for me meant being at peace with whatever was

before me. No action or movement needed. With this definition
now clarified, acceptance was something that was achievable
for me in every aspect of my life except, admittedly, true acceptance of self. This trait was brought to my attention by another
synchronistic event, thanks to Maureen, the captain's assistant
from the Whisky whose sofa had become my home.

One of the most profound gifts that I've ever received to
date was through Maureen. It was a free session with her friend
Katara Gara, who did healing through sounding out Tibetan
Bowls. After all that had happened in my life up to this point, I
was open to anything, so I made an appointment with Katara for
a private session at her home. From the moment that I entered
the grounds of her apartment complex, I felt a calm and inviting
spirit permeating every nook and cranny. She answered the door
and invited me in. Before taking off my boots, she said, "You are
a Queen but you don't realize it." She continued, "And, you have
a problem with receiving. Don't you know that this is your calling? Your gift to the world is receiving." Caught off guard by this
unusual post-introduction, I felt that everything that she'd just
stated didn't make any sense. However, she continued to clarify,
stating how arrogant it was for me to block others' blessings by
not allowing them to give, and soon the message began to hit
home loud and clear. From that point on, everything she did in
that healing session was directed at me realizing my place in
this life as a Queen. It was the ultimate lesson in self-acceptance.
We conversed at length, and she even brought out some cards
that resembled the tarot. Afterward, she had me lie on a massage
bed, where I closed my eyes, then she sounded out the bowls and
did something comparable to a reiki treatment, then we were
finished.

This piece of information regarding my purpose ultimately
made so much sense and answered so many unanswered questions from my "little princess" childhood. More than anything,

it cleared up what may have caused my solo career to shut down. Too often, the reoccurring theme of having to be the "responsible one" would overwhelm me, along with the negative connotations placed on being different in my household, which forced me to want to go unnoticed, to be in the "background." What better place for a singer from my experience to assume? Of course, it would be the position of a "background" singer. However, taking full responsibility for this, I understood more fully the resentments that would come my way from people who were frustrated with my career choices. It's possible they expected me to be "Queen." They saw it in me, but I never saw it in myself; at least, this is the story I told myself.

The "Queen theme" played itself out in one of my past lives as well, according to a reading that I received more than twenty years ago from Dr. June Gatlin, a past life regression therapist. After seeing Dr. Brian L. Weiss on "The Oprah Winfrey Show," talking about his book "Many Lives, Many Masters," then having the pleasure of meeting him in New York City, I sought an opportunity to receive this past life regression therapy, which was a type of hypnotherapy that allows people to re-enter past lifetimes that may answer and/or cure illnesses in their present life. I made my appointment with Dr. Gatlin and headed over to her home in the Los Feliz section of Los Angeles. She invited me into her apartment, then asked that we say prayers before beginning the session. Afterward, she seated me at a table and sat across from me. There was a cassette tape player in front of her. I sat quietly as she started the tape player. Then, she closed her eyes and commenced to read the "book of my life." It was as if she could literally see the book in her mind, reading page by page, including every punctuation. It was the most incredible and unusual experience I'd ever witnessed up to that point. It was as if the information was being channeled through her. In one of my past lives, I was a healer. People traveled from afar to see me and to be healed. I was treated and honored like a Queen. Yes, feeling the weight of being responsible for someone's life and wanting to avoid it in this lifetime, suddenly made complete sense.

I walked out of Katara's apartment feeling like a totally different human being. My stride was different; it felt, in my body, as if I'd had a chiropractic adjustment. I felt brand new, and at peace. Finally, complete acceptance. After all of the goal making, the running "things to do" lists, movement, and following my heart, there came a time for me when I had to STOP and LISTEN, which are intentional actions. This is what happens when one surrenders. Surrendering creates acceptance.

Sitting in the lobby of the Spa that day I lost my beloved Mini Cooper forced me to surrender. There was literally nothing else to be done except sit, cry, meditate, say prayers, then listen for answers with no other options or means of control. *I let go.* Praying over and over again as if not to be heard the first time was not the answer. This place, this most profound state, defined my very existence, for finally it came to my attention that this is where we should all reside, all the time. It is in this perpetual state of surrender, where we are given instructions by God on the right thing to do, listening with our hearts.

As humans, we have now come full circle in our existence on this planet, whether we realize it or not. The events of the day have forced us to wake up and rely on ourselves, which means relying on and accepting that God has ordained our destiny, for it is revealed through our dreams, which then ignites our desire to follow suit. Just like Dorothy in "The Wizard of Oz," we learn that the answers were always there inside of our hearts, directing our path the whole time. The key is to trust what our heart says, and to trust is to have faith. Don't allow your brain to cause you to second-guess. The heart *is* the God intelligence. It is all-knowing. This is the artist's way. This is what artists are faced with all the time. The confusion comes when the sub-conscious programming from childhood comes in to play devil's advocate. That's it. Now, when these feelings of uneasiness, worry, and doubt arise, I know their origin. Now I know that, regardless, even if it means learning things the hard way, I have to surrender everything. Let it go and the God in me will direct my path.

What happens when you don't surrender? Stress, pain, disease (dis-ease). My experience has been that you will get confusing results that can swing the pendulum very far in one horrific direction. But, as you continue to live your life, being still, there will be moments or experiences that come, forcing you to listen. When you do finally listen, notice the calming of the mind, soul, and heart. The result is pure bliss. Listening is reacting and how you react is everything.

PAST - 1998

At the beginning of my three-year return to Los Angeles in 1998, the Screen Actors Guild (SAG) went on strike, which had everyone in the music, film, and television industries in a frenzy. Many movie and TV projects were now being shot outside the U.S., mainly in Vancouver, British Columbia, Canada, and scores of working actors you would recognize on television commercials and series would soon be out of work. For singers, we would not be able to do any SAG-related work either, which translated into all of my commercials and television series work being taken off the air. This meant no residuals, and no residuals meant no income. Having just returned to L.A. to solely work as a session singer, I was again at a loss, not knowing how to consistently get work under these circumstances. Going on tour and leaving my daughter was not an option.

Initially, returning to L.A. to only do session work was a challenge. But, as work started to come in, things seemed to level off. My past relationships and work in the industry helped me

land a few significant jobs, working on movies, TV, and records
with prominent producers like Patrick Leonard, Bob Marlette,
and Don Was. I worked on the Disney animated film "Dinosaurs"
for composer and producer James Newton Howard, as well as
a DreamWorks animated film titled "The Road to El Dorado,"
doing all the background vocals for the opening theme, sung
by my previous employer Elton John and produced by Danny
Jacobs. Later, I would also do the soundtrack to that movie,
which was produced by Patrick Leonard. Then, I did backing
vocals for the movie "Ali," produced by Trevor Horn, with my
friend Niki Harris, a former backing vocalist with Madonna.
I attended the film's premiere, and midway through the film,
in a scene where Will Smith as boxing great Muhammad Ali is
walking through the streets of Zaire (the former Republic of The
Congo) with the townspeople all around him, I suddenly heard,
as the music was showcased, an ad lib sounding like my voice.
Then, I realized that it was in fact, my voice! It was a riff that was
on the background tracks of an original work that I recorded on
a Salif Keita album in New York City. I waited until the end of the
movie to read the credits and yes, there was my name. It was a
surprise. Fortunately, I did eventually receive a contingent scale
check from the union, which is a one-time payment that singers
receive for recordings that are used in films.

While I did sing on a project for the Black Crowes with Patrick
Leonard producing, I turned down the offer to tour with them. I
did one short weekend with Jeffrey Osborne in Connecticut at a
casino. Just leaving my daughter for even those few days threw
me into a state of depression. Then, I received a call to perform
on MTV's "Total Request Live" with Beck. This meant returning
to N.Y.C., which was cool since there were friends there to take
care of my child. After the taping of that show, Beck asked me
to do two outdoor festivals, one of them being Coachella out in
Indio, California, in the spring. Beck is one of the most creative,

artistic people I have ever met. The band was awesome and this was a style of rock that was eclectic, soulful, and just plain cool. I was such a huge fan of his artistry. He asked if I was also available to tour. Reluctantly, I turned him down, as my daughter came first. Leaving her was simply no longer an option for me. Things were financially tough. Doing these movies was paying union scale, which was good, but the real money was in the residuals, which depended on sales. It would be months before I'd be receiving any residual income. However, when it did come in, the residuals were low, possibly due to the agreed union contract negotiations that were affected by the onset of the strike.

My friend Bridgette Bryant called me to do a couple of Coca-Cola commercials. Now, this was promising. Finally, I could go ahead and settle into my own home again. I rented a house that was a lease with option to buy, once again in my beloved Topanga, the lovely, quaint town located in the mountains between Malibu and Santa Monica. Soon after moving into the house, the Screen Actors Guild strike went into full bloom, which meant that my newly booked Coca- Cola commercials would be taken off the air, which put my finances, already shaky from my brief return, into a complete tailspin.

It was as if I were walking around in the fog like a zombie. These were waters I had never traversed before. After two years of hitting the streets of Los Angeles, getting some significant work, it still was not enough to sustain and stabilize me. Having never been in a strike situation, I had no idea how bad things could get or how quickly they could turn. What I didn't realize until much later, was that my residuals would be extremely low and that eventually, there would be none. This was because all union members were taken off the air. That was the end of my high residual income. Sessions were few. I was in trouble. My landlord, who was a very kind man, had informed me that because of my delinquent rent status, he had no choice but to evict me, which of course, I understood. The problem was that I didn't even have enough money to move out.

Quickly, judgement day arrived as I stood before the court, asking the judge for an extra thirty days on top of the two weeks sentence awarded, hoping it would give me time to gather the cash to move out. Everyone in the courtroom snickered, as if what I'd asked for was ridiculous. In the end, the judge ordered that in approximately two weeks, I was to move out or marshals would come and kick me out. All that I remember of this time is my prayer walks up in the canyons of my neighborhood, when I asked God to just lead me in the direction I was to go. Thinking I was following my path, I began to question my judgement, as things were swerving out of control.

It was summer and my daughter was finishing up with summer camp. I decided not to inform her of our move, as she was too young to understand. In order to maintain as stress-free a move possible, I sent her to Memphis to visit my mother for the remainder of the summer. It was one of the most difficult things that I had ever done at this point, putting my young daughter on a plane to Memphis alone, under the care of the flight attendants. While this may be OK for some, it was hard for me. Still, I made the idea of going on this exciting adventure on an airplane alone so tantalizing that my daughter seemed excited to do it. Years later, she would tell me that once she got on that plane, she held tightly to her doll that looked like me and cried. That broke my heart, but under the circumstances, I couldn't think of a better way to deal with packing and moving out of our home at the time.

As the move-out date was fast approaching, a couple of my friends from New York, Sandra St. Victor and Jeff Smith of The Family Stand, happened to be in town doing a gig in Hollywood. When they called to check in on me, I was in the midst of packing my entire house on my own again. Sandra and Jeff came over, and in the midst of their tour, they found themselves up all night wrapping dishes, building boxes, moving furniture, and packing my U-Haul until dawn, which was when the marshals were scheduled to come. By daybreak, it was all done.

I ended up moving to the Oakwood Apartments in Woodland Hills, California. It was a lovely, transient, family-friendly place that was initially created by people who wanted to offer housing to musicians and other artists. It had grown to become a well-known long/short-term housing complex for companies that had employees with families who needed to relocate for work. You could rent for a few days, a week, month, or a year. Fully or partially furnished, unfurnished, with or without maid service, it had a playground, gym, tennis courts with a tennis pro on site, pool, jacuzzi, barbecue pits, and recreation room. Movie night was on Fridays and Sunday brunch was offered free for all residents and their guests. The people who worked there were like family. The residents were from all over the world. As in any community, there were the colorful eccentrics whose lives were spent keeping up with the latest gossip in the compound. They were always seated out by the pool every night, people watching, always eager to start up a conversation. There were tons of kids running around, and one weird guy that would hang out around the playground. Of course, I kept my eyes on him. Overall, it was a soft place to land. When my daughter returned from Memphis, it was a somewhat smooth transition. Having the pool and playground on the premises helped tremendously. Amazingly, she never really asked why we had to move out of our house. I can't recall exactly what was said. Evidently, it was enough to satisfy her at the time.

Session work in Los Angeles continued to be precarious, though the strike had finally been lifted. I began to do some work for John Powell on an Eddie Murphy movie called "Pluto Nash" and a lead vocal on a song titled "Your Time Will Come" for the Christina Applegate movie "Just Visiting." Soon, depression would hover, as this work was not enough to sustain me. My happiness no longer lay in singing other people's music. I was so busy trying to survive, making money to pay bills, there was zero space to create or write music of my own. The chances of ever being a solo artist were seeming to fade into oblivion. Struggling to make a life out of a few sessions would soon seem futile.

I ran into my friend Bridgette Bryant again. She was excited about a three-day seminar she had taken called the Landmark Forum, and strongly suggested that I do the same. At this point, I was completely exhausted, having depleted every resource available to get my life secured. I was ready to try anything. However, there was a cost and monies were tight. Literally, the very next day, I received a call from producer Camara Cambone to do a session for a PBS documentary. The pay was for the exact amount of the Landmark seminar. He paid me by check and I cashed it the same day. Afterward, I went straight to the offices of the Landmark Forum and signed up for my classes.

What an amazing experience. These classes were life-altering. Many of the fundamental principles taught in these courses became an integral part of my belief system and foundation for my own teaching philosophy. It gave me a perspective on my personal life that I never had before, and by the end of the seminar, I knew exactly what I wanted to do. Artistically, all I really wanted to do was my own music. My desire to go on tour or do sessions was gone. It was time to move on; for now, those became things I would do for money but not for my heart. Of course, I needed income to take care of myself and my child, but I would rather it come from something else, even if it were not music-related at this point. Then, it hit me. That was the answer. Leaving Los Angeles and the music business altogether and teaching college full-time became more attractive. Three years earlier, the chairman of the Voice Department at Berklee had offered me the opportunity to teach full-time. Had the time finally come for this consideration?

I called Jan Shapiro, chairman of the Voice Department, and asked if a full-time position was still available. Her answer was a resounding yes. Also, during my time away from Berklee, I had accrued three more years of experience to my résumé, allowing me to negotiate a higher salary. I decided to move to Boston. Any questions remaining about the decision to make this move back to the East Coast were settled by yet one more challenge that sealed the deal.

While residing at the Oakwood, I had met and made friends with a woman from Switzerland, whose name I can't recall, who was the manager for an African recording artist, whose name and country I also can't recall right now. At this time, I was having trouble paying the last installment of my daughter's school tuition at the private school in Topanga. The payments were divided into four installments. I made the first three payments on time with no problem. However, by the last installment, which was during the union strike, I was struggling. It was right at the end of the school year, and I was short the last $3,000 installment to complete payment for the school year. Having no idea why but for the pure, generously flowing grace of God, this woman from Switzerland gave me $1,500 toward that final installment of my daughter's tuition. No strings attached. No paying it back. Immediately, I paid the school with a balance of $1,500 pending. I had never been late with my payments before, so I felt the school would give me some leeway with this remaining balance. However, one day, about 30 minutes after the little school bus came to the Oakwood Apartments to pick up my child for school, which was approximately 25 minutes up the mountain from Woodland Hills to our previous hometown Topanga, I received a phone call from Page, the mother of one of my daughter's friends from school. She said my child was crying because they would not let her off the school bus due to the non-payment of tuition. I was horrified, and in tears, not believing the school would do this to a child. Page tried to calm me down and said she would handle the situation. She was there at the school with my daughter. What happened after that was simply a priceless showing of humanity. Page, who was also a board member of the school, along with two other moms from in my child's class, got together and paid $500 each to clear the $1,500 debt that was owed to the school. My daughter was able to attend class as usual and went ahead to finish out the school year. This would be one of the most painful yet beautiful memories of human kindness I have ever experienced.

This story is still painful for me to recall, though somehow I moved forward through it all. In the end, I prayed that this incident would not scar my child. It certainly scarred my psyche, though. The guilt of putting my child in that position weighed heavily on my consciousness. So that was the sign that alerted me that it was time to go and confirmed my decision to move back to the East Coast. After fighting to live in Los Angeles according to my plan, it was time to let go. It was time to surrender. Boston would be my destiny, an escape route to freedom from a flailing music business and from feeling stuck in a backing vocalist career. I was definitely ready to move away from financial uncertainty. The Landmark Forum Seminars had proven to be my version of The Underground Railroad, introduced to me by my very own Harriet Tubman, my singer/friend Bridgette Bryant, which was the vehicle that led me to Boston, the Promised Land.

THE PROCESS, OH THE PROCESS - PRESENT

For the next two weeks, I sat, slept, and ate on Maureen's sofa. Still numb from the experience, I totally surrendered to the process and allowed this stranger, who was a quirky, somewhat eccentric person, take over my affairs to get me back on my feet. She had a good heart and worked hard to do what she loved to do, singing and dancing. Pretty fearless, she created a life that seemed to work for her.

One of the things that she was great at doing was making calls to bill collectors and everyone affiliated with getting me help through MusiCares and the Actors Fund. This was not my strong suit, as it was difficult for me to even open my mail if I didn't have the money to pay the bills.

We would get up in the morning and make the calls to trace the paperwork regarding my repossessed car. It was obvious that the car auction company and my bank lender were not expecting me to be able to get my car back. Maureen made the calls and spoke on my behalf, over and over, every day, until it was all set. Luckily, all of my bank statements and other receipts were online and could be retrieved via my email or an app on my cell, as all of the hard copies of my letters and bills were in my car. Thank God for the Internet and the fact that I had set up a lot of my activities online. This made completing the applications easier.

So, first thing Wednesday morning, we started on the application for MusiCares. They needed proof of five years of music income. That was easy, as I'd never done anything else in my life. I have thirty years of proof. Still, much of the information that was needed – my W-2 forms, bank statements, invoices, receipts and more – was in my car. It was time to pull everything up online. I left messages with Chaka Khan's business managers to inquire about my W-2s. All of my teaching online was paid via PayPal, and luckily PayPal maintains statements via email to me. Great, I just downloaded those statements. Then, I went on Maureen's computer and downloaded my bank statements, which showed automatic deposits for teaching at the Los Angeles College of Music in Pasadena, oh yes! And Chaka! No need for the W-2s. Everything was online. Then, MusiCares wanted performance proof. Since everyone that I worked with were icons in the music industry, I could get this evidence online as well. I included my résumé, bio, and a commercial reel, a five-minute MP3 with excerpts from music performances with Elton John, Chaka Khan, Bette Midler, films I sang on, and even an excerpt from my original music EP. It felt good to get all of this done.

Maureen was also very good at speaking to the agencies and especially to the bank that had repossessed my car. That call was the most stressful call as sometimes, she would get people who were cruel or inept at their jobs. She finally found one person, Tatiana, who was very helpful and clear about what was needed and when. I was simply too overwhelmed to get it all done as efficiently as needed. Maureen kept a record of everything, emailed everyone affected, and followed up. She was a well-organized machine. I also called my auto insurance company to see if and how much it would be to re-instate coverage for my vehicle. I called the dealership to get an estimate on costs for brake pads, as my car had just alerted me that my front brakes were low and that it was time for a servicing.

On Thursday, Maureen and I got up and after our usual tea-and-toast breakfast, she informed me of several things. First, someone was offering me a car for free but it needed a gasket. She said that Adam, one of the founders of Ultimate Jam Night, suggested that I consider giving up my car and returning it to the dealer so that I wouldn't have a car payment. He said he may also be able to get the car fixed for free. I understood his reasoning here, but I also knew that the bank might still insist that I pay my car note even if I did voluntarily turn it in. In that case, I would not turn in my car. We'd been through too much together at that point. Next, someone offered a place for me to stay for free, but it was up in Palmdale. Not! Too far from everything. Next, I was given the name of a producer and UCLA professor who had produced Madonna and other singers and told that he was always looking for singers. That was a hell, yeah! I can work! Then, there was an offer to get me work as a deliverer for a catering company. I was open to that. Last, she told me that they were setting up a GoFundMe site and soliciting donations on my behalf. Oh, my God. I didn't know what to say but thank you.

Maureen contacted the people regarding the car, while I emailed the producer about work. Then, she and dropped me off in Burbank to the home of a new student to teach a voice lesson. The student was in town visiting her family while attending the Paul McCartney school in London. She was a lovely and talented young lady, which made teaching a joy. Her mother was exuberant and sweet. We got a lot done in an hour and fifteen minutes. She paid me via PayPal immediately as I'd instructed. It was a great lesson. Luckily, Maureen had a doctor's appointment in the area, which coincided with the time I'd be finished teaching, so she was able to pick me up. Everything was coming together as best as it could under these circumstances. Friday, I spent the day and night at Maureen's apartment, tying up loose ends with my applications to both MusiCares and the Actor's Fund. The bank informed me that my car would go to auction if I didn't get it by the 31st of the month. Right now, it was not clear exactly where my car was. I realized that I'd also left my asthma inhalers in my car. At this point, it was Friday the 13th. There was nothing else I could do toward my application. Everything had been turned in via email. Now, I just want to be rested and ready for my work on Sunday and Monday.

Rehearsal Sunday was for the rehearsal and taping of a new ABC television series called "Greatest Hits," which would be taped on Monday. My voice was still cruddy from crying and stress, so on Saturday, I decide to use my Wi Spa pass to get out of Maureen's way and rehabilitate my voice and my stress-filled body. First, since Maureen had to go for a few items at Trader Joe's market, I ask that she drop me off for a bite of vegan food.

Finally, I had food I could eat that was delicious. Then, Maureen dropped me off at the front door of the spa. Just as I entered, the Asian woman who managed the spa who had come to inform me about my car repossession, came out of the front door. "How is your car?" she inquired. "It's still repossessed, but I'm working on everything," I told her. She smiled and continued on her way. I continued to my locker where I took off all of my clothes, turned off my cell and iPad, put everything away, then proceeded to the hot tub, where I lay for at least an hour, going back and forth between the hot and cold tubs, then to the steam room until I was ready to pass out. I had leftovers from my vegan meal, so I got my food from the locker and sat at the table in the spa with iPad, playing my Words With Friends, snacking on leftovers. I was completely serene. I remembered that I could watch the season finale of "Scandal" on Hulu, so I went to the sleeping room at the spa, lay down on the heated jade floor, watched the show on my iPad, then drifted off into the deepest sleep ever. The physical healing had begun.

After a busy Sunday of rehearsing, I used Uber to get to Hollywood to attend my friend Gary Allen's fashion show titled "The Horrible Fantastic." He used his original music as runway music for his exquisite fashion showing. I sang on several of those tracks, which made me feel I was part of the show. What an experience. His fashion and his music were so avant-garde. The people who came to see his show were equally beautiful, avant-garde, eccentric, and artistic. I felt right at home. So many visual artists attended. They are a different breed and I loved being there with them. Afterward, Gary and a few of his friends and I went out to dinner in Beverly Hills, then returned to his house for a nightcap glass of wine and some weed. Yes. Just what I needed. He had no idea of my issues. I got a ride back to Maureen's and prepped for my TV show the next day.

Monday, I arranged a quick lunch with my friend Allen at

H.O.P.E. (Healthy Organic Positive Eating) restaurant, which is within walking distance of CBS television studios. We caught up on our lives and discussed the recent tragic loss of his daughter. I did not dare speak of my situation. I only discussed my upcoming work that day. Quickly we finished our delicious vegan meal and I walked over to CBS. Strangely, the show "Greatest Hits" is a new ABC network show, even though they are taping at CBS. It was set to air the summer of 2016. The host of the show is Arsenio Hall. My job was to sing backing vocals for the iconic rock group Foreigner as they sang their hit "I Want To Know What Love Is," which was a favorite of mine in my growing-up years. They were awesome guys. The lead singer, Kelly Hansen, was incredible. It was quite an experience. The television audience went crazy as we came out of the audience onto the stage as choreographed. It was a great show. That work was from 3 p.m. to about 9:30 p.m.; a long day, but a great day singing backgrounds with old friends. It was like old times, as this was my life regularly for years, years ago. Afterward, I took an Uber back to my sofa at Maureen's. Riding on the high of doing new singing work and feeling things were improving, I barely knew myself, as I was also feeling lost. Feeling good and lost at the same time.

As I settled in for the night and assembled my bedding on the sofa, a feeling of anxiety, suffocation, and heat came over me, as reality set in that I was in a strangers' home for an unknown length of time, having no idea where to go from here. I was taking one day at a time. One moment at a time. I stopped to meditate. What is happening right now? Right now, I am concerned about my status with the SAG/AFTRA union. While I knew that my friend who hired me for this show, knows that I am not financially paid up with the union, I know that I have included this payment in my application for assistance with the Actors Fund and MusiCares, which are both affiliated with the union. It's stressful to me, because in the past, the union has been known to reprimand producers by fining them for using non-union people. It's been so long since I've done consistent work with the union, I'm not certain of the rules, as they do change. I write a long text to my friend explaining that I am awaiting word from the help agencies on this matter and hope that it all works out in a timely fashion. I also know that the union will allow people to work under the Taft-Hartley Act without being financial. I had done this two years ago when I did the work on the "Rio II" movie. I wasn't certain what that would mean this second time. I was just grateful that the work opportunity came up and I was able to do it. I was sure it would all be fine.

By Tuesday morning, after my week of work, I was feeling emotional. I was here at Maureen's apartment, sleeping on her sofa, and it dawned on me: I really didn't know this woman. Maureen was eccentric, nice, helpful. But, I had opened myself to her as she was helping me traverse these waters through this application process, which means she now has all of my personal information, my social security number, everything. Suddenly, I was feeling helpless, naked, crazy. Was I crazy? What had I done? How was I getting out of this situation? Where was I going with my things? How was I getting out of her house? Where was I going? She had emailed me something called 211 information on places for housing. Now, I was really feeling homeless, as this speaks to me that I am about to go to a homeless shelter. I knew that I had the Airbnb woman in Pasadena I could go to if the room was available. But, that was $50 a night. Now I was stressing, uncertain about what to do, and beginning to feel a little suicidal for a moment, as that damned dark feeling always hits eventually. Luckily, I released the feeling quickly. Then, Kevin the background vocalist from the Whisky texted me, asking me how things are going. I started to cry as I texted back, telling him I was feeling overwhelmed and stuck. He responded, "Sometimes, someone wanting to help makes us feel helpless and that's not good either. There's a very fine line." I answered, "So true." He asked if I had money. I told him yes. Then, he said, "It's gonna be okay. You know that. Right?" "I know," I answered.

The process. Oh, the process.

HAPPY ENDINGS, NEW BEGINNINGS
CHAPTER NINE

THE VOICE

$\int$ tarting private voice lessons at age 10, and singing such a heavy operatic repertoire like Puccini at age 13, may have created what would become a slight vocal issue for me. While many experts preach that having classical training protects one from numerous vocal issues, pushing my voice in that genre at that age, I believe, proved to cause me more harm than good. Either it appeared and sounded as if I knew what I was doing technically with my voice, which I did not, or my teacher was so enamored with my voice that he neglected to make sure I knew exactly what I was doing, so as not to cause any harm. How do you explain classical technique to a 10-year-old, anyway?

In my sophomore year at Howard University, my vocal teacher, Mattiwilda Dobbs, placed me on complete vocal rest for an entire semester. She suggested that I see a laryngologist, which is a voice specialist, as she suspected I may have developed vocal nodules, which are raised callouses on the vocal cords caused by the cords rubbing together. This can happen when one pushes sound repeatedly in the same area of the cord, causing inflammation and eventually causing callous build up and preventing the vocal cords from vibrating efficiently. She could hear the airy quality in my voice when I sang in certain vocal registers, which meant something was blocking the flow of sound.

My mother took me to see the voice specialist when I returned to Memphis for winter vacation. The prognosis was that there was some slight indication of vocal nodules, but it was much too small to operate and remove. The remedy was complete vocal rest and speech therapy. I was enrolled in several speech therapy sessions during my winter vacation. This assessment also found that my speaking voice was overused, due to excessive volume on a regular basis. This made sense, as shouting in our household was a normal, everyday occurrence. The speech therapist also explained that one was more likely get nodules from negative speaking practices than from singing. I did a series of exercises to loosen tension, relaxing the tongue and jaw, and worked on using a more comfortable volume, along with making sound without an excessive glottal attack.

The exercises proved valuable, as this knowledge, in addition to sitting out the spring semester of my sophomore year, assisted in my recovery, which lasted for ten years, until the middle of my tenure with Elton John. At that time, I again solicited the help of a well-known laryngologist, this time in Los Angeles. Again, I was told that there was some inflammation that was inoperable. Again, I got speech therapy. Again, the issues disappeared. Again, it would be yet another ten years before any vocal issues resurfaced. This time, it was near the end of 1999, after 15 years of non-stop touring, when I was considering leaving the music industry all together. Exhausted, stressed, and ready for a change, I decided not to pursue another appointment with another voice doctor. Yes, there was concern and worry on my part, but perhaps this was a sign that my singing career should come to an end. Turning a blind eye to my vocal issues, I decided to focus instead on what my next move should be to ensure financial stability for myself and my daughter. It was time to consider college professor as a new vocation.

Just as the number nine is a symbol of completion, which coincidentally, is the assigned number to this chapter, my life as a session/tour singer was coming to a close, as the path of least resistance led me back to Boston, Massachusetts and Berklee College of Music. It was a happy ending and a new beginning.

PRESENT - 2016

Maureen had informed me that she needed her space back, which I was more than ready to relinquish. It had been almost two weeks since that fateful, traumatic day at the Korean spa when my car was repossessed. While I was extremely appreciative of the help received from Maureen, Kevin, and the Jam Fam at the Whisky, I was restless to move on and get my life on a better path. I needed my solitude to pray and meditate, to focus on listening for my "marching orders," the spiritual answers to my mantra of "what's the right thing to do today?" The energy in Maureen's house was a bit scattered and sometimes affected my ability to truly meditate and align with the universe. In my heart, I knew that it was time to go.

I had done some work on a couple of recording sessions, which paid immediately, affording me the opportunity to pay for a return to Margo's Airbnb in Pasadena for six days. I took an Uber over to Margo's home, explaining to her that my car was in ill repair. Again, she graciously accepted me into her home and I went right upstairs to my same room as before, and finally slept in that bed like a baby. There was a Zen energy in her home that was so calming to my spirit, as I would lock my door upon entering my room, then leave the door to my personal outdoor patio area wide open, giving me a feeling of connecting the beautiful garden/outdoor space with the indoors.

Having no idea where I would go once leaving Margo's home, on the night of day five, I closed my eyes and meditated, using the concepts of Dr. Len's Ho'Oponopono, first expressing sincere thanks to the Divine for giving me such a lovely serene place to live this week. Then, I apologized for ever doubting that things would not work out and for any stress that I placed on myself for not trusting the Divine to take care of everything. Then, I expressed love to the Divine, who always provided everything and to myself for persevering through this experience and being able to take care of myself in this process. I set my intention to have a place to go to from here, then I drifted off to sleep.

On the morning of day six, I was awakened at 8 a.m. by the ringing notification of a text message. It was Chad, one of the managers from the Crescent Hotel in Beverly Hills. He wrote, "Good morning! I hope your Friday is amazing!! #Goodvibes." I responded with a thank you, then for some reason, decided to tell him of my need for a place to live by the next day.

Now, telling Chad that I needed help was a clear indication that I was moving through life in a different way. For me to admit I needed help to anyone was confirmation that a huge shift had taken place in my life. He asked me to explain what happened. So, I wrote in detail, about the events that had taken place, leading me to my stay at Margo's Airbnb. Chad asked me if I had reached out to Susan, the owner of the Crescent Hotel. When I'd frequent the hotel every Monday night, I would sometimes meet the owner. Susan is a beautiful spirit, vivacious and fun. Many times, after the Cookies' show, we all would sit around and talk late into the night. Susan would offer hors d'oeuvres and drinks. We would laugh and talk about music all night.

It had not occurred to me to contact Susan. I had stayed there last Christmas with my daughter as a paying customer. However, at this time, I did not have enough cash to even consider such a thing. Then, I remembered that the gentleman handling my case at the Actor's Fund told me that they did offer payments towards move-in expenses. I thought that perhaps I could arrange for the Actor's Fund to pay for my stay at the hotel, which made me feel hopeful. Perhaps staying there was a possibility. Chad asked me if I was OK with him contacting Susan on my behalf. I texted back, replying "yes and thank you," then proceeded to call Kareem at the Actor's Fund to inquire about payment to the Crescent.

Well, Kareem did answer but the news was mixed. He informed me that the fund only had $700 maximum toward all bills. So, if I were to use $700 toward living expenses, then there would be nothing to use toward my auto insurance, repairs, registration, and other bills. For me, this meant that there was no money now toward my living expenses, since getting my auto insurance was my first priority. I already had a citation for my expired registration and I couldn't get my car registration renewed until showing proof of auto insurance. I told Kareem to go ahead and contact my auto insurance company and make the $647 payment that would allow me to reinstate my auto insurance. As for paying for my stay at the Crescent, that wasn't gonna happen. With some remorse, I texted Chad hours later, asking him if Susan was expecting me to contact her. He said yes, so I texted Susan, giving her the details of how my living situation tanked and how I was now at the end of my stay without money or residence.

Then, it happened. Susan texted back that she would gladly arrange for me to stay at her hotel for seven days at no charge. That was the answer. I texted Susan back, expressing my thanks and that I didn't know when I could repay her. She replied, "We'll do some recording or something fun, don't worry. Just be safe and I'll see you tomorrow!" I thanked her again when she replied, "I'm glad you reached out." Like magic, I had a place to stay.

I went downstairs to the kitchen for a croissant and coffee.

There was Margo, washing clothes and watering her garden out on the patio that was right off from the kitchen. She offered to heat up my croissant and make my coffee as I explained to her that I had worked out a place to stay in Beverly Hills. She expressed her happiness that everything had worked out for me, then we got into one of our conversations about kundalini yoga and meditations. She offered me information on a triple mantra sung by Nirinjan Kaur. Then she texted me the YouTube link, and printed out the words to the mantra. "This mantra gives you protection and sets you up to always be at the right place at the right time to receive your blessings," she explained.

Of all the things that Margo has shared with me via YouTube, this mantra really resonated with me. Something in my spirit was eager to try this mantra, so I ran upstairs to get my notebook, pen and phone. I returned to the kitchen then looked at the printed copy of the words, listening to the YouTube recording of the mantra. I rewrote the mantra in my notebook with phonetic symbols, making sure I pronounced the words correctly. Margo then instructed that I needed to keep my tongue in the roof of my mouth as much as possible while I'm singing the mantra. Then, she sent me another YouTube that shows the physical positions that should be executed as part of the chant. I got it! I went upstairs to my room and got my earbuds, placed my pillows against the headboard, and laid out my words so I could clearly see them, assuming my position.

Nirinjan Kaur's voice was so melodious. When I initially saw and heard the words, I thought they would be difficult to say. But, in moments, this mantra connected to my tongue with ease, as if I had always known it. I didn't know how long I was to recite this. The video felt short, so I played it back three times, which felt right for me. Afterward, I felt great. I noticed my eyes were relaxed and more open. My spirit had an overall feeling of gratitude as I contemplated how this information came to me today of all days. I knew there was a reason and I looked forward to seeing how all of this played out in my life from here on out.

I asked Margo if I could wash my clothes before leaving for the hotel. She graciously said yes and also inquired if I needed to get lunch somewhere and that she'd be happy to take me wherever I wanted to go. Accepting her offer, I suggested we go to the neighborhood Thai restaurant.

Finishing up with my laundry, packing everything, I was ready for Margo to drop me off at The Presidents Thai restaurant in Pasadena for a bite to eat before heading over to the Crescent hotel in Beverly Hills. After my delicious yellow curry and pineapple fried rice with tofu dinner, Margo picked me up and I returned to the house.

The time spent in Margo's home was such a healing and transformative experience. Again, I expressed my thanks to her and her son for their lovely energy and welcoming spirit. Then, I contacted Uber for my ride.

Returning to the Crescent hotel, I was welcomed with open arms by the staff as if I were an old friend. They remembered me as I remembered them, fondly. I had spent almost every Monday night there for two years and we had some great times.

For the first time in a while, I watched mindless television until the late hours of the night. Then, I performed my triple mantra at 3 a.m., then finally drifted off to sleep. In the late morning, closer to 12 noon actually, I left my room and went down to the lounge for a bite to eat and coffee. I was greeted by Arnold the bartender with excitement, again, as if I were an old friend. It was awesome. I ordered a soy latte and chopped salad, feeling right at home. My focus during my stay was now to move from the Crescent Hotel into my home, wherever that was. My vision had been in Malibu. I continued that vision. I repeated to myself: *I am open to the process. I am at zero and the Divine dictates my every movement.*

I decided to take a walk around downtown Beverly Hills on this beautiful day, proceeding down Brighton Way towards Beverly Drive, with no destination in mind. I was thinking that I could probably find a market to get some snacks for my hotel room. This was the cost-effective way to eat when you are living in hotels, as per my experience as a touring singer all those years.

This was the first time that I had walked around Beverly Hills without a purpose. Although it was the Memorial Day holiday weekend, this town had an empty spirit feeling to it. I have never wanted to live here for that very reason. The assumption has always been that like Hollywood, Beverly Hills was filled with fake, flaky people who live fake lives. Now, here I was walking the streets of Beverly Hills imagining that if someone were to drive by as I walked, I too would be labeled as one of those fake, flaky types. One should never judge.

Continuing down Beverly Drive, it dawned on me, Hey! I'm down the block from Whole Foods! That will work for a vegan like myself. So, I made a left at Dayton Way and headed back towards Crescent Drive to Whole Foods. As I walked toward the store, it reminded me of the last time that I was at this particular Whole Foods location, formerly called Mrs. Gooch's. It was during the Rodney King riots in 1992.

An unarmed African American man named Rodney King was stopped by members of the Los Angeles Police Department for drunk driving. Somehow, things escalated with Rodney King being completely surrounded by six cops who proceeded to taser and beat him unmercifully. Everything was caught on video and shown to the world. It was obviously excessive force. But, after a highly publicized trial, every officer involved was acquitted, causing a surge of racial unrest not witnessed in Los Angeles since the Watts Riots in 1965. The city was on fire and there were mass demonstrations all over the Los Angeles area. It was a tumultuous time with crazy, frenetic energy in the air. The day that everything came to a climax happened to be the day I was in Whole Foods/Mrs. Gooch's, shopping for groceries. As I walked through the aisles of the store, I could hear whispering amongst the white people in the store. I heard one woman say to another gentleman, "The gangs are coming." She looked completely terrified. As I continued to shop in the next aisle, I could see that same look of fear in almost everyone's face. I decided to just keep shopping, because if things were going to be that bad, there was a possibility that the city may be placed on a curfew, which meant no one would be allowed on the streets after dark. I was in between tour dates with Elton John and staying at my boyfriend's apartment in North Hollywood at the time. We needed food in the house, so regardless of the danger expressed by everyone in Whole Foods, I intended to finish shopping. When I first got to the store, there were long lines at the checkout counter. One would have thought everyone was preparing to store goods for the approaching apocalypse. But, by the time I was ready to check out, the lines had disappeared. The store looked like a ghost town. There were baskets filled with groceries left in the middle of aisles everywhere. The only person in my line, standing right behind me, was actor Clarence Williams III. He's better known as the character called Link in the hit '70s television show "The Mod Squad." He is also known for his portrayal of Prince's father in the movie 'Purple Rain." He is a tall, African-American man. We both looked at each other with smirks on our faces, as we calmly and confidently stood in line. I felt we both knew that if, in fact, the gangs were coming, they probably wouldn't bother us! We finished our grocery shopping. I laugh every time I think of that moment.

Anyway, I got my groceries and returned to my hotel room at The Crescent. For the rest of the evening, I watched "Keeping Up with the Kardashians," then settled in to my triple mantra. My intention remained as before, to move into a new home from this hotel room within seven days. The next few days were spent in solitude in my hotel room, as I wrote in my journal and just stayed in that space of zero.

After filling out forms over the phone, leaving messages, crying, and following up, I finally got word from MusiCares that they had spoken with my bank about my car repossession and they have agreed to pay more than $2,000 in car notes and repossession fees directly to the bank. Since the Actors Fund agreed to pay my delinquent insurance bill, it appeared that very soon, I would be able to get my car back. The vehicle was being housed in a holding facility almost two hours' drive away.

I contacted Maureen and asked if she could take me to pick up my car. I offered her money for gas for the trip and she agreed, so I made the appointment to pick up the car that following Monday.

Early that morning, Maureen arrived at The Crescent to pick me up. She was nervous about driving on the freeway that far, as she almost always seemed to be nervous when driving. Luckily, the traffic wasn't too bad in Los Angeles as we headed east on the 10, also known as the San Bernardino freeway, toward Fontana, to the holding facility, located somewhere in what appeared to be the middle of the desert.

We arrived and Maureen remained in the car as I went into the building to pay the fees for release of my vehicle. Once my car was pulled around to the front of the building, Maureen rolled down her window and wished me luck, then drove off. The car was dusty and the window on the driver's side where they bent the glass forward to get into the vehicle was seeping air. Otherwise, "Max" looked OK. The battery was dead, so the facility technician had to give me a jump. Before getting on the freeway, I pulled over, took a paper napkin from my purse, and meticulously cleaned the yellow and red crayon marks made on my windows from the repo yard, wanting no trace of the car's repossession.

The next step was to drive another hour and a half to Bellflower to get my things that had been taken out of the back of the car. Obviously, this had been in preparation for sale, as they were expecting to put my car on the auction block. Again, I had to make another payment but thankfully, I had the cash. I got to the address and there was nothing visible on the building indicating this was the right place. Then, I happened to notice an address on the building that was painted over, the same color as the building itself. This was an obvious attempt to make this address as inconspicuous as possible. I parked out front and walked past this guy who was standing outside of an open doorway, smoking a cigarette. There was something suspicious about him but not too scary, so I continued to go inside the open hallway of this rundown structure that had a door with mud brown paint over the windows. There was a doorbell to the right side of the door, which was odd, but something told me to go ahead and push the bell. It didn't make a sound that I could hear. Just as I was about to walk away, a voice came over a loud speaker, saying, "Place the money inside the small cupboard next to the door." I saw this compartment in the wall, resembling the box that one would use at a doctors' office to put a urine specimen. Strange. Since I had been instructed over the phone to only bring cash, I could only hope that this was the right place and that I was not just giving cash money to a stranger through a wall. I decided to go ahead and do as instructed. After I closed the small compartment door, I heard a sound coming from inside the compartment, as if something opened up on the other side of it. Finally, the mud painted door opened up and a woman came out with a pad and asked for my signature. Scanning the room behind her as she stood in the doorway, I could see it was a real office with people and desks. I signed the release documents, then she instructed me to walk outside to the end of the building and someone would come out with my belongings.

Needless to say, this entire scene was pure theater. It felt as if I were in the middle of a James Bond movie or some sort of police drama. I had no choice but to go along with the program, so I walked out to the end of the building. Sure enough, here comes this tattered-looking white dude with a large bag on a dolly. It was my things. I took everything out of the bag, as he just stood and watched me put the contents into the trunk of my car with no offer of assistance. I returned the bag to him, as he looked puzzled and asked me if I wanted to keep the bag. "No, I don't want anything from you guys in my car," I stated.

I thanked him, then got into my car and sped off as far away from that experience as I could. It was over. The horrific experience was over. Happy Ending.

BERKLEE – 2001

After making the decision to move to Massachusetts, everything clicked into place quickly. Berklee paid for my move, so I didn't have to worry about how to finance this. All that was left was to pick a moving company and pack. Even the events associated with choosing the moving company were fraught with synchronicity, as I found one that would move and store our furniture for thirty days at no cost before having to pay their reasonable storage fees until we found our own apartment in Massachusetts.

However, I still experienced some residual feelings of sadness and disappointment about leaving Los Angeles and the music business. It had been a long run on the road and a full career as a studio singer. I had learned so much about performing live and the music business from a solo artist's perspective. Each tour came with its own invaluable life lessons. Now I faced the new frontier, as a full-time college professor. What lessons did I have to learn here? It would soon become apparent that everything that I ever desired in life was contingent on me learning the lessons during my tenure in Massachusetts. It was huge.

My student Nura Creitz, whom I'd taught as a part-time professor at Berklee three years prior and had served as a babysitter for me, offered a room in her place for my daughter and me to live in until we could find an apartment in Cambridge, Massachusetts. We lived with her for three months before finally moving into our first home in Cambridge, which was on 17 Chilton Street, just off of Huron Avenue, in an area called Huron Village, which was walking distance from Harvard Square. We were on the top floor of a three-family Victorian house. My neighbors were Harvard students, lovely guys who loved my daughter, who was now entering third grade. We were one big happy family.

I did not bring a car to Massachusetts; instead, I relied on public transportation, as this was the East Coast lifestyle. The trolley stop to Harvard Square was right at the top of my street and I was three doors from the corner. It was a seven-minute ride into Harvard Square, then a transfer to the #1 bus down Massachusetts Avenue to Berklee, which was about a thirty-minutes ride, depending on traffic, an easy commute.

I enrolled my daughter into a Quaker School called the Cambridge Friends School, feeling this would be an easier transition for her from liberal Los Angeles, as Boston had a reputation among African-Americans as a racist city, having been the last to accept busing and school integration at the end of the Civil Rights Movement. In the mornings, I walked my daughter to the Quaker School, then walked back home to prep for work or catch the bus to Harvard Square, then on to Berklee.

The liberal politics and overall diverse culture and lifestyle of hyper-liberal Cambridge was the best place for a pseudo-hippie/artist like myself. The mayor of the city was an awesome gay, black man. It was the perfect match, as I felt right at home, loving the cobblestone streets and 200-year-old Victorian houses, with tiny mom-and-pop-owned shops everywhere. There was something magical about it.

Soon, I found New England as a whole to be the perfect place for us. My favorite seasons were fall and winter, and this is when New England really comes alive. It has an outdoor lifestyle and is a big sports town, which suited a huge snow-loving football fan like myself perfectly. In Cambridge, it felt as though a kid could still be just a kid, free to ride a bike safely everywhere, and everybody knows your name at the neighborhood market. My local market, known as the place where famous French chef Julia Child shopped, had a "running tab" system for their customers. People still trusted people. Most of my neighbors were professors like myself. This was the seat of the education industry and an ideal village for a single parent to raise a kid. Three years would pass before I realized that the area where we lived, Huron Village, was actually the exact same area that I had fallen in love with on that first day I decided to venture out into the neighborhoods of Cambridge in search of the perfect place to live should we ever move here permanently. Simply synchronistic, simply magical.

As the Fall 2001 semester approached, so did the birth of my own new beginning, this time in the music education industry. For the first time in my entire life, I had a "normal" job. It appeared everyone was happy, especially my mother. I even noticed a sense of pride in my own voice, as each time someone would ask me what my profession was, I could now answer without receiving any puzzled looks or a barrage of questions about how I made a living doing such a thing. For the first time, I didn't have to go through any long explanation or drop names about who I worked with to get people to understand that one could actually make a substantial, lucrative living as a singer without being a star. For the first time in my life, I was not an oddity or an exception, because now, inconspicuously, I fit in with everyone else around me in Boston. I was a college professor.

It was also a relief not to be under the magnifying glass of someone scrutinizing the size of my body, because no one cared what a teacher looked like. I came into the education profession at the top of my previous game with nothing to prove, having paid my dues in the music industry, so I was given a measure of respect by my superiors and some of the other professors at Berklee, especially those with my same vitae. I found a comfort zone amongst these colleagues, as we would get together from time to time, sharing road stories and noting many fellow acquaintances we had in common. We were all of one accord, ready to share our knowledge and experience with students, even though many of us didn't really know the depth of what we had to offer, for this was the first time we had been asked to teach these subjects in contemporary music education. It was all new territory for everyone in the college-level contemporary music education arena, as there really was no pedagogy for it, especially in contemporary vocal music. Berklee had always been on the cutting edge of contemporary music education, but as it moved from what some deemed a "trade school mentality" to a liberal arts college sensibility, the institution had to clear a number of hurdles before the curriculum was fine tuned. Soon, the richness of this opportunity to carve out new roads in contemporary music education would reveal itself, as we all were encouraged to explore our experiences, write curriculum for new classes, and put our own spin on pre-existing labs, ensembles, and other genre-specific labs and classes according to our own professional backgrounds. This was priceless, as the opportunity to learn and build such a program was immense, and the payoff for having this experience provided a level of credentials unmatched anywhere in the world.

After I'd spent fifteen years of touring and session work,

experiencing successes and failures in the music business, it was a relief to not be concerned with over-singing or maintaining the health of my voice, as I didn't have to perform at peak levels anymore. In fact, it was a relief not to sing at all, which was something that I never imagined would ever enter my thoughts. Reflecting on my journey, I could see that my path to singing had frequently been met with crazy resistance, and while I had never been one to give up, I had to acknowledge that things hadn't gone according to my plan and the disparity between my past life in the music business and my current music business life had worn me thin. Once I made the decision to let go, then the path to Berklee opened up, as it was the path of least resistance. Obviously, there was something here for me to learn. It was definitely something I had spoken into existence, as being a single mom, I prayed for a change. Whether all of this shift was solely for my daughter's sake, was uncertain. However, clarity was a welcomed friend, as I could finally exhale and just be a regular mom with a regular job.

While some professors continued performing in clubs around the Boston area to maintain their "chops" (vocal prowess), or just as a performance outlet, I had no desire to do so, completely content to just teach. And though it was also an option for me to maintain my professional relationships in N.Y.C. in order to do recording sessions, that would have posed a dilemma, as I would need to find a baby sitter for long nights or overnight stays, since New York was an hour flight or a four-hour drive or train ride away. After all of my experiences with leaving my daughter with sitters over the years, I was content to decline these opportunities, for I didn't have the heart or energy to pursue them. My singing career was completed. It was a new day, a new life.

Boston is a big bar town and many evenings were spent after work, especially after late-night auditions and concerts, drinking and laughing it up. Soon, we became a family. Most of my

MEMOIRS OF A BACK UP DIVA

students were eager to learn and quite talented. However, I was amazed to learn that Berklee did not have any entrance audition criteria at the time. All students who paid tuition or had scholarships were accepted. The only auditions held were placement auditions, which assigned students to their voice teacher, labs, and theory classes. It would be six years before Berklee finally established official Entrance Audition criteria. So, amidst these diamonds in the rough, many of whom are now established artists, pursuing successful careers in the industry, were students who had zero aptitude for singing. It was quite frustrating for me to grade them and debilitating to watch their self-esteem be torn to shreds as each semester, many failed their final vocal exams and/or couldn't pass Harmony I, and sometimes ended up being placed on academic probation.

The majority of the students matriculating through Berklee at this time were from all walks of life and many had made tremendous sacrifices to come to the U.S. for an education. These students had a different level of respect for artistry and a tremendous work ethic. It was rewarding to teach students who were so serious and committed to their art. On the other hand, it was frustrating to teach students who really had no true interest in becoming artists. They were just there to get a degree, a goal that was forced on them by their parents. They had little motivation to really learn a craft and they were not mature enough to see the value of the life lessons available to them by attending a university or being away from home. Perhaps, this experience of not applying themselves to their studies, only to have to deal with the aftermath at a later time, would indeed be their true learning experience. Regardless, it was frustrating to deal with, but, without fail, I continued my routine as a single mom and working college professor, ignoring my subconscious need to sing again.

Many students were impressed by my résumé, and often

asked why I was teaching at Berklee and not singing for a living. Many of them thought I was much younger than I was, and
frequently asked, "Why are you here? You should be singing."
I simply brushed off these comments, saying I had already ac-
cumulated a body of work and was not seeking to expand my
résumé in singing any further, and that I was perfectly happy
being a mom and mentor to them.

During my teaching stint, I never sang a note for anything
or anyone other than to demonstrate the exercises known as
"vocalises" during my private lessons. In addition to teaching,
my primary focus was to develop and fine-tune my own versions
of classes like background singing, vocal performance, and jazz
and non-jazz improvisation. Eventually, I would write a dream
curriculum of what a perfect contemporary vocal program
would look like, given my experiences at Berklee so far. It was
awesome to take a break from singing and from being under the
spotlight. Exploring this part of myself was enlightening. Using
other parts of my brain, I felt smart again, realizing that my
experiences on the road were great teaching moments, and that
what I had to offer my students at Berklee could not be found
at any Ivy League institution, or any college or university in the
world. This was empowering, and I soon realized it was priceless.
Also, my "ear" became the defining quality in how I taught my
private lessons and classes. In addition to having perfect pitch,
it was highly developed from all those years as a professional
tour/session singer and set me apart as an instructor. Along with
the technical pedagogy learned from my early opera company
training and Metropolitan Opera star teachers, I could hear and
fine-tune vocal issues without even looking at my students as
they sang. This was a job any teacher who was classically trained
could do. The difference between myself and teachers with my
background was that I could hear and adjust stylistically because I knew what it sounded and felt like to authentically make

that particular sound. Having several musical genres under my belt broadened my knowledge and my appeal to all students.

Also, after watching students deliver heartfelt performances, which always won out over the more technically astute, I was able to develop what would soon become my signature class, Vocal Performance Workshop, which was quite popular and produced some of the best performances I'd ever seen.

The first Vocal Performance classes were created by Vivian Reed, former Berklee professor and star of the hit Broadway play, Bubbling Brown Sugar, among other things. I had the honor of watching her teach this class. She inspired me to trust my instincts and taught me how to bring my own performance experiences into the classroom. This class alone assisted me in addressing my own issues of self confidence in front of a crowd. I learned the art of validating my own experiences and accepting my gift by watching and witnessing my students do the same. It was the epitome of the definition of a mentor/disciple relationship. Being a part of this progress in my student's artist life was rewarding. However, as I continued this teaching path, I knew there was still something amiss in my life.

As 2004 rolled around, my need to sing again grew exponentially and could no longer be ignored. I inquired around the Music Production and Engineering Department (MP&E) for a producer to work with, as now songs were stirring around inside my head, fighting to be written and be heard. Professor Carl Beatty was a good friend who suggested Zoux Bluestein, a producer and Berklee grad, to record my music. I spoke with Zoux over the phone and we worked out a reasonable plan of monthly payments until his fee was paid in full. Once a week, I caught a ride with his engineer, out to his studio in Bedford, Massachusetts, to record my EP. It was awesome and exhilarating to be back in the studio, especially doing my own music. It was heavy rock and I would push my voice relentlessly, fearlessly, even though I was aware of my slight vocal issues. I felt it was worth taking the chance on getting hoarse. I wanted to finally solidify my true rock voice.

After finishing four songs, I decided to release the EP, titling it "Confessions." The next step was to do some performances to promote it. The Chair of the Voice Department had asked that I do a special clinic or seminar for the department. I thought this would be a great opportunity to perform one of my original songs. I called it "Staying True To Your Style," and the session showcased me speaking about my tour experiences and how to maintain vocal health, culminating with a concert that featured me singing a number of different styles, including a jazz standard, a singer-songwriter pop original, and ending with a heavy metal tune from my new EP, which blew the wigs off of everyone in the auditorium. The clinic gave all the attendees, including my Berklee colleagues, a chance to hear my music, and it was a success. But, this performance created a tidal wave of anxiety for me, as once more I became super anxious to shift my focus back to my own artistry. After taking a summer vacation with my daughter to Paris and Amsterdam, I decided it was time to move on. After four and a half years of teaching, it was time to quit Berklee.

In 2004, I took my daughter to Paris and Amsterdam for summer vacation during the entire month of August. We stayed with my longtime friend Sandra St. Victor and her family. Sandra had rebooted her entire life and career in Holland which included a new husband and baby. We all biked the dykes of the small town of Arnhem, located about an hour from Amsterdam, visiting castles and seeing parts of the countryside most tourists don't get to see. It was a glorious experience. One evening Sandra brought up in conversation that I should consider getting married. I mentioned to her that the only one that "got away" was Brian. He was my friend that I'd met through an ex-boyfriend, who was actually the same Brian I mentioned earlier who lent me the sweat pants and kept my car the night before my daughter was born.

When we returned home to Cambridge, I decided to contact Brian. It had been twelve years since we first met. Although we had run into each numerous times whenever I visited Los Angeles over the years, for some reason this time was different. After several phone calls and visits to each other's homes, the relationship evolved. We decided to get married.

At Brian's suggestion, we moved to Northern California, actually back to Marin County, where his mother also lived. Since I had prior connections from living there before and working with Narada Michael Walden in 1995, I did some research and sent out résumés, which landed a small job teaching at the Jazz School in Berkeley, California. I was already familiar with Mill Valley, which was near Narada's recording studio, so I decided to look for housing there. So, in 2005, I resigned from my full-time teaching position at Berklee College of Music and, with daughter in tow, we returned to Mill Valley.

MILL VALLEY AGAIN?

Here we were: Another beautiful rented house, and a richly resourced middle school for my daughter. But there was no work for my new husband and my job at the Jazz School left a lot to be desired. The school simply didn't have enough students to fill the classes they proposed that I teach. After one semester, the job ended due to low enrollment. A couple of my students asked for private lessons soon after, and eventually I would get another job, teaching voice lessons at the Blue Bear School of Music in the Fort Mason area of San Francisco. The pay was incredibly low, as I was making $320 every two weeks, which barely took care of food and gas. While my daughter prospered at school and continued her dance studies at San Francisco Ballet, financially, we were suffering, and so was my marriage. Narada did a few concerts around the Bay Area that I was part of, but they didn't pay enough to sustain a household. I did get the opportunity to do a couple of great gigs with rock icons like Chuck Lovell, former keyboard player for The Rolling Stones. A friend and colleague from Berklee hired me to go to Maputo, Mozambique, in Africa, to do some clinics at the University of Mozambique and some jazz performances at a couple of clubs in Maputo. It was an awesome experience, realizing how the classes I had previously developed at Berklee translated so well with the students in Maputo. I returned to California knowing that if I was going to teach, it needed to be at that level, in an area where I could best serve, which I believed should be through clinics and workshops at the collegiate level.

Knowing that I had to maintain some level of continuity for my daughter, as she was preparing for high school, I recognized that it was time to place my own musical endeavors on hold again. My professional strengths, gained from the experience as a professor at Berklee, were reflected in doing clinics and workshops, which also gave me the flexibility to do what I had chosen to ignore for the moment, to sing. However, I knew that once my daughter graduated middle school, something had to change in preparation for the next level in her life. So, with a crumbling marriage, no real income or artistic outlet in San Francisco, I contacted my former boss at Berklee once again and asked if my job was available. Happily, she offered my full-time position back and I accepted. Once again, across the country I moved, back to Cambridge, literally back to my old neighborhood, just in time for my daughter to enroll in high school and rejoin her friends from elementary school. The timing could not have been more perfect for both of us.

BACK TO BERKLEE

This return to Berklee was special, as both I and the college had experienced some significant growth. It was now 2007, and Berklee had established a Diversity Initiative, a Liberal Arts Department, a campus in Spain, and finally, a desperately needed audition criteria, raising the bar on the talent that entered the college. The Voice Department alone had grown exponentially since my first tenure there, expanding from 600 students and 15 voice faculty to 1,200 students and 55 faculty. It was a huge machine.

Jumping with full force back into my teaching position, I set my mind on doing things that were more impactful, em powering, and tailor-made to my persona, and also exploited my relationships in the music industry. First, I authored a three day Artist-In-Residence program titled "Black Women In Rock," inviting some of the top Black women in the field in-cluding drummer Cindy Blackman from Lenny Kravitz's band; singer-songwriter Nona Hendryx, formerly of LaBelle; Joyce Kennedy, lead singer from the iconic rock group Mother's Finest; Siedah Garett, singer-songwriter of Michael Jackson's "Man In The Mirror"; singer, songwriter and bassist Me'shell Ndegeocello; and guitarist, Felicia Collins from David Letterman's show band. It was a huge success. Afterward, I received invitations to teach in other departments, culminating with me accepting a position teaching a Women In Rock Ensemble. With the installation of the Liberal Arts Department, I contacted the Chair, Camille Colatosti, proposing to teach a history course that I authored titled "Women In Rock History." It was a research paper-driven class that allowed me to explore history and sociology in a way that I felt would be more compelling to a classroom of creative minds. Marrying the artistry of rock music with an exploration of the personalities and sociology of female rock artists and juxtaposing their lives and experiences with the perils of society for women and the repetition of history, the course was exhilarating and just what I envisioned teaching. This course became an elective for the students and allowed me to utilize areas in my brain that were screaming to be heard. It was an overall success.

Two to three years into my return to Berklee, almost like clockwork, my need to sing again began to beckon at the doors of my heart. My daughter was nearing the end of high school, which meant the time to really focus on how to really fine-tune my life to my own needs was approaching. However, I was still having some residual vocal issues, as my voice started to become hoarse, this time for no reason as I was not singing enough to warrant any issues. I made an appointment with famed laryngologist Dr. Steve Zeitels in Boston. I had been his patient once before, when I first had a vocal cord check-up. His schedule was full, so he suggested that I see his partner, Dr. James Burns. I made the appointment and had my vocal cords looked at with the strobe scope. Finally, those vocal nodules that had wreaked havoc off and on since I was seventeen were finally operable. The doctor felt confident that surgery would end my vocal issues.

I sat down and had a heart-to-heart talk with Dr. Burns, as I wanted to get to the bottom of what could have caused the nodules to get to this point. Just as the previous doctors and speech therapists had noted, he explained that my nodules were so small that they could have always been there for a number of reasons. They could have developed from singing such heavy classical repertoire as a child, or simple overuse due to a combination of how I taught singing via example and lack of sleep. However, there was no redness, bleeding, or indication of a broken blood vessel, so singing incorrectly was the least likely cause. He also clearly stated that the level that I used my voice to teach and talk, in addition to attempting to sing professionally as I did before, was high, and that at some point, I would have to choose between teaching and singing. Doing both full time was too much. He encouraged me to work with the speech therapist again and said that the surgery would be successful, should I decide to do it. I am a huge proponent of speech therapy and believe that the work I had done through sessions taken while in my sophomore year of college helped develop a vocal muscle memory that alleviated most of my glottal attack usage in my speaking voice. I believe this contributed greatly to the health of my voice over the years. Even professional singers talk more than they sing during the course of a day, so how you practice and speak regularly is key to maintaining a healthy instrument.

So, the time had finally come to make a huge decision, and this decision was a serious one. My life has always been about my voice. It is a risky surgery, as several singers who have had the surgery – both famous solo artists and famous backing vocalists – had successful outcomes while others had not-so-successful outcomes. A couple of my friends had this surgery, which ended, unfortunately, with them losing their singing voice permanently. However, one of the most successful results that I have ever witnessed was Chaka Khan.

In the 1990s, when I resumed my road gig with her, I noticed her voice. She sounded more amazing than ever; her voice was simply incredible. I complimented her, saying she had never sounded better. She said that she had the surgery to remove nodules from her cords. I asked her what she did to recover from her surgery, as obviously she was fully confident, unafraid to sing whatever sound or note came in her mind, and even to this day, she sings all of her songs full on, in their original key. Her answer was pure Chaka. She said, "Your voice is a muscle. You have to work it and you cannot be afraid to use it. You got to just kick it out yo ass!!" I will never, ever forget that. "You got to kick it out yo ass" is exactly what she does every time she gets in front of a microphone. She gives it everything she has, all energy.

So, in 2009, I had the vocal nodule removal surgery at
Massachusetts General Hospital, and it was successful, just as
the doctor said it would be. It took two weeks of total quiet before I could try out my newly healed vocal cords. Afterward, I
completed several sessions of speech therapy. So far, everything
was going just as the doctor had hoped it would.

The first day that I went into my office at Berklee and did a
few vocal warmups, my voice was rough and cracking in that
register where the surgery took place. Yes, it was scary to push
that area, to feel mentally the delicacy of my vocal cords' recent healing. I decided to solicit help from one of my colleagues,
Kathryn Wright, to give me voice lessons, as I felt I needed another person's trained ear to assess me. Kathryn was a graduate of Yale University and former student of Phyllis Curtain,
with whom I also studied at Tanglewood. She assured me that
my voice sounded fine and my technique was intact. I trusted
her ear implicitly. I began a regimen of vocal exercises, each
time pushing through my cracks and crevices, making sure my
breath support was perfect, to eliminate as much pressure from
my cords as possible and create no glottal attack on notes or spoken words during my practices. Remembering Chaka's words, I
took chances and pushed my upper-to-middle mix register. It
was getting a little better, but the slight cracking and roughness
in my tone was not going away. Then, I remembered my very first
tour with Chaka Khan when developing my mix register, how I
had to sing more consistently, balancing vocal rest and steam
therapy until my voice acclimated. It was clear that the best
thing for me to do to get my voice back was to get back on the
road. The consistency in singing every week would rebuild my
voice to where it was before. But, how was this going to happen?
I was a college professor in Boston now, far removed from the
possibility of even getting called to go on the road with anyone.

I made some calls to friends, telling them of my interest and asking them to inform me should any gigs come up. My daughter was graduating high school soon and was now old enough to handle me going on the road at this point, so my possibilities were open. Then, it happened. At the beginning of the Fall 2012 semester, my friend Lisa Vaughn from Chaka Khan's tour, called to check my availability to do a seven-week tour with Chaka and famed songwriter and producer David Foster, best known for his hits with Whitney Houston and Earth, Wind & Fire. This was my chance, my opportunity to get my voice back, to reconnect with the music business, and meet new artists. My first call was to the laryngologist, to consult with him one last time. This last meeting with the doctor was quite telling, as he had told me earlier in no certain terms, "at some point, you're going to have to choose whether to sing or teach. For you, doing both is too much on your vocal cords." I knew in the recesses of my spirit that he was correct. Right here, right now, I knew that there was only one thing that I had to do. I had to sing!!

FULL CIRCLE
CHAPTER TEN

TOO LOW FOR ZERO

Just when things were going well or leveling out, it seemed that something would come out of the blue, causing a shift that would literally send me spinning out of control again. At least, that's how it initially felt, as it has now been a three-year struggle to set up my diamond-hard foundation in this new music industry.

Whenever these shifts occurred, I became a sort of shape-shifter, as I accepted and adapted to my circumstances. Some would call it a re-invention, as I traversed a constantly changing landscape while maintaining my own integrity as an artist. It was challenging yet still a natural progression for me. I was no longer looking for work as a backing vocalist, but as a solo artist, songwriter, and clinician, and still accepting work as a vocal coach and session singer. Constantly twirling the plates of these streams of income, whether the return was immediate or in the future, was formidable and challenging. However, these shifts spoke to everything I wanted to accomplish, so the energy it took to maintain this pace was well worth the struggle. All that was needed was my continued razor-sharp focus, the ability to act on all possibilities, an air-tight faith in God, and a healthy, spiritual grounding maintained through a consistent meditation practice.

I held firmly to the concepts stated in the "Zero Limits" book by living in the present moment, doing nothing, planning nothing, just remaining silent as I enacted Dr. Lin's concept of "cleaning the subconscious" by forgiving myself for erroneous thoughts, being grateful, and expressing love. I used this practice at every chance. It became my mantra, staying in that zero space each morning by starting my meditation asking, "What's the right thing to do today?" then releasing the question into the universe with no provocation. Each time, the answers flowed with ease, and my days and nights were filled with what was important and needed to be addressed. It was literally God running every second-to-second movement of my life, like magic. At the end of each day, I knew that everything that could be done, had been accomplished. Worry would disappear from my consciousness, as I was now living in the moment and consistently feeling more content with my life.

Soon, constants began to spring up in the form of business relationships and all forms of work, as I was finally connecting with the people associated with all of the projects I had aspired to do.

Through a friend who is not in the music or music education business, I was introduced via email to the owner of an online company who would market one of my online class ideas. Through a "work for hire" rehearsal, I met a producer who was looking to co-write music to be placed in films and television with a major music licensing company. There was an offer to submit my music to an upcoming cable television series, which gave me the opportunity to submit my songs for review. After doing a session for a friend, the producer asked if he could submit the song and any of my other songs to Atlantic Records for a possible record deal. Also, after participating in a mentoring program with the School Of Rock, an independent music education school, one of my colleagues asked if I could send in a résumé for consideration to return to The New School for Social Research in New York City, this time as a visiting professor, to do a clinic or residency. All of these things came unsolicited.

These shifts in my life, I soon realized, had occurred as a result of a death, change or ending of some kind, and were an indication that new, positive beginnings were being born. Still, there were days when I had no money for food, I was still sleeping in my car, and work was simply inconsistent. My energy and stamina were fraying away as again depression and self-doubt reappeared. Moving through these shifts by working through my issues, never avoiding them, was a key component to a more peaceful solution, and the pendulum of my life began to swing a little more evenly. However, as reoccurring thoughts of suicide – which still rose up when things got tough – started to resurface, the "elephant in the room" issue that needed to be addressed, showed itself, this time with more clarity. It was my upbringing.

PARENT/CHILD

That parent/child or mentor/disciple relationship is a complex one, and in its early stages, the parent or mentor authority figure is expected and assumed by the child/disciple to have all of life's answers. As the learner or child/disciple, you trust and accept their leadership, which naturally places you in a position of always wanting to please them. However, when you mature and come into your own, fully realizing who you are and discovering your purpose, your expectations can conflict with the vision the parent/mentor/authority figure has of you. Even when you know what's best for you, the subconscious programming installed by your parent/mentor and surrounding society still runs its story, causing all forms of self-doubt. When adversity arises, your reaction to it can cause you to question your own intuition, which may allow what your parent/mentor believes is in your best interest to supersede your own beliefs about what is best.

Many friends of mine at Howard University were uber-talented musicians. Some of them had total emotional and financial support from their parents, while others were not allowed to study or get a degree in music because their parents would not allow it or financially support them. In their parents' eyes, music was not a "real job" and studying it was a waste of time and college tuition. While one would think that my childhood classical training and university degree in music meant I had garnered support from my parents, this was not true. They told me that all of my training and my college degree were supposed to prepare me for the vocation of Minister of Music at my church in Memphis. It never occurred to them that I would ever seriously pursue a career as a singer in the music industry. Therefore, they never supported such a life, thinking it was foolish. I ignored their suggestions, and yes, they even attempted to force me to abandon my pursuits by saying they would not financially support me in any way unless I returned to Memphis and the church, but I pursued my dreams anyway. However, inside I felt there was always that sub-conscious programming running amok, reiterating, "You can't sing anything but classical music. You'll never make it in this business," creating even more deep-seated self-doubt.

One would think that as we get older, living on one's own, we would mature from the "trying to please" mode. For a long time, I was one of them. Whenever things got rough for me in the music industry, and doubt reared its ugly head, conflicting thoughts arose as I tried to figure out how to do what made me happy and what was pleasing to my parents so they would be proud of my accomplishments. Even with the success I had garnered so far, touring the world with Elton John and other major artists, did not matter, as doubt was still there. Any pride in my accomplishments that was expressed by my parents, specifically my mother, was soon followed with the words, "So, when are you going to get a real job? You can't depend on singing." Passively, I never responded to her rhetoric. Internally, my feelings would be hurt, but still I pursued my dreams and yes, I paid a price.

Einstein said, "The definition of insanity is doing the same thing over and over again, expecting a different result." Was I insane to keep pursuing my dreams? Was returning to Los Angeles a full-circle move? Full-circle, 360-degree turns felt as though I was either starting the same scenario over and over again, like the running theme in the 1993 movie "Groundhog Day," or just running in place and never advancing, neither of which I was interested in doing. Regardless, as these events would happen and appear to wreak havoc on my life, then a waterfall of tears would spew from my eyes, rendering me lifeless and lethargic, as each night I would park my car in front of Cafe Gratitude, then cry myself into a deep sleep, sometimes praying to die. This was my reoccurring theme, as any time things got unbearably difficult, my response included suicidal tendencies. However, when I awakened, a sense of calm, peace, even happiness welled inside of me, filling up those depressive, empty spaces from the night before, and it felt re-energizing. Crying brought clarity, erasing all erroneous thoughts of "maybe this struggle is a sign that it's time to give up my dreams," or "Why is this happening to me? What's wrong with me? Shouldn't this path be met with lesser resistance?" So, it became my final decision to believe that, if I awakened the next morning, then this was my cue, indicating that I was gifted with yet another chance to remain focused on my goals and make everything right, and that these stressful, sometimes painful events were all part of the cycle of my life, alerting me to what needed to be addressed, fixed, and changed.

This valuable lesson was discovered as a result of my first suicide attempt, at the age of 18.

It was during my final spring term of high school before attending undergraduate school at Howard University. I held the position of vice president of the gospel choir at my high school and we were asked to perform at Southwestern College, which for kids like us was a big deal. After much rehearsal and preparation, we were ready and excited to perform. All that was needed was to make sure that everyone had transportation to get to the college. My parents had two cars, so there was no problem with me driving one of them. Many of our members were from families that did not have cars, so they needed a ride to our concert. As the VP of the choir, I felt responsible for assisting them, as I had the means to help. I was happy to pick them up. However, my mother refused to allow me to pick them up, even though she was not driving nor would she be attending the concert. "I am not a taxi!" she insisted. I felt as if I were letting everyone down and knew they were counting on me to help. In my high-strung, teenaged mind, I couldn't do anything right. My mother hated gospel music, didn't believe in supporting it, and she didn't care to help anyone who was economically disadvantaged. All of those times when nothing I did was enough or suitable for her came rushing to the surface and this singular event became the jumping-off point.

We did the concert that night, even with a deficit number of members who had no way to get there. I could not get over the shame of feeling as though I was the privileged one who couldn't help my friends. I came home that night feeling angry, worthless, and powerless. I got the medicine that had been prescribed to me earlier that year to treat an allergic reaction to ragweed and swallowed twenty pills. My intention was to force my mother to notice that she was doing something wrong in our relationship, that this was a call out for help that said, "If you don't pay attention and try to address this, then it's your fault that I am dead." It was my last response to feeling that there was nothing I could do to make my mother happy, as I felt she would always find fault in everything I did for most of my life. This was my 18-year-old reasoning of this situation.

I thought that I would fall asleep, but the pills had the reverse effect, as I couldn't be still. I decided to awaken my parents and tell them what I did. My father got up immediately, went to the waste basket in my bedroom, and pulled out every wrapper from every pill that was ingested, meticulously reassembling the paper and counting each one. Then, he took me to the car in my night gown, and we all went to the Baptist Hospital emergency room. I recall the nurse fighting to get the tube down my nose into my stomach for the stomach pumping, because my nostril passages were small. As I flailed around on the gurney, the nurse said in a sharp, abrupt tone, "You had no business doing this in the first place." I remember how hurt and helpless her remarks made me feel. After the first pumping session, they filled my stomach with activated charcoal water. Soon after this treatment, I regurgitated it all as black water splattered against the white hospital walls. After that episode, I fell asleep.

I awakened the next day to my mother walking into my hospital room. The impact of my actions was not at all what I bargained for, as she whispered in my ear, "Your godmother is on her way to see you. I told her that you accidentally took too much of your medication. You better not tell her or anyone that you did this on purpose. They will think you're crazy and lock you up!" That was her answer. That was her reasoning. No discussion, no therapy, nothing. My mother and father never inquired or brought up this incident again. Ever. I went away to college that fall thinking that if I ever considered suicide again, it would only hurt me and not anyone else. That was a true wake-up call. Still, it obviously was not enough to shift my love toward myself first, as there were other suicide attempts throughout my life. Each time, as I survived, I experienced some growth along my learning curve. However, it would take something even greater before I spiritually awakened.

PRESENT - TOO LOW BELOW A ZERO

It was my last day of a week at the Crescent Hotel. I got up around 11 a.m. and went down to the restaurant of the hotel for coffee. I sat at the bar, as one of the servers, my friend Marcus, was running things that morning. Today, I was scheduled to attend the graduate recital of my friend Valerie's son at University of California-Los Angeles. It started at 4 p.m., so there was plenty of time.

Everyone at the hotel was cheerful and busy, as again, they treated me like an old friend, which at this point, I guess I am. One of the hotel managers came into the bar. As we greeted each other and began our conversation, I mentioned the recital at UCLA. "You're going to UCLA today? Didn't you hear? There was a murder/suicide shooting this morning!" she said. I had never turned on the television that morning, so I quickly checked the news on my cellphone, then I called Valerie. She informed me that she was awaiting word to see if the recital was still happening as scheduled and would get back to me. Ten minutes later, she called back, stating that the college had informed her that the recital would go on as scheduled. They believed the incident was contained, and that at that point, the campus was not in danger. Thank God. I finished my coffee, checked out of the hotel, and headed on to UCLA.

I arrived early, as I was not familiar with this expansive campus. You really need a car to get around UCLA. Since I skipped breakfast, I decided to grab a protein smoothie in Westwood Village, then drive up the hill to the parking area. Just as I parked my car, a call came in from my daughter.

She sounded agitated and asked if I had purchased a Galaxy cellphone. "No," I responded, as she knows I have an iPhone. In the background, a woman's voice could be faintly heard. Obviously, my daughter was not alone. She then said, "I'll call you back" and hung up. Approximately three minutes later, she called back, screaming, cursing, and angry. "Don't ever speak to me again. I am shutting off the phone service!" she screamed and hung up again. Click! Quickly assessing in my mind what could possibly be happening, I went down my list. First, our phone bill was paid up until the next bill, which was due next week. Second, I knew nothing about a Galaxy phone. We hadn't had a disagreement, so there was no reason to be angry with me about anything else. I tried to phone her, but she wouldn't answer my calls, so I started texting her, "What happened? Did someone compromise the account?" She texted back, "YOU ARE A LIAR, I CAN'T DEAL ANYMORE, DON'T CALL ME EVER, FOR ANYTHING, OR TEXT, JUST LEAVE ME ALONE." Then, BAM! The phone service was shut off! It felt as if I was in a crazy nightmare. Her behavior was bizarre and irrational.

I remembered passing by a T-Mobile store in Westwood Village, so I pulled out of my parking spot and drove down to Westwood Boulevard again. It took a few minutes, but finally I found the store, parked, then I went inside to make my inquiry. First, they restored my service. They were surprised that my daughter could have it shut down since she was not authorized to do so. They didn't know that she knew my social security number and could call in, using my number to pay the bill, which is why I gave it to her in the first place. They noted that I had been wrongfully overcharged for an old phone that had been turned in a year before. However, that overage cost was only seven dollars per month, and should not have warranted her bizarre behavior. Now, noticing the time, I rushed back to my car and drove up the hill, hoping to retrieve my parking space, as it was time for the recital to begin.

At this point, I arrived five minutes late, missing the first song. Though I was trying my best to just enjoy the music, deep inside of my heart, I was screaming with worry that my daughter was honestly having what appeared to be a nervous breakdown. My first thought was to call the police, as I had experienced two friends having nervous breakdowns at Howard University. It was a horrible thing to witness. I texted her, informing her of my worry and that I would contact the police if she didn't at least tell me what was going on. She texted back, "If you send the police here, I will be homeless, kicked out of my apartment. I just paid my rent." She went on to rave about how I shouldn't call the police, and how this shouldn't be my response when I couldn't reach her. She was right. Being a parent who lived 3,000 miles away, I never knew how to respond to issues that were out of my control regarding my child. Many times, the worst scenarios would infiltrate my consciousness, leaving me sick with worry, and not knowing what else to do but to contact the authorities. Was she really losing her mind or was she just upset? It had all happened so fast this morning, with zero warning.

Ever since my daughter has been in this world, one of my ongoing mantras has always been, "If the kid is all right, then I'm all right." It didn't matter what was happening in my life, as long as she was taken care of and happy, there was a sense of calm in the middle of all of my storms. Today, this was not the case. This event with my daughter left me feeling suicidal again, powerless, and scared. For the next several days, I walked around in a daze, not knowing how to react or act at this point. I contacted one of my daughter's girlfriend's in N.Y.C. After receiving a text, assuring me that my daughter was probably OK and just needed space, I felt a little relieved. Struggling to keep my sanity, I decided to listen to her friend and pray that she did know what she was talking about, as I could not afford to fly to N.Y.C. Her friend texted again, saying that she had experience as a medical assistant and had dealt with suicides and breakdowns in her own family, etc., and that she was certain this was not a breakdown. After reading the details of the friend's background in the last text, I felt a little better. Still, it would be more than three weeks before I would hear a word from my daughter.

On June 30, I was scheduled to sing at the Rainbow Room on the Sunset Strip in West Hollywood. I decided to check my mail in Malibu first, then head out to the beach. As soon as I parked my car, my phone rang. It was my daughter. Finally! I answered. She was nasty, angry and just plain mean. She told me that she was calling to tell me to stop contacting her friend to inquire about her. She then proceeded to curse at me, saying, "You are a piece of shit, I hope you fucking die of cancer, better yet, why don't you just kill yourself. I won't come to your funeral. I fucking hate you, you are not my mother, you piece of shit." I sat in my car and listened to her scream to the top of her lungs, calling me a "fucking bitch" for what felt like half an hour. I constantly tried to intervene, asking her why she was angry. What did I do to make her angry? She would not respond to any of my questions. Instead, she just kept calling me names.

Finally, she started to cry and asked what it would take for me never to contact her again. I told her she needed to tell me what I had done wrong. She then said that all she wanted was a break from everyone. Then, she admitted that when she turned off the phone service, it was because someone had compromised the lines and added another phone line, making the bill higher. I told her that she had never told me this, and that I had gone to T-Mobile that day to restore the service and they said nothing about an extra line being added. But, they did have a Galaxy cell phone that was mistakenly being charged to my account. She mentioned that she was angry that I contacted her friend inquiring about her. I apologized for that and told her that her behavior was so bizarre that even her friend was concerned about her.

By the end of my daughter's conversation, it came into my thoughts that she might be angry at me for being homeless. Possibly, the stress of my life weighed heavily on her, and there was nothing I could do about this. Referring to the book "Zero Limits," its concepts state that I am 100 percent responsible for everything that happened to me, which meant my daughter's ranting and raving was brought on by me. With this in mind, it dawned on me that she was my mirror. This is 100 percent how I felt about myself and my circumstances. This was the ultimate display of a lack of self-love. I was not wholly taking care of myself or putting myself first. My child unequivocally came first, before me, before anyone. Then, I remembered one day when she was around 6 or 7 years old, she came to me crying and said, "Mommy, I feel bad that I had all of these beautiful clothes and your clothes have holes in them." At that time, shopping for me was the very last thing on my list. All money went to everything my daughter needed. I recall kissing her and assuring her that I was fine, and was never really a fan of shopping, which was true. From that moment on, I made a point of showing her how I took care of myself, by getting more manicures and pedicures, or going out to dinner. Somehow, I felt this was enough evidence of my self-love. Again, I was wrong. Again, this current event brought this issue full force to my attention, and my God, it was a hell of a way to learn a lesson.

Now, it was time to completely let go. It was time to put that mask over my mouth first. There is nothing to be done to help her or anyone, if I am not OK. This means I must put myself first. I cannot control whatever is going on in her life, and worrying about it or getting upset, even sick, about this is not the way to help her or myself. My daughter had her own journey to traverse now, and how she reacted to her circumstances would incite her own lessons to be learned. This was one of the most difficult things that a parent must face, letting go. I imagined some parents made a smoother transition. However, this was not the case for me. While I understood in theory the need to let go and allow my daughter to enforce her independence, even though she chose to assert it in a negative way, it still took another six months and two more conversations before accepting this new state of being. Acceptance. There's that word again.

The shift in this relationship with my daughter, the death of our previous relationship or my conception of our relationship, was the ultimate lesson. Slowly, it began to sink in, bringing everything to full circle, that my lesson in true self love must be learned now. As my daughter fiercely sought her independence, I had to fiercely install my own self-love.

Now, coming to an understanding of the role pain played in my life, I looked forward to the tears. I knew they were a sign that there were lessons to acknowledge, changes in perspectives and attitudes to address, and some growth needed, moving me closer to realizing my dreams, closer to my full becoming, and this was a good thing.

In the end, sometimes under the most horrific of circumstances, you learn awesome lessons that move you closer to your truth, aligning your purpose with the universe. I understand all of this in theory, yet this is something that, currently, I work through every day. It would be a lie to say that my heart was not broken behind this event with my daughter. It still hurts.

BACKING VOCALIST FULL CIRCLE - 2012

Returning to the road with Chaka Khan for a month, including three more weeks with David Foster & Friends in Asia, was an incredible way to re-enter the real music scene, though in some ways, it felt as if I were repeating my backing vocalist career and not moving forward as a solo artist. While it was never my intention to simply return to this life exclusively, this was the path of least resistance that led me out of the Berklee College of Music "Bermuda Triangle," and that was all that mattered.

Before joining the David Foster tour of Asia, Chaka did a month-long tour in Europe via tour bus, which is by far my favorite mode of transportation on the planet, especially driving through Europe. It was like a month-long pajama party.

As always, the buses were pretty luxurious, with all of the accoutrements of a great apartment. On this tour, Chaka had two buses, one for the guys and one for us girls. The beauty of traveling this way is that you can monitor what you eat. We bought lots of fruit and healthy snacks, and yes, we also had some junk food like chips and popcorn. Best of all, we watched movies or TV shows. On this trip, everyone was obsessed with the Showtime original series "Carnivale." This was our after-gig addiction, as we couldn't wait to get on the bus after a show and binge-watch episode after episode. There were no showers for band members on the bus, so we lounged around in our pajamas until we reached our hotel, checked in to our respective rooms, showered, ate, or did whatever until showtime. We checked out of the hotel right before we boarded the bus for the show. After the show, we hopped on the bus, got back into our PJs, then it was movie/TV and popcorn time. Eventually, we fell asleep. While most everyone went to their bunks, I slept in the living room area on the sofa or in the loft, located above the driver, as I was very claustrophobic in those bunks, especially when they shut the doors between the living room and the bunk sleeping area. The door to Chaka's suite, which was at the other end of the bunk sleeping quarters, in the back of the bus, was almost always shut. Everyone knew that my bunk always housed my things, not me. This kind of travel promoted a feeling of family, as we were literally living together on that bus. Many times, we played card games. Our favorite game on this tour was the Uno card games, which we also played in airport lounges and dressing rooms. It was so much fun, and we had lots of laughs as we traveled the countryside of just about every country in Europe.

Our last tour stop in Europe before meeting up with David Foster in Singapore for the Asia portion of the tour, was the city of Berlin in Germany, where we were scheduled to perform at the GQ Awards. It was a star-studded event and we were the headline performers for this televised show. Among the stars who attended were the band Simply Red and actor John Cusack. I sat next to Mr. Cusack while getting my makeup done for the show. Lovely guy. We chatted briefly, as it was always nice to meet artists in their relaxed, non-working state.

After the GQ Awards show, there was a huge after-party. These parties were almost always very boring. There was no one there to really talk to and everyone was just sitting around looking at everyone else. It was really crazy. My friends who aren't in this business seem to believe these parties would be exciting. Not. Most times, including this one, we housed together as a band, in our sectioned-off VIP area, eating, drinking, and watching everyone else watch us until we couldn't take the noise, as most times our ears were exhausted from doing the show, which entailed listening to our own music in detail, which was considered "work." The gift bags were cool, though. However, even these gift bags end up in the hands of a friend, the maid, or with strangers, because when traveling on the road, there's limited space to carry extra items unless you choose to pay for over-weighted luggage. Besides, I had already shopped, which can become a tour addiction. You end up shipping things back to the U.S. to avoid luggage overages, which is still not cost effective. But, it's what many musicians do out of boredom.

After more than twenty-five years on the road, the schedule is pretty much the same. I woke up at my leisure, checked out what there was to see historically in the city, went sight-seeing, then hit the gym to work out. Ate. Then laid down and rested up for the show. After the show, usually, we met in the bar of the hotel for a couple of drinks, then off to bed. After having toured so extensively, especially in Europe, my addiction to just shopping like crazy wore off. My weekly paycheck for the tour was deposited automatically into my bank account at home and was never touched. I used my per diem to shop but had to be careful, as that money was designated for food and other needs on the road, not shopping. Some musicians balanced out extra cash from their per diem by taking advantage of free band dinners, which are part of the riders/contract agreement between artist and promoters on the details of what the band members like to have in dressing rooms, etc., or eating at the venue with the crew, which is always an option.

We arrived in Singapore first to rehearse with our new band mates for this portion of the tour, the David Foster Band. The musical director sent out an email ahead of time, inquiring if the three of us could read music. This was awesome, as it meant we would be able to have charts to perform this show, which included the music of Babyface, Peter Cetera, Paul Young, Chaka, a couple of other artists, and, of course, the huge catalogue of David Foster music. I'm a good sight-reader, but the other two singers didn't read music. No worries, as the three of us could get together on our own and I could help them learn the music. But, I never received a single chart before getting to Singapore. The musical director only sent audio files of the songs, so it was left up to us to use our ears. Since our performance schedule with Chaka was pretty consistent all the way up to our flight to Singapore, there wasn't much time to go over the large set list of songs for the DF tour in detail. We got together and worked out the songs as best as we could but were partially prepared.

In our first rehearsal, I noticed that every band member had a chart except us. This made me angry, as there was a bit of scrutiny when we missed a part. Basically, this meant that we had to know our parts by memory while the rest of the band were reading charts, which was not fair. The musical director had recorded vocals on a track that he played while we were rehearsing. They did not match our voices at all, yet I knew that he intended on using them, which meant we would be singing but the audience would be hearing these pre-recorded vocals, which were not well done. This was insane, but he was willing to use them because he was not confident we would know our parts. It was a frustrating situation. After missing another cue, I informed the musical director that I never received the charts. He made a snide comment, saying, "I didn't know you could read." I retorted, "I told you in my email that I could read." There was an uncomfortable silence on stage as he dismissed what I said by reiterating that they would just use the recorded vocals. "Fuck it, then," I thought. We would get paid for just standing there, mouthing lyrics, and just sing during Chaka's segment of the show. What a way to start a tour.

In addition, we were using ear monitors instead of the floor monitors we were used to and had been using for the past four weeks on tour with Chaka. Not a major problem at all, as we knew how to adjust. However, the setup the monitor engineer used only allowed one single mix for all three backing vocalists. In most ear monitor setups, each musician/singer on the stage has their own combination of instruments with independent volume to control what they wish to hear on stage in their ear monitors to assist them in their job performance. Everyone is different, requiring different things. In this case, the background singers had ONE mix between the three of us, so we were stuck with working with whatever the other two needed to hear. This was problematic and only added to the stress of our job performance. Hearing music in a certain fashion is essential to doing your job well. Obviously, they were not prepared or thoughtful when it came to backing vocals, as every other musician on that stage had their own individual ear monitor mix, which I took as a sign of disrespect. As a backup singer, this unfortunate event happens often, and is one of the things that I abhor about the treatment of people in my profession. We still rose to the occasion, doing our job. Professionals like myself can make it look easy to overcome these hurdles, which is probably why it continues to happen. In accordance with my passive personality, thanks to my upbringing, when such situations arose, I found it was best to not try to make an example of the disrespect, but to simply do the best job, under the conditions. I can't say that my reaction was right or wrong. Simply, it was my reaction.

Regardless, the first show with David Foster was great. In a mood of spontaneity, David sat down at the piano and began to sing and play some of his hit songs. Many of his songs were the blueprint of my life, as I knew all of them. The other singers knew them also, and in a fit of spontaneity, we chimed in with him, singing the background parts to every song he chose at his whim. After the show, he came off stage, congratulating us, saying, "You girls had my back!" From that moment on, we were treated differently. We earned our respect. We were golden.

In between Bangkok, Thailand, and Jakarta, Indonesia, Chaka was asked to sing in Jaipur, India, for a birthday party given by supermodel Naomi Campbell for her boyfriend. They flew Chaka, the background singers, her tour and personal managers, and stylist on private jet to India to do the show.

India was incredible and, yes, cows roamed the streets like stray dogs. When we arrived at what was to be the hotel, it was an unmarked, pink stucco wall with cracks in it. After idling there for a few minutes, this wooden fence next to the cracked wall opened up electronically like in a James Bond movie, and we drove inside to what I witnessed as the most lavish hotel I've ever seen. There were peacocks walking the grounds, grounds keepers sweeping the walkways with old-world, authentic, hand-made brooms, and the property was beautifully situated at the base of a hill with a huge, medieval-looking castle at the top. The Castle was our venue!

Castle in Jaipur, India

Guests arrived to the party on the backs of camels, beautifully decorated with marigolds and colorful linens, coverings
and pillows. It was extravagant. We sang to pre-recorded tracks
at around 1 a.m., then returned to our hotel. The atmosphere
on the main grounds at that hour was still quite festive, with
twinkling white fairy lights and the sounds of a party coming
from the upper level of the restaurant located in the center of the
garden. There was a snake charming show going on with cobras.
This was absolutely not my thing, so I excused myself, continuing on to my room for a long hot bath and on to bed, as our
wake-up call time was at 8 a.m. Our next private flight took us
on to Jakarta, where we reconnected with the David Foster tour.

The entire seven-week tour was a total success, ending in
China with a lovely dinner for band, crew, and family members
only at an exclusive restaurant in Shanghai, owned by a friend
of David Foster. As the only patrons that night, we were served
an incredible world-class meal. The next morning, it was time
to return to the U.S.

Six months after my return, I decided to resign from my
position at Berklee College of Music for the third and final time,
returning to Los Angeles also for the third time.

Then, after two years of returning to the road with Chaka
Khan, the indications were clear that her tour was not assisting
me in gaining any financial ground nor was it promoting my
current dreams as songwriter and rock singer. It was the summer of 2015 and it was time to move on. My life with Chaka had
gone full circle and as much as I enjoyed every minute, I knew
it was time to go. My last performance with her and the band
was in Johannesburg, South Africa. It was an awesome way to
end a legacy.

It was time to finally focus on my dreams and take that leap
for myself as a solo artist and songwriter, among other vocations
of interest.

ZERO IS A FULL CIRCLE - THE PAST IS NOW PROLOGUE

It had been two weeks that I'd been sleeping in a bed! I wasn't ready to return to sleeping in my car just yet. Since Kevin, the backing vocalist at the Whisky, and his boyfriend David constantly offered accommodations at their home, I thought it would be fun to spend some quality time with the two of them. I really enjoyed every minute hanging out and conversing with them, not to mention that their offer represented the path of least resistance once again.

Kevin is this sweet man; I also fell in love with David, his partner, the first day that I met him, he's such an awesome guy. That night when I arrived at the Whisky with no car and no place to go, David shared with me his story, which was quite a tumultuous one. He spoke of having endured three major deaths in his immediate family in a very short amount of time: His child, due to illness; his mother, who was murdered by his step-father; and his previous partner, due to illness. He'd lost everything and then, somehow, was able to come back to life. I tell you, you never know what people have endured.

Anyway, Kevin had said on several occasions that he knew I needed a place to live, but only had a trailer, which he would comically say in a silly voice, "a tra-lor," as in "tra-la-la." Now, I did hear him when he made this whimsical statement, but since I had never, ever known anyone who ever lived in a trailer or "tra-lor," I never took what he said literally, always thinking he just said this as a commentary on the fact that his place was just too small.

It was awfully kind of Kevin and David to offer their home, and I didn't mind that what he offered would be a small place. I decided to take him up on his offer after leaving the Crescent Hotel, so I got directions out to their place. They lived in Apple Valley, which is about ninety miles, or about an hour and forty-five minutes by car with zero traffic from Los Angeles, to get there. I got off of the 15 freeway onto Highway 18 with less than a quarter of a tank of gas, thinking I'd better stop at the nearest station, since I had no idea how much longer it would take me to get to his house from the freeway. I stopped at the first station that I saw, which was an ARCO station surrounded by desert, mountains, and not much else. Wide open spaces. A guy at the station offered to clean my windshield for tips. I told him I had no cash on me, which was true. He quickly turned in the other direction to someone else. I could hear Jevetta Steele's song "I'm Calling You" from the movie "Baghdad Café" in the back of my head: "... a desert road on the way to nowhere ..."

It was at least another five miles before I arrived to Kevin and David's street. Then a text came in, saying they could see me on their Waze app, indicating that I was almost there. When I pulled up into what appeared to be some kind of an entrance, Kevin and David were standing outside, waving me toward a parking space. I parked and got out to greet them, and as I looked around, it hit me: This was a real, honest-to-God trailer park. OK, if my father were alive, he would kill me if he even suspected I would be near such a place with two white men, gay or straight. My arrogant, bourgeois, sorority-girl upbringing did a double-take. Personally, I felt safe and could have cared less. While I was a little taken aback only because this experience was a new one, I loved and trusted Kevin and David so much that it didn't matter. They led me inside their one-bedroom trailer, which they shared with a lesbian couple. They lived in the living room and the lesbians lived in the bedroom. I chuckled to myself, thinking, "This could make for some great reality TV right here. Here's the cast: A white gay man with his Mexican lover, a white lesbian woman with her East Indian lover, and the straight black chick who comes to visit. That's must-see TV!"

As usual. Kevin was happy, joking around, and of course,

very hospitable. Oodles of jokes ran through my head as I looked around, wondering, where am I gonna sleep? In the bed with Kevin and David? Definitely not with the lesbians, since I didn't know them at all. Excusing myself to the bathroom, I decided to take a shower. Kevin shouted out, "David and I didn't know what kind of soap you would like, so we bought some Dove flowery smelling shower gel. Hope you like it!" How thoughtful of them both, I thought. I went in and hopped into the shower and right in front of me in the shower caddy was a bottle of Massengil Douche. Laughing to myself, I thought, "I wonder which couple is using this?" Just the thought of this made me giggle out loud, though I knew the thoughts were ignorant and politically incorrect, but hilarious.

When I came out of the bathroom, there my bed awaited, a twin-sized air mattress in the kitchen area, blocking the front of the refrigerator. I hopped in, wearing my leopard onesie. It was quite comfortable. We laughed and talked, as we always did, and I was feeling right at home, actually. They also had two poodles in a doggy crate that slept right across from me. As it was fast approaching 3 or 4 a.m., we all finally decided to go to sleep. I tell you, we were one, big, happy modern family.

The time spent out in that desert was priceless. Kevin and David took care of me the entire time, treating me to meals, going to the gym, driving around looking at houses for them to purchase one day, and taking me up to Big Bear to meet their friends – which, once again, could be a separate book all unto itself. We sincerely enjoyed one another's company. Kevin is a great singer, having had success on the '80s rock scene in Los Angeles. He, like so many other musicians, had been struggling to find footing in this new music industry. While we were diametrically opposed politically – he was a total conservative and I was a total liberal – we managed to come together in love, for the love of music. It truly is a universal language, bringing every being together as one entity, no matter who you are or what you believe. If only the rest of the world could be that way.

After a couple of days of traversing the desert landscape amidst the beauty of a very simple yet unconventional life with friends, I decided it was time to return to L.A. Treasuring every moment, taking in the dusty scenery of cacti, rock formations, and tumbleweeds, I began my hour-and-a-half drive back to what I termed civilization. But, what is civilization? Los Angeles County? Returning to the Korean spa? Sleeping in my car in front of Cafe Gratitude? A true definition of civilization escaped me at the moment, for it could mean one thing at one time, then another thing to someone totally different at another time. I had made no real decision on exactly where to go, as my habit of living in the moment gave the resounding answer, "It is yet to be determined."

CHAPTER ELEVEN

As always, taking these long drives gave me a chance to think out loud. More than anything, a road trip gave me a chance to listen to my heart. On this trip, the landscape was very different from what I was used to. Unlike the beauty of the ocean or the rolling hills and greenery of the mountains on my drive up the coast to San Francisco, this time the landscape was of the desert, which provided a different aesthetic and level of energy. I recalled reading a book back in the '90s about the effects of receiving this energy through one's environment in a book titled "The Celestine Prophecy." In this book, the main character finds a manuscript in Peru that details nine insights. As he studies and experiences them, they assist him in his spiritual awakening. One of the insights explains how everything in our environment is alive, vibrating with energy that, when we access it, can heal and aid us in our life's journey.

As I drove along the eastern corridor of the San Bernardino Forest, through the multiple rock formations and stacked boulders of the desert, I reminisced about my own past spiritual journeys and the teachers who have assisted me over these last thirty years, and my former Elton John bandmate Mortonette Jenkins-Stevens came to mind. Thanks to the guidance of Mortonette, who was heavily involved in several scientific disciplines, she and my other EJ bandmate, Marlena Jeter, and I spent countless hours together off stage, practicing kinesiology, quantum physics exercises, and all things metaphysical. Marlena and I had been Mortonette's guinea pigs, happily so, as it felt as though we were performing magic. It was all in the name of healing our minds, spirits, and bodies, and obliterating negative patterns in order to live more full and productive lives. I treasured every moment and credit many of those principles learned as the reasons I am alive and well today. It was amazing how the post-traumatic stress of my childhood wreaked havoc on my life. Through the study and practice of these concepts suggested by Mortonette and other spiritual teachers, I had been able to process most of it and move on. However, as always, I am a work in progress.

One day, Mortonette invited me to come and visit with her and her husband in Las Vegas. We stayed up all night, binge-watching "Cosmos," the TV series on science and the environment hosted by astrophysicist Neil DeGrasse-Tyson. Afterward, Mortonette spoke of the healing effects of living in Las Vegas. She said that living in the desert promoted a healing of the intellect, which she found to be stimulating and not so emotionally based, which suited her needs at the time. She said that the physically open spaces of the landscape there allowed her to think things through more clearly.

I found this to be interesting, as there was a time in my life when, on the way to a personal vacation in Santa Fe, New Mexico, I decided to stop and spend a couple of nights at Graham's Bed & Breakfast Inn in Sedona, Arizona, near a well-known energy vortex in an area called Bell Canyon. As I drove down the winding, two-lane highway through the mountains to Sedona, the beauty of that region, with its deep-red clay, tall, dark-green pines, and overall majestic landscape, left me speechless. I attributed that

entire experience there in Sedona to my being mentally, physically, and emotionally prepared to deal with my father's illness
and death while I was on tour with Elton John in 1993. The inn
was located right behind the vortex. Each night, I said my prayers
and meditated, opening myself to its healing energy field.

DADDY'S GIRL - 1993

From that moment on, my schedule went into overdrive as I, a
true "daddy's girl," flew to Memphis to assist my father who, at
this point, was hospitalized with two broken arms, a result of
his bone cancer. While in Memphis, we spent countless hours
in conversation, maximizing the quality of our time together.
My schedule included playing tennis early every morning, then
going to the gym and working out for two hours every afternoon. Afterward, I grabbed a bite of food, then went to my father's hospital room and talked through the night until we both
fell asleep. This schedule went on for about two or three weeks.
Eventually, he was released from the hospital for the Christmas
holidays. Soon after, in January 1993, he re-entered the hospital
as his health began to deteriorate, leading him into a coma. At
this point, though I chose not to spend the night with him at
the hospital, I came every evening and sang jazz classics to him,
as they were his favorites. As February approached, it was time
for me to return to the Australia/New Zealand portion of the
Elton John tour. I arrived in Auckland, New Zealand, at 6 a.m.
on February 6; by 2 p.m. that same day, I received word that my
father passed away. By six p.m. that same evening, Elton John's
office paid and arranged for my flight back to Memphis. I arrived there just in time to make funeral arrangements with my
mother. I returned to the tour the day after my father's funeral,
never missing a beat, moving through these emotionally strenuous events effortlessly, remaining healthy and calm throughout

the entire ordeal. I believe that was the God energy of that desert vortex working on my behalf.

Mortonette also spoke of the energy of a mountainous environment, and how the grassy areas were in fact, "grounding" and when standing on this earth on bare feet, the energy of the landmass healing and cleansed you of negativity. In light of this, I reminisced about the time I'd spent living in Topanga when my daughter was born. At that time, it was the perfect place for me to bring a child into this world, and certainly a loving, positive, and grounding environment for me after having been on the road, flying for the last ten years. Grounding and nesting were the best prescribed medicine for my life at that time, a necessary environment for me to sustain as a new, single mom. Even when I moved to northern California almost two years later, I was tucked away in that magical forest of tall redwood trees in downtown Mill Valley. I could definitely see how healing that green, mountainous environment had been for myself and for my daughter as well. Recalling the time when my heart instructed me to move back to New York, to the more rural Dutchess County area, I now realize that was divine intervention, for the necessity of maintaining the "grounding/nesting" energy of my surroundings assisted and prepared me for my life as a single parent to a teenager and a college professor in Boston.

Now the time had come for me to be on the ocean, as this location now spoke to my heart. I love the beach, and as far back as 1986, when I bought my first car, I spent quality time driving up to Malibu at every opportunity. However, I had never felt the need to actually live on the beach with the ocean as my backyard until now. Mortonette said that water represents emotional healing, which is also connected with the limbic system of the brain. It aligns one's vibration and gets rid of negative ionization, promoting feelings of peace. Yes, the goal of setting up a foundation here in Los Angeles for this third installment of my life and being at peace truly resonated with me. After all of the chatter, the traveling, moving back and forth across the United States, and finally finding self-love and emotional healing, finding peace was key.

It all made sense now, as this energetic attraction to various environments, possibly defines the role vacations play in all of our lives. Human beings need to recalibrate in these different levels of energy restoration stations. Artists who travel the world are especially sensitive and understanding of how certain environments can affect one's spirit. It is funny and probably not a coincidence that the home base of the music, television, and film industries is found in the state of California, which provides all of these different levels of energetic existence. When my spirit needs the ocean, it's here. When my spirit needs a view of the green mountains, it's here. When my spirit needs the desert, it's here. Every climate is here, and my being placed here as my foundation is Gods' gift, preparing me for my work in industries that reside right here outside of my front door.

I started out as a singer, as was prophesied by a woman to my parents when I was six months old. But, there is much more to me than singing, as I now realized that my voice has evolved into being a vehicle for a more expansive purpose that may very well be the defining legacy of my life. I am so glad that I listened to my heart. Listening is everything. However, it took the bird's eye view of a background singing career to see, feel, hear, and experience all of these things and understand their depth and beauty. What a life.

IT'S UNIVERSAL IN SPITE OF IT ALL

It is virtually impossible to speak on anything that has occurred in this country without including the issue of race, as it is a prevailing issue that permeates every aspect of existence of every

American in the United States. I was aware of the aftermath of
Jim Crow Laws where Black musicians could not enter a front
door of a club or stay at the same hotel as their white counter-
parts in America through the fifties. In the '60s, the racial lines
did fade away, as most everyone acknowledged and spoke the
universal language of music, succumbing to its emotional and
unifying influences.

As a child who was raised in the Deep South in the late '60s
and early '70s, I was no stranger to racism. However, my experiences would be equally balanced, positive and negative, on
both sides of the black and white fence. I grew up in a black,
middle-class atmosphere, filled with black doctors, lawyers,
judges, and other white-collar professionals. My father was the
first African-American to be hired by the United States Post
Office in the state of Tennessee. Coincidentally, it was a gentleman from Howard University, my alma mater, who was the cat-
alyst in my father's hiring. My mother was an elementary school
teacher who later moved on to become the librarian. There were
no white people in my community, except for that second-grade
teacher who had me sing at her wedding when I was seven. The
only other experience I had communicating with white people
was with my voice teacher when I began studying privately at
the age of 10. Both experiences were positive ones.

My first recollection of racism happened when I was about
6 or 7 years of age. My mother took my sister and I with her to
a doctor's appointment. Her doctor was a white man whose office was in a refurbished house, with a living room containing
a floor model, console color television. When my mother was
called into the examination room, she instructed us to go sit in
the living room area where the television was located and watch
cartoons. Happily, we went in and sat on the floor and watched
TV. Shortly after my mother left, the receptionist approached
us and said, "Y'all have to sit in the back. You can't sit here."

Respecting authority, my sister and I followed her directions, as she led us to the back door of the office, which had a small, enclosed porch that was just wide enough to fit two hard, up-right, white, wooden church benches, which faced each other. We sat there quietly and a little stunned, definitely upset that we couldn't watch cartoons. It felt as if we sat there forever before my mother came out of the doctor's office. She was furious with us. "What are you doing back here? Didn't I tell you to sit up front and watch cartoons?" I told my mother that we were instructed to sit back here. She told us not to follow her, then went up to the front to the receptionist's desk while we remained on the back porch. I have no idea what she said or what she did. All that I know is, we never went there ever again.

While I understood later in life that this event happened be-cause I was a black child who was not allowed to sit with other white people in that doctor's office, a couple of years later I found myself in an opera company completely surrounded by white people. My voice teacher, who was also the director of the com-pany, was a tall, robust, rather flamboyant white man who wore a funny, unusual hair style that I later realized was a toupee. My parents never attended any of my rehearsals, so I was left to my own devices in this world at the of 11. Not once did anyone ever treat me badly or make me feel as if I didn't belong or that something was wrong with me. I was one of two black members of the opera company and the youngest one there, but for the most part, I was a singer. I was an equal. Therefore, my overall experience growing up was that, as my father had taught me, not all white people were bad. More than anything, my experiences clearly demonstrated that music and musicians spoke a universal language that was accepted by all, in spite of any racial barrier.

It wasn't until my six-year stint with Elton John, where the issue of race ever came up again. There were three racially ques-tionable, eye-opening incidents.

The first one happened on a trip to Auckland, New Zealand, traveling from Sydney, Australia. We were all sitting in the lobby of the international terminal of the airport along with the opening act's band. As usual, the road manager went to the counter to check us in and get our boarding passes. It appeared that this time, things were taking longer and the boarding time was fast approaching. One by one, each band member was called up to get their passport and boarding pass to continue on to the gate. Suddenly, the road manager began shouting angrily at the woman at the ticket counter. As I looked around, it became obvious that the only band members left in the terminal were my black mates from Elton's band. At first, there was no thought of this being unusual or that it meant anything. The road manager finally returned with our passports and boarding passes, completely apologetic, saying, "I am so sorry, they didn't have any more first-class seats." This was unusual since we always flew first class with Elton, still, we didn't think much about this. It was a short flight to New Zealand from Australia, so we could manage. However, when we boarded the plane, we realized why the road manager was so upset. As we walked through the first-class cabin we saw that Elton's music director, our other band mates, and every member of the opening act were all in first class. Only the black band members were in economy. It was obvious that something discriminatory had occurred, judging from everyone's reaction. None of them would even look us in the eyes as we walked past them. One of the members of the opening-act band offered his seat to Marlena, obviously feeling uncomfortable about the whole situation, but she declined. No one ever spoke to us about it, ever. While no one openly admitted this was racially motivated, it was obviously an upsetting and uncomfortably quiet ride to Auckland.

When we got ready to leave New Zealand to return to the United States, again, there was a problem at the airline counter and again, the road manager lost his composure. Just as we had before, we sat and waited for our boarding passes and passports. Again, it was only the black members of the band who were left waiting to be assigned seats. This time, we were all seated in first class. However, the black band members were seated in the last row of the first-class cabin. Again, it was never discussed among our band mates, only among the ones whom were affected, the black members. We never spoke about the incidents to anyone of any authority nor did we speak amongst ourselves about it after that day. Again, there was silence. However, to say these incidents didn't affect our psyches would be a lie.

The other two events were similar. In Sydney, Australia, as usual, I hired a tennis pro every morning to hit balls and play a few games, this time at the prestigious White City arena, home of the Australian Open. The tennis pro was a very nice guy who befriended me, offering to take me around to see some of the sights of Sydney after our game. We got into his car and he drove me around the city to various locations. It was really lovely. Obviously intrigued by my connection to Elton John, he wanted to spend more time together, and asked my availability for dinner. I kindly turned down the offer.

As we talked, I asked him, "Where are the Aborigines? I haven't seen a single one since I've been here." His answer shocked me as he said, "Oh, you don't want to see them. They are lazy and shiftless people who are ignorant. They steal and their neighborhoods aren't safe." "Hmmm," I said, "This is the exact same thing they said about my people in the United States." His eyes grew large and he exclaimed, "Oh, no, it's not the same. You are American. You have been civilized." I really didn't know how to respond to his answer. He sincerely did not see me as an African-American, he saw me as an American. It was an odd position to be in, as in the U.S., I am not recognized by most white people as an American without the hyphenated "African" attached.

He went on to add that Aborigines were given houses to live in and didn't know how to care for them, even setting fires to them, trying to build a fire inside. They were not used to living in such a structure. He seemed to feel as though the Aborigines should be content with being given houses to live in in the first place and couldn't understand why they would be opposed to the rhetoric that had dubbed them as being " ungrateful."

My answer to him was this: "Just think about this, sir. If it were you, how would you feel if you owned your house for years and your family owned it for generations before you. Then, one day, someone came and knocked on your door and said, 'Hello, we love your house and we are going to take it. But, you can live in the bathroom. ' How would you feel about that? Would you feel grateful?"

The tennis pro looked at me sideways, like a dog. It was as if I were speaking another language. I don't think he ever thought that anything he said was racist or demeaning. It was mind-boggling. He never really responded to my questions. That was the end of the conversation, as we continued our visit, which concluded in him dropping me off at my hotel. It was an eye-opening day to say the least.

The last event happened in Rome, Italy, where Bernie Taupin, Elton's writing partner, treated the three backing vocalists to a day of touring the major sights of the city with a private limo driver and tour guide. Halfway through the day we all went out for lunch, which included the best pasta I had ever tasted, from a small restaurant located not too far from the Trevi Fountain. As we sat there, I asked the tour guide, "What is the southern part of Italy like?" as I had never toured there at this point. She answered, "Oh, they are simple, lazy, shiftless black people who" – here we go again – "are backwards, country and uncultured." I am certain there was a look of shock on my face. As I turned to look at everyone else at the table to see if they heard what

I heard, Marlena and Mortonette's heads were bowed down. Bernie just ignored what was said and quickly changed the subject, so I followed suit, not saying anything as well. When we returned to the hotel, I asked Mortonette if she heard the woman's answer. She said yes, as we further discussed how the tour guide didn't see us as black at all, but American. It never occurred to her that what she said could be construed as offensive. Again, it was mind-boggling.

In all cases, while traveling as a musician, staying at five-star hotels, and performing at world-class venues, we were always treated like kings and queens. However, the fabric making up the foundation of humanity is so complex when it comes to race. Most times, music supersedes any ill feelings. Once the music starts and our voices are heard, on some emotional level it connects with the souls of all people. Just the sound, the tone, even without words or language, can erase racial fear yet incite emotions of all kinds. It is amazing to witness. Traveling the globe as a black musician is tricky. It's sometimes like walking through a mine field. You never know what you're gonna run into and, sometimes, the best reaction is not to react. Overall, the whole issue is a sociological study that can just be more than a notion on a Saturday night before a show. Growing up in a passive, conservative environment definitely played a major role in my responses.

As a black solo artist singing rock music, I saw the other side of discrimination occur, when black people made fun of me and/or put me down because of my choosing to sing this style of music. Many friends, associates, and colleagues expressed how much farther my career would have gone if only I had chosen to sing R&B or jazz. While to a certain extent this might have been true only because a machine had been established, allowing black people to develop a following in these genres, this is not what spoke to my heart. Many times, I was viewed as a black person trying to fit into a "white people's music" society, which is what they labeled rock music as, and frankly, many felt I had no business trying to get into. "Always establish your fan base, and for black people, that would be the black audience," seemed to be their advice. So, what does one do when the music they perform is not in alignment with the black audience? It was a precarious position to be in at the time. Standing in integrity with myself had been the one thing that I felt was necessary to sustain my soul. I had observed the careers of other artists who allowed themselves to be led down a musical path not in alignment with their spirits, with some of them indulging in drug addiction and other negative behaviors to cope with their decision to please others rather than themselves. They made a lot of money. However, money did not buy them happiness. In fact, money bought them incredible amounts of sadness.

At this point, it is my hope that if my music is meant to be heard, then it will be heard, regardless of what was acceptable in the past. The main thing for me is to remain true to myself, to keep my integrity and accept whatever levels of success may come of it. Timing is everything and, perhaps, in the scheme of this newly realized multi-racial society we now live in, a larger audience may be ready to hear what I'm saying. You never know unless you try. There is nothing to lose here. The irony of it all is that rock music *is* an African-American art form. Unfortunately, even some black people are not aware of this. Regardless, rock speaks to my heart. I always listen to my heart.

THE CURRENT MUSIC BUSINESS

Just as the popular club in the '80s At My Place in Santa Monica was one of the venues "to be seen" as a networking place for professional musicians, currently, there are several spots like The Whisky's Ultimate Jam night in West Hollywood; or the Sofitel in Beverly Hills; or Sayers Club, The Viper Room, Lucky Strike's Soundcheck Live, or Jason Joseph's Super Soul Monday's over on Hudson Street in Hollywood, to name a few, that are some of the noted networking places for musicians seeking to connect with current professionals. These are great places to be seen and heard, and while there is no pay to play, many connections to paid work have been made in these venues. This is still a viable way to get started developing relationships in the music industry. Still, maintaining relationships is everything.

While union session work as it was known, went down in flames during the late '90s and early 2000s, it has risen under a different identity, and there are a number of producers out there, still hiring singers for a reasonable, negotiable scale, to do sessions for records, video games, and other projects. Technology cannot totally replace what a true session singer can do. Thanks to the internet, singers can get session work from producers from all over the world, by receiving music files via email. All that is needed is a connection to a studio to record and Wi-Fi to receive and send music files. These days, most people have recording studios in their homes, which is cost effective. You can get electronically paid for this work via PayPal, Venmo, or other online applications.

As for movies and television, those sessions are still available and are done through the union. With shows like The Voice and American Idol who use live union singers, this viable stream of income is to also be considered. Connecting with the people that do those sessions can be challenging, as sometimes you need to know the vocal contractor, producer, or music supervisor. While some have joined special choral groups to meet and connect with the union members that do this work, others have simply kept a visible profile, singing in front of people at every opportunity, to meet and establish relationships/friendships. Joining the union, which for singers would be SAG-AFTRA, would eventually be necessary once you commence doing sessions more consistently for television and film. However, joining the union does not assure that you will be called in for session work. It only assures you a basic rate. Again, relationships are everything, which simply means that you have to meet the singers or producers that are in this aspect of the industry. Just stay visual, singing at every opportunity and trust that the meeting will happen because you desired it to be so.

Being well-versed in a number of different self-employed vocations like writing charts and studio rental (if you have one), is key to maintaining these different streams of income. Again, thanks to the Internet, developing your own YouTube channel, and other social media branding can generate several streams of income if you are business savvy, and keep you in the spotlight to be seen by fellow musicians. Always, record your own music and put it out there on the internet. It is pure profit for the artist and you never know who is out there listening. The Internet has global ears. Unlike the environment that I grew up in, today is a "do it yourself" society, which means you must be expansive and entrepreneurial in your thinking. You will be amazed at how many other talents you possess and are called upon to utilize. In this pursuit, you may find an even higher purpose that had not even been considered. That is what happened to me.

Remembering the profound words of Maya Angelou, "At our best, we are all teachers," my advice is that once you have mastered your craft, then share it through teaching. All of this happens through being ahead of the curve, by being silent, meditating, listening, then executing. Following your heart will guide you accordingly. Also, there are invaluable lessons learned in the mentor/disciple relationship.

Lastly, as a singer, I encourage everyone to write their own story, their own music. Not only is song writing and journaling good for the soul, it helps with the shaping and molding of your own voice, your artistry, solidifying your identity, and it inspires and encourages others who hear your words. While this can also be another source of income, you don't do it for the money, you do it as an outward expression of who you are. The money will come. Music is a universal language, spoken by everyone on the planet. Your music is your means of communication.

The book "Zero Limits" and the concepts offered by Dr. Hew Len saved my life. Staying in the moment, cleaning the sub-conscious, being silent, listening, then following my heart, kept me sane. Finding self-love and letting everything go, not thinking or second guessing, propelled me forward and un-leashed work in the form of recording sessions, clinics, and solo artist performance opportunities. Going to the Korean Spa in-stalled the next level of my self-confidence and kept me healthy, physically clean, relaxed, and at peace. Yoga kept me physically strong, moving, breathing, and connected my body to my spirit. Soon, some level of consistency/routine developed and happi-ness appeared. No more worrying or concern about my current state of life existed. In fact, there was no more judgement at all, as I was no longer attracting such a thing. This was revealed in my interactions with people and their new response to my situation.

Stability and housing were at my feet, as I ran into an old friend at a concert, who offered me a place to live for a few weeks, free of charge. She lived with her boyfriend, so her apartment was vacant. Synchronistically, another chance meeting with a guy who said he owned income property, happened while hang-ing out at a sports bar during the 2017 NBA Finals, which I took as an indication that I'm energetically closer to settling into my "Malibu home."

After everything that has happened these last three years, establishing the next level in my life, thinking the way to go about this process of receiving what I want, was to list my goals

and desires, then figure out a plan to get them, helped me realize that I had it all backwards. Desires are an indication that
it has already happened, appearing in dreams simply as a reminder that the time to focus and act on these desires has come.
Listen for the signs, act accordingly, and accept it. Acceptance
was a *huge* lesson for me. Acceptance, Surrender, and Self Love
were personally, the learned lessons that defined the shift in my
consciousness.

At the end of the day, what became real for me as a person
pursuing my dreams, was that need for connection and love. It
is what drives every human being, everything on this planet. It
starts with self-love, which is something many are not naturally
taught.

In our society, we are told that we need exterior things in
order to be loved. We need a certain car, lipstick, clothes from
certain designers, lashes, breast and butt implants, etcetera. In
our pursuit to be loved and accepted, when it gets overwhelming
and we can't afford to maintain these things, then we seek place-
bos, or things that give us a false sense of love or we anesthetize
ourselves with drugs and alcohol to cope with our feelings of
inadequacy, for not having those things. All of this happens because we don't love and accept ourselves for who we are. We are
never good enough. Some of us seek the support of family and
friends when we are having these feelings. However, because of
their own "lack of love" upbringing, they may not have the tools
to help us. This was my experience, and the answer for me was to
totally place my trust in God, not a religion or minister, but God.
At the end of my day, that was all that I had, the only relationship
that mattered and could assist me. This meant that I had to listen and know it was God speaking through my heart and not me
second-guessing my moves through my brain. As a singer pursuing this career, there was no other way to live but by faith that a
Higher Source would dictate every move that led to a successful

career in this music business. A life of constantly being in touch with my feelings so that I could convey them through song, is an emotional adventure. It's eye-opening, it's exciting, it's draining, it's scary, and it's healing. It is a roller coaster ride, and as I said earlier, "You've got to love the roller coaster!"

It took me while, through experiences I wasn't certain I'd survive. But, my waking up this morning was my indication that yes, I get another chance to make this life work, so don't give up.

This back up diva FINALLY got it!

CRY

"BABY GIRL, BABY GIRL
WHAT'S YOUR CLAIM TO FAME?"
I'D ASK THAT QUESTION OVER AND OVER AGAIN.
YOU CAN SEE BEHIND MY SMILE
I'VE BEEN THROUGH SOME THINGS,
BUT IN THE END, I FOUND STRENGTH
THROUGH MY PAIN.

AND I JUST WANT TO CRY.
BUT, NOT FROM ALL THE SADNESS.
I JUST WANT TO CRY
A RELEASE FROM ALL THIS HAPPINESS.
I JUST WANT TO CRY.
MY HEART IS FILLED WITH GLADNESS.
I FOLLOWED MY BLISS
AND I JUST WANT TO CRY
I JUST WANT TO CRY

NEVER BEEN THE ONE
TOO AFRAID TO FLY.
DODGING STICKS AND STONES

AS I'D FLOAT THROUGH THE SKY.
EVEN BROKE SOME BONES
BUT KEPT MY EYES OPENED WIDE.
"WHERE DO I BELONG?"
HAS BEEN MY SOUL'S DESIRE.

HEY, LOOK AT ME,
NOW I'M LIVING MY DREAM.
AND ALL THIS STRESSING OUT
IS JUST A FAINT MEMORY
AND I'M SO HAPPY,
OH I'M FEELING SO FREE.
WHAT A BEAUTIFUL PLACE TO BE.

AND I JUST WANT TO CRY,
BUT NOT FROM ALL THE SADNESS.
I JUST WANT TO CRY
A RELEASE FROM ALL THIS HAPPINESS.
I JUST WANT TO CRY.
MY HEART IS FILLED WITH GLADNESS.
I FOLLOWED MY BLISS
AND I JUST WANT TO CRY,
I JUST WANT TO CRY.

I JUST WANT TO CRY
I JUST WANT TO CRY
I JUST WANT TO CRY

Words and Music by Kudisan Kai

THE ULTIMATE JOURNEY
EPILOGUE

O ne of the things that I noticed every time I went to the Korean spa, was how every woman, regardless of age, ethnicity, socio-economic status, or living circumstances, loved getting in that hot tub. There was a universal look of total release and bliss on every woman's face, as they entered the spa, submerging into that hot water, closing their eyes, allowing every ounce of stress, worry, or concern to gently float from their bodies, disintegrating into the air with the steam. It was one of the few places where everyone could truly exhale and for me, it became the center of my joy and a necessary medicine. In addition to its relaxing qualities, breathing in the steam room and going back and forth between the hot and cold tubs, removed all inflammation from my body, including my vocal chords. It was a great way to recuperate from a day's work in the studio or on stage.

I began to wonder, what if these spas were a foundational part of the fabric of the United States, as they are in Asian culture? Imagine how healing and rehabilitating it would be, especially for those re-acclimating themselves into society after some horrific life experience? This became a main focal point for me, so I decided to do some writing and research on what the benefits of living a "spa life" would be after having post-traumatic experiences. Like magic, creating a proposal to build a healing lifestyle facility organically evolved, helping me to find an even higher purpose that could be fed by my music. Developing a cooperative living environment that included spas as an integral part of the lifestyle was just what a healing place of rehabilitation needed. This was a priceless gift given by my present circumstance.

These past three years of living out on the periphery, taught me that regardless of our political or cultural differences, whether you are enlightened or unenlightened, at the end of the day, human beings are all the same when it comes to wanting the basic needs of acceptance, happiness, to love and be loved, and to independently take care of themselves and others both at home and at work. We all have dreams but, somehow understanding that our dreams are our reality, ready to materialize and awaken us to what our intention should now focus on, got lost in translation.

That Audrey Hepburn "Breakfast at Tiffany's" picture is timeless, speaking volumes now louder than ever of this changing landscape called an artist's life. Like the Mona Lisa, the eyes in this image revealed the soul of a dreamer with desires, strength, audacity, freedom, independence, endurance, and pure perseverance. No wonder it hangs in the bar lounge of the Crescent Hotel in Beverly Hills and at the Korean Spa. It is representative of the stories of just about everyone who comes through those halls and doorways.

After spending quality time and developing relationships with many of the regulars who frequented the hotel and spa, it was obvious that some of these people, much like Holly Golightly and the other characters in the movie, took on the persona of that old television commercial slogan, "never let them see you sweat, as you could not guess in a million years, just by looking at them, what they had gone through and overcome. My quality

Crescent Hotel Final AH image

time spent in conversation with so many of them, taught me that they were willing to step out on that ledge of possibilities and jump, taking chances at living their dream fearlessly at the expense of being different. All of them rode life's roller coaster up to its apex, then down to the bottom, to that impasse in their lives where there was nothing left to do but stop, be silent, and listen. Some of them learned to be completely present, only living in the moment, while others were still struggling with their choices. Above all, each and every one of them courageously persevered, still moving forward in spite of adversity, in spite of their fears. Loving, vulnerable, flawed, and defiant are the words that describe and define these true artists living out there dream instead of living inside of a box. Others, however, struggled with their circumstances, as you could see it in their faces and feel it in their demeanor.

This was my state three years ago, when I first arrived in L.A. and started attending the spa. Many nights, as I slept on the heated jade floor, with eyes filled with tears, heart filled with meditation and prayers, my mind spoke loudly, regurgitating my circumstances, never giving me a moment of peace. However, as always in life, everything changed, and as my mind exhausted itself, finally giving in to my heart, I found a silence that placed me in a constant state of pure gratitude. It became my spiritual home.

Now, when I look at that portrait, I see every woman, every man striving, thriving, and transcending. to live a life far beyond their own dreams and desires. That's when I realized that there is artistry in everything and we are all artists. However, only some of us choose to pursue it.

The artistry of tour/session singing is relatively new to the ears of the public. Thanks to the academy award-winning documentary "20 Feet From Stardom," a light has shined on the backing vocalist profession, revealing its existence. While I didn't spend a lot of time writing about developing dance skills or taking movement classes, it is also a key factor, specifically in the life of a touring back up vocalist. Musicians and singers condition their bodies like athletes do, which is one of the things they both have in common, their work ethic. Singing is physically exerting and movement while singing requires stamina. There are so many stories to tell, as it is such an expansive career in and out of the recording studios, on television, film, radio, and live performances across the globe in every venue ranging from clubs to theaters, to stadiums. The preparation for such a career is as weighted as any professional solo artist career with the included skill of possessing a gifted ear.

In addition to the natural gift, the years of studying music, the hours of practicing, and body conditioning and developing muscle memory (this includes the voice, as it is a muscle), musicians and singers can make what they do for a living, look so easy, it causes many to take what they do for granted. Adding in the emotional toll it takes to be vulnerable on stage in front of an audience, makes this quite a formidable profession, as this aspect of performance is rarely discussed at any length. Thus, emotional connection exercises became the foundation of my teaching philosophy, and an integral part of what I teach in my clinics at various colleges and universities. Preparing for this instruction infers that I be open and vulnerable to my own experiences, which has been rewarding and quite challenging. So, my endurance through all of these events in the last three years, has only created more power for the course, a test I hope to have passed.

Music is effective in healing people psychologically, emotionally, even physically as now music therapy is one of the burgeoning professions that have proven to be an intricate part of healing a list of illnesses such as restoring speech loss in stroke patients and reducing side effects in cancer therapy, just to name a few. As a society, we already recognize the affects music has on people who may use its powers to incite emotions of unity, love, and action. So, singing is healing through the sound of the voice, through music. In essence, the music business is the healing business.

Maya Angelou expresses, "At our best, we are all teachers." I totally agree. However, after singing for a living for over 34 years, my experience so far has taught that in addition to being teachers, "At our best, we are all healers."

The landscape of today's music business, uses Auto-Tune to correct pitch and other possible flaws in a vocal performance. While this can be viewed as a good and helpful thing, the misuse of this device gives inexperienced singers a false sense of abilities, suggesting that they don't need to really hone any skills in this profession. This is not true. Use of this technology on vocals, gives a robotic quality to the voice, which is popular right now, and is a current standard sound among many well-known pop singers. However, this may not be the case later, as sound production in the music industry constantly changes. At the end of the day, the truth comes out when the artist has to perform live. Rarely are non-singers able to replicate the voice on their recording. Singing exclusively to a pre-recorded track is tricky, leaving you at the mercy of technology, which is not always dependable. There have been numerous videos of artists who have experienced equipment failure during a concert performance. These issues have exposed flaws, revealing what is lacking in vocal production, and can sometimes break a career. After an audience pays for concert tickets, aren't they worthy of receiving a real, complete, live, non-prerecorded performance? A true singer will always possess a certain level of skill that only comes from study, practice, and putting in the work required for longevity in this industry. This is the hallmark of a true artist. Are you in this business merely for the money and celebrity, or are you driven by your talent to persevere and succeed in this business? Know your purpose. Even if your motivation is to simply "be famous or be a celebrity," know that while you incur a fan base, and may fool them for a moment with poorly rehearsed performances and uninspired imitations, at the end of the day, the audience will eventually seek to connect with the truth. Seeking the truth is what initiates the changing landscape of the music business. Be true to yourself and know who you are as an artist.

The ultimate learning curve in this journey came via relationships. One of my coping mechanisms whenever I felt overwhelmed by my homeless situation, was to busy myself with helping others. That way, my mind and energies would be completely wrapped up in the tasks at hand, negating all things that caused me to contemplate my own issues and feelings. It was a great way to stay in a giving mode and my friends loved it, as I helped organize garages, packed and moved houses, did spring cleaning, all of the above. Always in this constant state of giving, rarely receiving, the imbalance of it all, frayed the edges of my life. I was wasting away, giving my energy with nothing being reciprocated. The constant judgement and ridicule from my family over how I was living, only exacerbated things as I struggled to get my footing into the new music business. Soon, I realized that I had to disconnect from their chaos to stay focused. This was difficult but proved to be necessary if I was to survive and move on past my present circumstances.

Whatever words or judgements spoken to me, good or bad, were direct reflections of how I felt about myself. This was the ultimate teacher. As stated in chapter two, "relationships are everything." Soon, I realized that the first relationship that needed to be addressed was the one with myself. It had come to my attention that my physical life and body were the mirrored reflections of my subconscious, which played back all of those ugly stories and painful experiences of not being able to sing anything but classical music, not being thin or pretty enough, not being the right race for rock music, all those negatives. Unfortunately, I bought into society's hype because I didn't love myself enough to brush these opinions off my shoulders. Constantly, on the defensive, I still continued to do everything in my power to please everyone, hoping that if they were happy, then perhaps, they would allow me to be also, and not judge my choices or belittle my differences. Raised to believe that being different was bad, it was an internal struggle between me fighting to be myself, the free-spirited rocker with gauges and tattoos, and still fit into the society that wanted me to be more universal or conservative in my dress and approach to life. I walked this line for my parents, boyfriends, child, husband, even friends, at the expense of taking care of and acknowledging myself first. I was a jack of all trades and a master of all, which made me a great background singer, but a lost solo artist. This recent re-acclimation to LA's music scene, gave me the opportunity to find that confidence, that self-love to move forward in my career, with my life. In the end, I found my artistry.

As for my looks and physical body, I learned a valuable lesson during my stint with Elton John. After having lost 65 pounds at the time, I felt that everything would fall in place, including my personal life, which meant, now I was pretty enough to attract the man of my dreams. In my mind, I was thin enough to be considered for that record deal. But, when none of those things happened, my spirit was devastated and disappointed. The reality was that none of those things really mattered. Acceptance was in order here. It is not about having "the look," it's about having "a look," which means creating a vibe or concept that feels organic and suits your personae. Accepting and loving yourself is key here, no matter what you look like. If you feel good in your skin, so will everyone around you. Continuing a healthy life and being able to function at the highest level in my profession should have been the goal here. Now, eating foods that nourish and promote healing in my body and exercises that I enjoy, dictates my weight, whatever that may be. Nothing else. The spa experience was predominant in showing me that being beautiful was in how you sincerely felt about yourself. My weight is simply a by-product of excellent health. Beauty, as always, is in the eyes of the beholder, the mirror, and comes in all shapes and sizes.

Then, it all came to a screeching halt when my daughter decided to end our relationship out of the blue. It was that singular act that propelled me into a depression, frankly, I thought I'd never survive. Today, I find myself feeling overwhelmed sometimes, as if my child has died and it suffocates me. This is when I hit the beach to meditate, to breathe again, to let go of what I can't control. This is a major lesson in surrendering, understanding that love and time heals. Experience has taught me this. In the meantime, I can first, take care of myself and secure my foundation by getting settled in a home. That way, I am prepared and am in a position to truly take care of everything. Thankfully, my spiritual path kept me aligned with the universe, and my purpose on this planet could not be denied, even by me. As a suicide survivor, I knew I had to let even that relationship go, giving it to God, in pure love, in order to move forward with my life, in the name of self-love upon which everyone including my child, would benefit. After all, even she has her own path to walk. I cannot walk it for her. At this point, it was not for me to direct, for it was out of my hands now. It was actually, never in my hands in the first place. Although, this has been the challenge of my life, being at zero, doing nothing, being silent, hearing and adhering to my instructions from God, has saved me. Finally, I am finding peace.

These life experiences in the last three years have prepared me for this next episode, as now everything that I had been working on to advance my career, has finally come into fruition.

From striving to thriving, and now transcending, I am an artist. I love and accept myself. I know my purpose. I align myself with the Universe to receive my highest good, each morning, listening and awaiting my instruction. This is my transcending, my becoming. So far, it's been an incredible journey. This career as a back-up singer, gave me a premiere view of all of the intricacies of several aspects of the music and other entertainment industries, including a level of life experiences, most people rarely get to participate in. Challenging, non-stop comedy, and drama? Absolutely! This life keeps your eyes wide open behind the steering wheel, no matter how tired you are. This life is not for everyone, but I wouldn't have it any other way, and for it, I am truly grateful.

ACKNOWLEDGEMENTS

First of all, I acknowledge the Universe for carrying me through this journey. As always, I align myself with the Universe to receive my highest good.

Thank you, Valerie Pinkston, for your beautiful work on the cover of my book and your photography. You are a woman of many talents and I am so grateful to be your friend.

To Maxayn Lewis, I owe my life for all of the struggles that were encountered during this journey, she was able to assist and many times, carry me through. When the tears came, your shoulder was there for me to cry on. In addition, she introduced me to the Korean Spa. That was a game changer for me.

My friends Tanya O'Calleghan and Robbie Angelucci, thank you for the many sofa stays, dinners, and just plain fun.

Stephanie Jeffries, you are a born life coach. What an extraordinary person, and I thank you for your guidance. Those Friday morning meditations and painting, helped me find my center in the middle of this storm. I am forever grateful.

Thanks to Lisa Vaughn and her family for giving me a place to live when I first returned to a Los Angeles.

Thank you, Sandy and Tony Simmons-Williams, for offering your home temporarily for a respite, much appreciated.

Thanks to Guy at Mel's Diner for food when I couldn't afford to eat, for a safe place to sleep in my car, and for the many conversations, arguments, and comic relief that is Mel's Diner. We had so much fun. Thanks to my family for giving me something to push up against. This is necessary in life and my journey would not be complete without it.

Thank you, Nell Walker, for helping me put this book together for my publisher and for giving me a bed to sleep in for a while. It was temporary, but every moment that I was indoors in a bed, was a gift.

Thanks to my friend Tracy Blackman for giving me work singing with her in San Francisco, housing me, sometimes sending money when I was broke, most of all, for making me feel like family.

Thank you, Ebony Rucker, for the financial assistance that allowed me to still have my car and phone services, food, and gas. There is no way I could have made it through this without you.

Thank you, Maureen Davis, for taking me, a complete stranger, into your home to sleep on your sofa and assist me in filling out those papers for MusicCares. You knew how to traverse those waters, and it was during a time when I thought I would die. Thank you.

Thank you, Adam Mandel and Chuck Wright, at the Whisky's Ultimate Jam Night for your support. You provided a way for me to sustain during a really tough time. You both have hearts of gold.

To Kevin Parker-Robinson and your partner David, thank you for my trailer home away from the madness of my life in LA. So many laughs, so much fun amidst a time when things were down right crazy. Thank you for feeding and caring for me. You saved my life many times.

Thank you, Katara Gara, for your insight and revealing who I truly am. It was the defining shift that changed the trajectory of my life.

Thank you, Gary Allen, for your friendship, giving me a place to lay my head, eat popcorn, and visit regroup from my days in the air.

Thank you, Johannes Raasina, for your amazing production on my music project that was inspired by this book. You were able to bring my music to life, sharing the same vision, which is a rare find. We are truly a match made in heaven. Also, much love and thanks to the lovely Luna Achiary, your wife, for her musical genius and infectious, loving, supportive energy throughout this project.

Thank you, Miles Jeffries, for being the incredible hair stylist and friend. What a gifted person you are.

Thank you, Janine Coveney, for editing my book. It was a challenge but you gracefully flowed right on through. Thank you for being so patient with me.

Printed in the United States
By Bookmasters